LADIES
OF THE
ROPE

LADIES

OF THE

ROPE

GURDJIEFF'S SPECIAL
LEFT BANK WOMEN'S GROUP

WILLIAM PATRICK PATTERSON

Edited by Barbara Allen Patterson
Arete Communications, Publishers
Fairfax, California

Ladies of the Rope
© 1999 by William Patrick Patterson
All rights reserved

Design by WordPlay Consulting, Berkeley, CA

Library of Congress Catalog Number is 98-70220
Patterson, William Patrick
Ladies of the Rope
Bibliography: Includes notes, references, and index
1. G. I. Gurdjieff
2. Fourth Way
3. Jane Heap
4. Solita Solano
5. Kathryn Hulme
6. Margaret Anderson

First printing 1999

ISBN: 1-879514-41-9

*Arete Communications, Box 58, 773 Center Boulevard
Fairfax, California 94978-0058*

*email: telos9@aol.com
Web Site: http://members.aol.com/telos9*

For
Vitvitskaïa

Acknowledgments

This book has taken a tremendous amount of energy and time and could not have been published without the help and support of a great many friends. I would like to thank Henry Korman for the cover and book design and preparation of the final text; his wife Mary Ellen for inputting the text and inserting accurately and without complaint what I am sure seemed like—and was—a monumental number of changes; and to Teresa Adams for the creation of the index and her steadfast help in researching the archives. Henry, Mary Ellen and Teresa also made many useful comments and additions to the many drafts of the manuscript. I thank also Leanne Francis, Kathy Keers, Mike Miller and Dave Seymour for proofreading the text; and, as always, my gratitude to my wife Barbara for bringing her professional editing skills, sensibility, and long standing support to this project. A special thanks, as well, to the many people who helped my research at the Beinecke Library, Yale University, Golda Meir Library at the University of Minnesota, the Special Collections Department at the University of Delaware, and the Library of Congress. Lastly, I would like to express my gratitude to Solita Solano for her notes of the Rope's many luncheons with Mr. Gurdjieff and generously giving the copyright to the Library of Congress.

Contents

Introduction

I N A LIFE THAT IS IN MANY WAYS AS ENIGMATIC TODAY AS IT WAS DURING THE THIRTY-SEVEN YEARS HE WAS IN THE WEST, George Ivanovitch Gurdjieff's formation of the special women-only group known as the Rope stands as perhaps his most unusual creation. The ancient teaching that it was his mission to bring to the West and the man himself were solidly rooted in Tradition. To form a group composed only of women, and of those, all but one lesbian, was simply without precedence. But as much as he stood for Tradition, Mr. Gurdjieff was clearly breaking with it in opening up the esoteric teaching of the Fourth Way to the uninitiated.

In doing so, he took on a tremendous responsibility, but apparently he felt the conditions of ordinary life had become so abnormal that only a desperate gamble might avert the certain societal breakdown that awaited. The gamble was the introduction of the esoteric into the spiritual wilderness that was and is worldly life. Breaking vows of secrecy, he delivered the shock of the esoteric in the hopes that it would arouse enough people to undergo the rigorous adventure of self-awakening so that the world as we know it might not be destroyed. For this, of course—and he expected it—he was castigated both by initiates and the uninitiated.

Having attempted to document Gurdjieff's life and activity in the West in my book *Struggle of the Magicians,* one part in particular stood out, that was his creation of the Rope. Other than

Kathryn Hulme's *Undiscovered Country* and Margaret Anderson's *The Unknowable Gurdjieff*, there was little information on the Rope. It was either not spoken of or given little more than passing mention. The Rope didn't fit. It not only went against Tradition but against Gurdjieff's own teaching. So why the Rope? To answer that, if only in part, I made a number of trips to read the papers of four of the women of the Rope archived in various libraries across America: Solita Solano's at the Library of Congress, Washington D. C.; Margaret Anderson's at the Golda Meir Library, University of Minnesota; Kathryn Hulme's at the Beinecke Library, Yale University; and Jane Heap's at the Special Collections Department of the University of Delaware.

In reading the diaries, correspondence and notes, I was struck by the women's intelligence, creativity and sensitivity. They had all led amazing lives and, most importantly, had sat at Gurdjieff's table. He had taught them directly. No small thing—very often an ordeal, a test of fire not for the weak. As I got more of a feeling for the world of the Rope (admittedly, of course, only in reflection), I wondered if it might be possible through first a diligent researching and then an articulation of this material in the form of a book that my original question—*why did Gurdjieff create the Rope?*—would make a call strong enough that an answer might reveal itself. I leave it to the reader's judgment as to whether or not, and to what extent, this has occurred.

Once the initial research was completed and the book begun I was suddenly struck with a most obvious question but one I had never asked. Namely, what was I as a man, a heterosexual man at that, doing writing about lesbian women? What evoked the question was reading Mathilda Hills' introduction to Margaret Anderson's novella *Forbidden Fires* and coming upon this sentence: "In a deeply expressive voice colored by warm tones and varied inflections, Lib [Solita Solano's companion] spoke candidly yet with subtlety, as one accustomed to saying what she meant, but paying the listener the compliment of not spelling it out. She allowed for silence and she connected." The sensitivity alluded to seemed very special and a characteristic that I felt most, if not all, the women of the Rope shared. Later, reading a lesbian writer speaking of Gertrude Stein and the lesbian women of that era as "ancestors" gave another shock. From that point of view, I wasn't just writing about eight women but, in a sense, exploring "ancestral ground."

I had never considered it before, but until the twentieth century lesbian women had virtually no public voice. Feminine love was draped in societal silence. Having no history, it had no authenticity. This is no longer the case. The subject is now a regular part of media coverage. That lesbian life partnerships, for example, are now so accepted in certain areas of the country that they are noted in society columns is a sign of the times. The significance of that sign remains a matter of hot societal dispute.

The women of the Rope do have a voice and speak so well for themselves, their lives, and their interactions with Gurdjieff that whenever possible I have let them speak. I have tried to present them in accordance with the facts as known and in a way that speaks to their determination to live their sexuality in the face of what was then total condemnation. It should be noted that other than a discussion about the nature of lesbianism and another concerning ecstasy, there is no mention of sexuality whatever in the papers these women chose to leave behind. They did this, I believe, from the desire that their lives be taken seriously.

There are also a number of significant events that must have been discussed but the women have deleted these from their papers. Among them: the extent of Margaret Anderson's nervous breakdown in 1923; the taking in and adoption of Tom and Fritz Peters; Gurdjieff's sending of Jane Heap to London; Solita Solano's lack of notes after June 1938—Margaret Anderson said the luncheons with Gurdjieff continued through the summer of 1939; why Solita Solano waited until October 1948 to visit Gurdjieff in Paris; and, finally, the reaction of the Rope, and especially Jane Heap, to Fritz Peters' book *Boyhood with Gurdjieff* (published the same year that Jane Heap died).

At the beginning of the book the women tell their life stories. It is documented that they did so, but what they chose to tell of their lives and how they told it is not known. All material given in the luncheons and dinners the Rope had with Gurdjieff is taken in abridged form from the notes of Solita Solano. The only change made is "voice," using third person rather than first. In certain places in the meetings with Gurdjieff a highlight here and there has been added to give a better sense of what was taking place, but quotes and situations are sourced and can be found in the Reference Section—nothing has been invented. Finally, biographical material concerning Alice Rohrer and Louise Davidson is slight, hence the gaps in what is presented.

For those interested in Gurdjieff's teaching, it should be pointed out that his giving the women animal names—Margaret Anderson he called "Yakina"; Kathryn Hulme, "Kroko*deel*"; Solita Solano, "Kanari"; Louise Davidson, "Sardine"—is unique in the teaching, as far as I know. While it is generally accepted that each person wears a societal persona, or mask, that there exists an inner animal is a much deeper recognition and a genuine contribution to the study of oneself and the teaching of the Fourth Way.

Prologue

O<small>N</small> O<small>CTOBER</small> 21, 1935, G<small>EORGE</small> I<small>VANOVITCH</small> G<small>URDJIEFF</small> FORMED A SPECIAL WOMEN-ONLY GROUP OF SPIRITUAL SEEK-ERS. It began with four women and eventually grew to seven, all lesbians but one. Of Mr. Gurdjieff's many and varied activities during his work to establish the ancient teaching of the Fourth Way, his creation of this group is the least understood.

First appearing in Russia in 1912, it was Gurdjieff's mission to introduce the Fourth Way, reformulated for our time, to the West. Gurdjieff came because he believed that *unless the 'wisdom' of the East and the 'energy' of the West are harnessed and used harmoniously the world will destroy itself.*

In Russia he intended to establish the Institute for the Harmonious Development of Man for the practice and dissemination of the teaching. However, the sudden rise of the black tide of Bolshevism in 1917 made this impossible. After a number of attempts to establish it elsewhere, Gurdjieff opened the Institute in France in November 1922 at a château called the Prieuré des Basses-Loges at Fontainebleau-en-Avon, some forty miles southeast of Paris.

Though his early lectures were heard by Western audiences only in translation, Gurdjieff immediately attracted people of a very high level; many highly intelligent, creative and successful in ordinary life. Foremost among them was Alfred Richard Orage, founder and editor of the *New Age,* a prominent London literary and political review, who gave up his editorship to follow Gurdjieff. What attracted Orage and people like him was not only the exceptional depth of Gurdjieff's understanding and knowledge, his Being, but the originality, scale and practicality of teaching itself. Nothing like it had ever been seen in the West. In fact, as Gurdjieff said—*"The teaching whose theory is here being set out is completely self-supporting and independent of other lines and it has been completely unknown up to the present time."*

In the 1920s, a number of more traditional teachings were making their appearance in the West as well. Hindu gurus, such as Vivekananda and Parmahansa Yogananda, Sufis, such as Hazrat Inayat Khan, and Buddhist monks had all come to the West. And, of course, there were the occult teachings of Madame Blavatsky's "Himalayan masters." But the Fourth Way had no antecedent.

In Left Bank expatriate circles the teaching—and Gurdjieff—generated a great deal of talk, even scandalous rumor. But for those having a serious interest no authoritative, substantial source of information was available. The teaching had no books. There were no lectures, no seminars. It had no center and no teacher for, following his serious car crash in July 1924, Gurdjieff had dissolved the Institute and no longer taught.

"Since I had not," Gurdjieff explained, "when in full strength and health, succeeded in introducing in practice into the life of people the beneficial truths elucidated for them by me, then I must at least, at any cost, succeed in doing this in theory, before my death." And so he had decided to give all his time to writing what he termed a *Legominism,* that is, a means by which initiates could transmit esoteric knowledge to future generations. Although he finished the final draft of the manuscript of *All and Everything, First Series,* before 1930, he would not authorize its publication until 1950.

For the first half of the twentieth century, then, all that was commonly known about the Fourth Way was that it was not a religion per se. There was no dogma, no belief system. Like traditional teachings, the Fourth Way was rooted in Tradition, yet, uniquely, it both appeared and disappeared. By thus avoiding a stultifying monolithic structure, it was free to take on a form correspondent with the time. Whatever form it might take, its principles remained unchanged. Rather than withdraw into a monastery or an ashram, the student of the Fourth Way stayed in life, learned to use life—use the uncertainty, shocks, suffering and negativity it produced—to come to real life. One learned, for example, to extend intentionally the inner process of the conscious absorption of impressions, putting energy and faith only in consciousness and direct experience. Every idea and practice was to be verified by one's own intentional observation and experimentation. What was necessary was not devotion but effort; not belief, but self-study, self-sacrifice and understanding. And the effort had to be voluntary. It was not an effort made by the willful ego, but an effort of a special quality, one both psychological and organic, the aim being to impartially observe one's manifestations. In turn, this observation of self *as it is*—not as *imagined*—brings a genuine suffering, also of a different quality (one unlike the personal psychological, emotional or physical suffering usually attributed to the word). It is a suffering that only the seeing of the stark impersonal truth can evoke. It is only this intentional self-remembering and self-observation, repeated again and again, which can build sufficient pressure to crack the imprisoning shell of false personality so that essence can develop and higher-being bodies be formed, and a soul created.

While this brief sketch can only be unsatisfactory, it will hopefully give some taste for the special teaching that Gurdjieff brought. It is a teaching that, if one understands Gurdjieff correctly, predates all the teachings we know and whose origin points, amazingly, toward prehistoric Egypt.

All Gurdjieff's work in the West was undertaken with one aim in mind: to establish the teaching for future generations. This he accomplished with *All and Everything,* comprised of three series of books, *Beelzebub's Tales to His Grandson, Meetings with Remarkable Men,* and *Life is real only then when 'I am.'* In the knowledge that everything Gurdjieff did was to further his aim, a question has remained as to why he created the Rope. What place did it have, if any, in establishing the teaching? How to understand this? Who were these women and how did the teaching affect their lives? And lastly, how did Gurdjieff regard the women and what antecedent, if any, was there in his work with them? It is with these questions in mind that we attempt to return in time to look at the embryo of the group as it existed in 1930, and how later it evolved into a full-fledged group under Gurdjieff's direct instruction.

The First Growl

Paris. 1930. Every monday evening a small group of women—all intelligent, talented, some strikingly beautiful—walked through the narrow, winding streets of the Left Bank to a small apartment in Montparnasse. What brought these women together, the aim they shared in common, was an ancient esoteric teaching of awakening called the Fourth Way. George Ivanovitch Gurdjieff, the man who had introduced it, no longer taught and the only way to learn about it was from someone he had authorized. He had authorized very few, and these only at the introductory level.

One was the occupant of the Montparnasse apartment to which the group of women came every week. Her name was Jane Heap. She was an artist working in collage and jewelry, and the former co-editor of the *Little Review,* an avant-garde arts magazine famous for having published James Joyce's *Ulysses,* as well as the work of Ezra Pound, T. S. Eliot, Ernest Hemingway and many others. She was forty-seven years old, heavy-set with dark close-cropped hair, and a broad forehead. Her brown eyes were both warm and observant. Her mouth was large, always painted with a bright red lipstick. The initial physical impression of her could be jarring, for she appeared to be two genders at once. She had a strong sense of herself; her energy was magnetic, and her mind powerful, clear, capable of making fine distinctions and seeing

5

broad patterns. Though she had studied the teaching for only six years, Gurdjieff had given her permission to lead the group.

Among the women who knocked at Jane's door was her old friend and former lover Margaret Anderson, the founder and co-editor with Jane of the *Little Review;* Georgette Leblanc, a well-known diva, actress and former mistress of the Belgian playwright and poet, Maurice Maeterlinck; Solita Solano, novelist and editor; Janet Flanner, foreign correspondent for *The New Yorker;* and Louise Davidson, an actress. Also, for varying periods of time, a number of other women attended the meetings at Jane's apartment. Among them was Jane's good friend the modernist writer Gertrude Stein and her companion Alice B. Toklas, as well as the novelist Djuna Barnes, author of *Ryder* and the *Ladies Almanack.*

It was autumn. Jane Heap's group had been meeting and studying the ideas of the teaching for some time. It was still too early really but the group had jelled and so Jane had given the task for each woman to speak sincerely and completely about her life. Of course, this was what everyone was always talking about—*themselves*—in one way or another. But none did it consciously, with intention. Stories were told piecemeal, either spewing out in uncontrollable outpourings, or furtively, in small cameos, always framed in rationality or justified with grand generalizations. There was a kind of inner taboo about being truthful in talking about oneself. The anecdotes were really little pieces of personal propaganda meant to polish the self image, or to destroy another's.

One's life story, one's belief in and worship of one's fabrication, was what held everyone in place. It was the mirror in which the reflection of everything was seen, and categorized, and judged. In this way the mirror—one's life story—made anything new instantly old. So no matter what "improvements" one might make ... all were made within the borders of the mirror. People lived and died within the mirror and never knew it. To begin to know oneself, one had to know one's mirror, one's life story.

Jane asked the women to work on making what she called "kaleidoscopes" of their lives, past and present. They were to examine each colored piece of "glass"—their influences, memories, attitudes, and beliefs—as if in a kaleidoscope and see the patterns the pieces formed. If one gave enough attention, patterns would begin to emerge. Each one was then to tell the group about her life. The person who spoke was to speak as sincerely as possible and, at the same time, listen to herself inside, her own feelings, reactions, judgments. Those listening were to give their attention to the speaker and, at the same time, to their feelings, reactions, judgments.

Gurdjieff had given this same exercise to his first groups in Russia: *In order to know one's type, one must make a good study of one's life, one's whole life from the very beginning; one must know why, and how, things have happened.... Let every one of you in the group tell about his life.*

To tell one's life story naturally brought up a great deal of charged and dark material, that which no one wants to touch, much less deal with. In giving people the task of telling the story of their lives, Gurdjieff had given no exemptions, no way out:

Everything must be told in detail without embellishment, and without suppressing anything. Emphasize the principal and essential things without dwelling on trifles and details. You must be sincere and not be afraid that others will take anything in a wrong way, because everyone must show himself as he is ... and nothing must be taken outside the group.

As an example, Jane told the story of her early life.

She said she was born November 1, 1883, in Kansas. Her mother was Norwegian; her father English. She had grown up on the grounds of an insane asylum. Her father George worked as a civil engineer at the Topeka Asylum for the Insane [now the world-famous Menninger Clinic]. Said Jane:

> When I was a little child I lived in a great asylum for the insane. It was a world outside of the world, where realities had to be imagined and where, even through those excursions in illusions and hallucinations, there ran a strange loneliness. The world can never be so lonely in those places where the mind has never come as in a place where the mind has gone.... There was no one to ask about anything. There was no way to make a connec-

tion with 'life'.... Very early I had given up everyone except the
Insane. The others knew nothing about anything, or knew only
uninteresting facts. From the Insane I could get everything.
They knew everything about nothing and were my authority;
but beyond that there was silence. Who had made the pictures,
the books and the music of the world? And how had they made
them? And how could you tell the makers from just people? Did
they have a light around their heads? Were there any of them in
the world now? And would I ever see one?

Once she had written to a friend that she had seen "a little bit of
life that is hard to forget. A man, once handsome and robust, a
leader of men—now a shrunken doddering idiot—being led from
an outing back into his ward—his white-haired wife standing with
eyes shaded from the setting sun, watching him go. She comes
every day at this time and follows him about, hoping he may sometime recognize her, but he only curses and jabbers at her."

Early on Jane had shown artistic talent and after high school had
studied painting and jewelry design at the Art and Lewis Institutes of
Chicago. She acted in plays and did set design. Then she heard of the
Cordon—whose bylaws stated the group was "formed for the purpose of establishing a common meeting ground for lovers of independence and self-expression, whose vocations permit excursions beyond
domestic bonds"—and immediately joined. The Cordon, meaning
rope, was composed of young women from affluent families who had
an interest in the arts and other women.

In 1908 Jane met the first love of her life at a meeting of the
Cordon. She was Florence Reynolds, an alumnus of the art institute. They immediately formed a bond. It was about this time,
said Jane, that she began wearing men's clothes.

During the summers or when she was away, Jane wrote constantly to Florence, addressing her as "Tiny Heart." The letters
often spoke of the great love she felt for Florence. Once she
chided Florence for calling "our Love—Friendship—it has not
got to that has it? Isn't it very like the Love our friends the poets
sing about. I think it very strange and different from friendship or
just love with a little letter—don't you?"

As both were interested in art, it was always one focus of conversation. Presaging her role as co-editor with Margaret of the *Little Review*, Jane once wrote to Reynolds saying that artists would find relief from life if they "would seek within their own souls and create in their work a new beauty and a new idealism—one far and away beyond the reach of our contemporary life. They would find their relief [there] and not in religion—I don't believe there is relief there." In another letter she added, "I have been thinking very much these days of Beauty (poor name for anything so Holy). I know that if everyone felt Beauty strongly, felt that everything beautiful was God and all things not beautiful not God. That woman was the nearest symbol for Beauty. If one could see this—there would be no sin, or squalor, or unhappiness in the world."

In 1910 they decided to go to Europe and visit all the art museums. As Florence had a private income, they were able to stay for a year. Returning to Chicago, Jane got a job at the Art and Lewis Institutes teaching art. She continued to act and design sets for a local theater. After a time, her relationship with Florence wound down—though she and Reynolds remained good friends and even now often wrote to one another. Jane then fell in love with Alixe Bradley, a gorgeous woman who spurned her. Rejected and downcast, she had then met Margaret.

Georgette Leblanc told her story next. Georgette spoke in faltering English and so Margaret translated. Georgette was born in Rouen, France, in 1869. Her early life was as dramatic as her later life would be. Until recently, she said, she seemed to be unlucky in love. For example, when she was only sixteen her mother, dressing for a ball, had suddenly died in her arms. Some time later, a young suitor proposed to her but her father objected. The young man drank poison and died. She then married a Spaniard who squandered her dowry to pay off a gambling debt. But her greatest loss of love was to come much later.

Despite such horrible events, she had been blessed with a clear soprano voice and so in 1887 when she left Rouen for Paris, she was soon singing in the *Opéra Comique* in Paris. She was only eighteen.

Jean Cocteau had said of her—"Georgette was the model for a lyric saint—one of those strange great beings who move through the crowd, headless and armless, propelled only by the power of their souls, as immutable as the Victory of Samothrace."

Georgette had read an essay about Ralph Waldo Emerson, the American Transcendentalist, by the Belgian playwright Maurice Maeterlinck. She soon found she could think of nothing else but Maeterlinck's mystic vision and poetic style. In him, Georgette said, "I had discovered a tendency of mind, a vision, ideas and even a being whose secret inner existence corresponded to my own. I had not tried to find out what he was like, how he lived .... I had staked my life on a purely spiritual intention." Relinquishing a promising position with the opera, she confided to a friend she was "going to Belgium to become the wife of the great Maeterlinck."

In Brussels, she arranged an invitation to a supper party at which Maeterlinck would be present. Adorning her forehead with a blue diamond, which she regarded as a symbol of happiness, she quickly captivated the sober and reclusive playwright. Shortly thereafter, the twosome moved to Paris and launched a salon which attracted the front ranks of writers, composers and sculptors. In their living room could be found people like Anatole France, Mallarmé, Debussy and Rodin. Georgette acted in Maeterlinck's plays and, being of a philosophical and mystical bent herself, provided him with both inspiration and ideas.

But with the passage of years their differences grew. He began to criticize her theatricality and taste for picturesque costumes. For her part, she found him "in perpetual flight before emotion, before disturbances, before the unexpected."

In 1911, while acting in his play *The Blue Bird,* Georgette noticed Maeterlinck's attention was drawn to another member of the cast, an eighteen year old, Renée Dahon. At the playwright's invitation, the young woman moved in with them. Finally, in 1919, having spent some twenty years with Maeterlinck—the most productive of his career—Georgette finally left him. He soon married Dahon.

In 1923 when Georgette came to America, though her life with Maeterlinck had ended twelve years before, she still had not freed herself. She had come at the invitation of the Hearst newspapers which had offered a large sum for her memoirs and wanted her to become well-known to American audiences. Though she had been much acclaimed in Europe, particularly for singing *Thaïs* and *Carmen* and for her roles in Maeterlinck's plays, her career of late had begun to falter. When her poetry and singing recitals in Boston and elsewhere failed to win acclaim, Hearst withdrew its offer for her memoirs, as well as all financial support. She was stranded. It was 1924.

When she and Margaret first met, she was fifty-five and Margaret thirty-eight. Despite their age difference, she and Margaret had fallen in love and had been companions ever since. Margaret, who loved music and played well enough to have considered a career as a concert pianist, gave Georgette the encouragement she needed to resume giving recitals and accompanied her on the piano.

George Ivanovitch Gurdjieff she had first seen in February 1924, at a performance of his dance troupe. The following June she had gone with Margaret, Jane and Louise Davidson to meet him at his Institute for the Harmonious Development of Man at the Prieuré, located in Fontainebleau-en-Avon. However, no sooner had Georgette arrived than she left. Gurdjieff and his demands for work on oneself—to see oneself as one really is and not as one imagines—had been too great a shock. Within a few days, though, she saw she was in reaction and returned. Now, more open, Gurdjieff's being made an indelible impression on her. Said Georgette:

> He resided on the earth as a planet too limited for his own needs and function. Where did he manifest his real existence? In his teaching, in his writings, not at all in ordinary social life which he seemed to regard as a vast plague and manipulated with resignation or impatience.
>
> I was not astonished that he was little known, that he was not surrounded by thousands of followers. Neither money nor influence could open the doors of the Prieuré—

Gurdjieff created all possible obstacles to discourage any idler-spirits who might push their way into a world where they did not belong.

What astonished me was not to understand a little, but to see that some people—newcomers to the Prieuré—did not understand at all. I sometimes had flashes of 'consciousness' so strong that a heat invaded me. Every hour I became aware of a soul I had not nurtured.

Now with Gurdjieff no longer teaching, Georgette had joined Jane's group in the hope of learning about herself and becoming more present to life, rather than continuing her imaginings.

Jane told Georgette that by attempting to put her life into words, she had objectified what had heretofore been unexamined. What had been said was no longer buried, could no longer be dismissed. By her truthfulness she had made the past—her past—come alive. She had brought it into the present, made it active and real. With it came a vulnerability, a certain chaos, a feeling of being adrift at sea, alone and unprotected—what she had been avoiding all along because of the suffering it caused. And so her psychological structure, with all its defenses and buffers, had been shaken and had begun to break down. She no longer could calm herself with the idea that *she knew.* Now, she could be spoken to.

Jane said she would attempt to speak about the idea and experience of love. However, it would not be addressed in the usual indiscriminate way in which love is taken as being indivisible. Instead, she recounted how Gurdjieff had spoken of three types of love—instinctive, emotional and conscious. It is rare, Jane told Georgette and the rest of the group, that all three centers—physical, emotional, mental—function when one is in love. Usually, one is instinctively in love, emotionally in love or mentally in love. This love is fragmented, personal and subjective. It is the "love" of one center, not the love of three centers. Hence, it is not whole, impersonal, objective.

Jane asked Georgette: "Which of your three centers—intellectual, emotional, instinctive—was in love with Maeterlinck? How much did you love the image of yourself that he created with his words?—love yourself in him? The 'woman on a pedestal?'" Jane explained that "Infidelity is a sign that the physical center has grown indifferent." There could be a shift in the center of gravity so that "one was not, at the moment, mentally or perhaps emotionally in love with the beloved, thus taking one off one's guard and making one's organism unfaithful."

Jane continued—"Dismiss Maeterlinck from your mind and memory—*consciously.* You are allowing a mortgage to stand against your own development. When you speak of resentment, calumny, hatred shown towards you ... they are only the negative side of something you thought divine when it was manifesting itself positively. Do not stand back and register horror, surprise, or the inability to understand."

Janet Flanner spoke next. She was thirty-eight years old, her hair prematurely white, her face with its observant eyes and large nose giving her the countenance of a wise owl. She was born March 13, 1892, in Indianapolis, Indiana. The second of three sisters, her father was a mortician. His suicide a month before her twenty-first birthday had been a shock so deep that she had spoken of it seriously only to Solita and Hemingway, whose own father had committed suicide. Her Quaker religion had given her no answers, or at least no answers she could accept, and so she supposed she had become an agnostic. She had gone to college for a while but dropped out. She felt trapped. What passed for thinking in Indianapolis was too small, its life too ordinary. She had needed to leave, but how? Then along came William Lane Rehm, nicknamed "Rube," a high school classmate. He was then living in New York and had come home on a visit to see his parents. She had convinced Rehm to marry her, moved to New York with him, became pregnant, and then lost the baby.

That winter in New York, she had met Solita Solano, a drama critic for the *New York Tribune*. She was an exotic dark-haired beauty with intense blue eyes and a shapely figure. But what really resonated was Solita's independence of mind, her literary interests—both she and Janet wanted to become writers—and their joint belief that in romantic relationships each must give the other "absolute freedom." They quickly became inseparable partners. At some point Janet and Rehm separated but, because of the way it would look back home, did not divorce.

Because she had deceived Rehm, she judged herself "criminally guilty." Her actions, she felt, could not be defended. In the late 1920s, he had come to Paris and they had gotten a divorce. He seemed quite happy. Whatever face he might put on it, nevertheless, she knew what she had done. It was a blot she continued to be ashamed of.

After separating from Rehm, Janet had moved into Solita's Greenwich Village apartment. Life was wonderful but they both came to feel they needed a fresh start. So in 1921 when *National Geographic* sent Solita on assignment to Constantinople there was no question but that Janet would accompany her. From Turkey they travelled to Crete and then around Europe before eventually settling in Paris. In 1925 Janet became a foreign correspondent for *The New Yorker*, writing a regular column called "Letter from Paris" under the name of Genêt.

In 1926 Janet published a novel *The Cubical City*. It received mixed reviews and she started another novel but couldn't sustain the interest, and so gave all her time and attention to her Genêt articles for *The New Yorker*. Janet ended her story by saying that she and Solita continued to live together at the Hôtel Napoleon Bonaparte.

Jane tried to work with Janet but it never evolved beyond intellectual jousts. Though raised a Quaker, Janet was a materialist, putting all her belief in science. She wanted concrete, factual answers and when feelings and emotions arose, as her friends often noted, she tended to rationalize them. Intellectually centered, Janet was defended at all times against feelings (possibly strengthened as a reaction to her father's suicide).

By 1932 Janet Flanner had stopped coming to meetings. She had fallen in love with Noel Haskins Murphy, a stunning widow nearly six feet tall with high cheekbones and hay-colored hair.

Noel was well off, her family being involved with high finance and politics, and she spoke and acted in what Janet teased as Noel's "Pahk Avenue mahner." Noel lived in a stone house surrounded by eight-foot walls in the village of Orgeval just thirteen kilometers from St.-Germain-des-Prés.

Soon, Janet was spending more and more of her time with Noel in Orgeval. As Solita said—"Genêt... lives with me when she remembers it." Solita saw Noel as "a careless, flamboyant Amazon in bright shorts and skirts—or something the peasants had never seen before, either for costumes or formidable motoring energy."

Solita Solano talked next. She spoke French, Italian and Spanish fluently as well as a number of Malay languages. She had a passion for etymology. She tried to speak using words precisely and economically, but with her intensity she often talked rapidly, the impression being that at any moment her emotions might fly away with her. Not as defended as Janet, more questioning of her point of view, Solita was sensitive to herself and others, perhaps too much so. She enjoyed the experience of her emotions, even if the tendency was always to romanticize them.

She was born on October 30, 1888, in Troy, New York, and christened Sarah Wilkinson. Of an independent and rebellious nature, she had changed her name to Salita after her Spanish grandmother, although no legal record of the change exists, then changed it again to Solita. Her father was a lawyer who found his daughter's desire to be a writer-poet inappropriate and kept his library locked. When she was fifteen he died, leaving a will stipulating that if Solita married without her mother's written consent or, should she die, her younger brothers' consent, then Solita would lose her entire inheritance. On her sixteenth birthday, in rebellion, Solita married a local engineer and ran off with him to Shanghai. After four years of marriage, she ran away to New York City with hopes of making it in the theater. Only passable as an actress, in 1910 she moved to Boston and became a rookie reporter for the *Traveler*. Eight years later, in December 1918 she returned to New York as drama critic for the *New York Tribune*.

That winter she had met Janet Flanner. Three years later they had gone to Constantinople together and after some travel had arrived in Paris in the fall of 1922. Taken with the city's legendary beauty, culture and tolerance, she and Janet decided to make it their home. After several moves they finally found the Hôtel Napoleon Bonaparte, a five-story walk-up at 36 rue Bonaparte on the Left Bank. Here Solita and Janet would live together, though having a number of separate relationships, until the approach of the Second World War. They quickly fell in with the literary crowd. They became friends with Ernest Hemingway and F. Scott Fitzgerald, who often visited them at the Bonaparte and slept drunk in the hallway. Jean Cocteau lived at the hotel for a time, as did Sergei Nabokov, cousin of the writer, Vladimir. They attended not only the millionairess Natalie Barney's Friday afternoon salon but Gertrude Stein's Saturday salon (both Americans, one originally from Dayton, Ohio, the other from Allegheny, Pennsylvania) and, of course, regularly visiting Sylvia Beach's bookstore Shakespeare & Company and Adrienne Monnier's *La Maison des Amis des Livres*.

Solita and Janet made many friends, among them Nancy Cunard. Slender as a rapier, her long arms covered with ivory bracelets, Nancy was the exotic and rebellious poet, the daughter of the founder of the great English shipping line, and mistress of Louis Aragon, the Surrealist poet. Her face reminded Solita of Nefertiti's, with its proud eyes and fine taut mouth, the lips painted scarlet with a lipstick known as "The Eternal Wound," Though always ready to share her endearing gaiety, she "functioned best," said Solita, "in a state of fury in which, in order to defend, she attacked every windmill in a landscape of windmills." Angry at the injustice of the world, Nancy would proclaim—"I am not a Communist—I am an anarchist!" The women shared recipes, gossip, Nancy's mother's ("the Ladyship's) Vionnet and Poiret gowns sent to Nancy twice yearly from London, and literary opinions. And Nancy, though heterosexual, even convinced them to go "brotheling" with her.

Solita and Janet had both intended to support themselves writing free-lance articles while working on their novels. Solita's two novels, *The Uncertain Feast* (1924) and *The Happy Failure* (1925), warning of the destructive nature of jealousy and championing sexual freedom, while critically praised, had only slight sales. Janet continued to work on her novel, *The Cubical City*, but she wrote slowly and, while good at description, tended toward a preciousness of style. In the fall of 1925 Janet took a job as foreign correspondent for Harold Ross' start-up magazine, *The New Yorker*. Solita began to devote her time to editing Janet's articles and acting as her secretary. In 1929 Solita would publish one last novel, *The Way Up*, but sales were no better than they had been for her first two novels. Though she still continued to write free-lance articles, she never again seriously wrote for publication.

Living their belief in "absolute freedom," both Solita and Janet had a number of flings with other women, but nothing too serious. That changed on February 19, 1927. It was on that day Solita said that she had met Margaret Anderson. From the very first, it was an intense relationship. Solita brought Margaret to her and Janet's rooms on the top floor of the Hôtel Bonaparte. Though surprised, Janet had been quite kind to Margaret and understanding of their relationship.

Margaret often spoke to Solita about Gurdjieff and this new Fourth Way teaching he had brought. Finally, Solita's curiosity aroused, she gave in to Margaret's urging, and accompanied her to the Prieuré to meet Gurdjieff. Solita, who believed herself a keen judge of men, was monumentally unimpressed:

> I hoped for a demigod, a superman of saintly countenance, not this 'strange' *écru* man about whom I could see nothing extraordinary except the size and power of his eyes. The impact everyone expected him to make upon me did not arrive. In the evening I listened to a reading from his vaunted book [*All and Everything, First Series*]. It bored me. Thereupon I rejected him intellectually, although with good humor. Later in the study house (how annoyed I was that women were not allowed to smoke there). I heard the famous music, played, I believe, by Monsieur de Hartmann. This, almost from the first measures, I also rejected. A week or so later in Paris I accompanied Margaret and

Jane, who had not quite given me up, to a restaurant where *écrevisses* were the specialty which Mr. Gurdjieff was coming to eat with about twenty of his followers. He seated me next to him and for two hours muttered in broken English. I rejected his language, the suit he was wearing and his table manners; I decided that I rather disliked him.

Still, the ideas of the teaching interested her. Solita liked Jane Heap, finding in her everything she had not found in Gurdjieff, and so when it became known that Jane was starting a study group, she readily asked to join.

With that Solita ended her story.

Solita and Janet having finished their attempts to tell their life stories, Jane spoke to them of some of their more glaring self-deceptions. She wrote to Margaret:

> While you were away, I spoke to your backward friends. They will tell you that I was harsh. Harsh! If I had had a bath of acids and lye I would have scrubbed them through and through. I didn't mean to be brutal, but my feelings were so intense and so full of rejections that I hope the force carried. They won't show the letter, but I said I was afraid that the fret and friction of their one-dimensional, straight-jacket code of life would exhaust you. I said that they may call me any names they choose; that if my agony of spirit produced a seeming cruelty, at least cruelty was better than nagging insensitiveness, lack of realization, pettiness of life, and so on. If I could only get my hands on them and bang their heads together until they had some cause to be so unseeing and unthinking! Physical force is the only way through some unawarenesses.

Margaret Anderson spoke next. She lived for ideas, ecstatic experience, challenge, and conversation. She believed absolutely in her feelings, her intuition, her aesthetic judgment. And she loved firing questions, baiting, goading everyone to go beyond themselves. Margaret flew into everything like a Valkyrie, giving a sparkle and energy entirely hers. For Margaret, words came effortlessly, her voice having a light huskiness which in some way gave to the edges of her words an uncommon softness.

Margaret was born of Scotch-Dutch ancestry, Scotch on her father's side, Dutch on her mother's. She had been born Margaret Carolyn Anderson in Youngstown, Ohio, on November 24, 1886, and was the eldest of three daughters. Her father Arthur managed the city's utilities and trolley system. She grew up adoring her father and hating her mother, Jessie.

In Margaret's eyes her father was "a poignant man [who] talked like Lincoln" and cared very much for his family. Her father was kind, gentle and hard-working, mild mannered and ever accommodating to his wife who was given to nervousness and hypochondria and an obsessive need to control others. Her mother she saw as enjoying being a "victim of nerves." She did so, Margaret believed, because "it made everything disagreeable, and she was one of those persons who gets an infinite pleasure out of making things disagreeable." Margaret saw her sister Lois, who was considered the family humorist, as intelligent and sensitive but lacking her confidence and self-esteem. Jean, the youngest, who everyone called "Venus de Milo," Margaret saw as perpetually living in an adolescent world. A rebel to the bone, Margaret was always fighting for or about something and never admitted defeat. She was known to family members as "the Victory." She and her mother, alike in temperament but completely unlike in how they interpreted the world, clashed constantly, filling the home with tension.

As a child, Margaret remembered insisting to her mother that the word *ball* was spelled with the letter *o* and not an *a*. Her mother was equally insistent that she was wrong. Margaret was absolutely certain she was right because that was the way the word sounded. "My conviction was so intense," she said, "that I began to have a fearful pain in the heart. I thought I was going to choke or faint. To relieve this feeling I began to cry and shake my fists at the ceiling."

When her mother showed her the word's spelling in the dictionary, Margaret said, "for hours afterward I was so depressed that everyone was frightened. I couldn't very well explain, but I felt a resentment against God or man for having imposed an incredible stupidity upon the world. And the world had accepted it...."

Not only extremely combative, Margaret was also given to great enthusiasms, both characteristics rankling her mother— "Mother had always said that my enthusiasm on any subject sickened her." A Christian Scientist, her mother and she debated the merits of Mary Baker Eddy's teaching and of anarchism, Margaret's interest. Of course to no avail. "I would seriously waste hours," Margaret said, "contrasting the unchallengeable loftiness of anarchism with the virtues of Christian Science. I would urge her to remain a Christian Scientist if she would allow me to remain an anarchist. This would be considered illogical. Mother would spend the rest of the night denying the existence of evil but finding me very evil...."

Margaret said she left Western College for Women in Oxford, Ohio, the end of her freshman year to pursue a career as a pianist. In the fall of 1908 she, along with her sister Lois, moved to Chicago. Margaret supported herself by reviewing books for a religious weekly. These were not reviews as much as brief summaries for she said, "One afternoon I reviewed a hundred books in three hours—books I had never seen and of course had not time to read. One glance at the cover notes, another at the style, and I dictated sentence criticisms as follows: 'The alleged adventures of the supposedly typical American in foreign parts; execrable style but well adapted to family fireside reading.' And to think I was being paid for doing this kind of thing."

Next, Margaret landed a job as poetry editor with *The Dial,* a literary review founded by Edgar Allan Poe and then edited by Francis F. Browne. Here she learned the mechanics of magazine publishing—type composition, proofreading and make-up. She left because, as she said, "our poetry society had become too lyrical for Mr. Browne [the editor], who one day had been moved to kiss me. He was full of sincere and touching apologies the next day, but I was as sincerely displeased as he was contrite."

As part of the city's literary society, twenty-year-old Margaret was a regular at the literary salon of Floyd Dell, literary editor of the *Chicago Evening Post*. There she met Sherwood Anderson, John Cowper Powys and Theodore Dreiser. She liked Anderson for his storytelling but found Dreiser uninteresting. "Dreiser was never any good," Margaret opined, "until some exchange of sex magnetism put him at his ease." Margaret said that she remembered herself in those days as "a very unrelaxed person ... all my sex manifestations were expended in ideas." She said that when she listened to Dreiser speaking with other women, ones with whom he could a establish "a quick sex sympathy," even then his conversation bored her. "Sex display," she said, "puts you at your best if you're a tempered human being—becomes responsible for wit. But Dreiser had not more wit than a cow."

By 1913 Margaret had become book critic for the *Chicago Evening Post*. She soon found herself bored but didn't know what was wrong. "I had been curiously depressed all day. In the night I wakened. First precise thought: I know why I'm depressed—nothing inspired is going on. Second: I demand that life be inspired every moment. Third: the only way to guarantee this is to have inspired conversation every moment. Fourth: most people never get so far as conversation; they haven't the stamina, and there is no time. Fifth: if I had a magazine I could spend my time filling it up with the best conversation the world has to offer. Sixth: marvelous idea—salvation. Seventh: decision to do it. Deep sleep."

At a party at Floyd Dell's, she met Dewitt Wing, a young man who liked her idea of starting a magazine and agreed to pay the office rent and printing costs from his small salary. And so in March 1914 Margaret Anderson published the first edition of the *Little Review*. Its logo read, "A Magazine of the Arts, Making No Compromise with the Public Taste." The magazine was to be "a crusade which would prove the superiority of the artist mind over the intellectual mind." She saw a war between emotion and intellect throughout society and she clearly was on the side of emotion. Said Margaret:

> I didn't consider intellectuals intelligent. I never liked them or their thoughts about life. I defined them as people who care nothing for argument, who are interested only in

information; or as people who have a preference for learning things rather than experiencing them. They have opinions but no point of view. They are so articulate that you wonder if their words reflect their thoughts.... I am indifferent to acquisition, I value experience—a receiving station. This is the gulf between intellectuals and me—the reason why they consider my type dilettante and amateur, why my type considers them dilettante and amateur.

When Margaret believed in something she was irrepressible and so quickly sold some $450 in ads for the new magazine. Writers and artists soon flocked to it, though the magazine could never afford to pay for contributions. The *Little Review* published poets and writers like James Joyce, Djuna Barnes, William Butler Yeats, Ezra Pound, Ernest Hemingway, Sherwood Anderson and Gertrude Stein; artists like Pablo Picasso, Constantin Brancusi, Marcel Duchamp, and Jean Cocteau; and anarchists like Emma Goldman.

"I was born to be an editor," Margaret said. "I always edit everything." This included rooms, people's clothes, tones of voice, laughter, words, gestures and so forth. She was always remaking the world in her own perception. "It is this incessant, unavoidable observation, this need to distinguish and impose, that has made me an editor. I can't make things. I can only revise what has been made. And it is this eternal revising that has given me my nervous face."

In June, three months after the first edition of the *Little Review,* her father, mother and sister Jean had moved to Chicago, taking an apartment across the hall from Margaret's. Family life went on as usual. Then came the first day of September. It was her father's fiftieth birthday, a date he had always feared. His life, he felt, had come to nothing. Though he made good money, his wife and daughters had lived a life of extravagance, so the family had no savings. How would they get on? One evening while playing bridge with his wife and another couple in their apartment he had suddenly thrown his cards on the table and laughed foolishly and for a full minute had talked incomprehensibly... then picked up the cards again as if nothing had happened and acted normally.

He had no memory of the outburst of his subconscious. Soon he was in a sanitarium and the following June, 1915, he died.

Of her mother, Margaret said: "She wanted *nothing in particular* and *got that* by trying and succeeding to foil *everything in particular* that any one else wanted. By this charming little system she killed my father." Of her father:

> He was at least "conscious" to the degree of knowing that he was a "wanter" but that he was not destined to be a "getter." He fought for a long time... but when he finally saw that he could not succeed, and when he foresaw the disaster that could easily come upon us all he took the only escape that was offered him: insanity.
>
> His sense of responsibility was just a terrible and terrifying instinct. It had never been trained into a preservation or a defense—never given a moment's intelligent help by anybody. His mother put it upon him before he was born (she had just been deserted by a delightful husband minus a sense of responsibility). Dad, *at birth,* was to be her solution and savior!
>
> Talk of cruelty! This is why Dad spent the day of his fiftieth birthday in an agony that none of us could understand—except dimly. Fifty stood for age. Age was coming upon him and he had not done, and was now really afraid that he could not do, the things necessary to insure our protection and happiness. The "thing he wanted" was *happiness for everybody.* It was the obsession of his life: ran through every gesture he made.

When he went insane, said Margaret, "All his first delusions were that he was hiring all his friends and all the husbands of mother's friends, and even the family washer-woman's husband, etc., on salaries of a million dollars a year—so that all their problems would be solved and the result [would be] eternal happiness."

A month after his death Margaret said she and her mother had a final confrontation. It went on and on for hours. "Her ultimatum," Margaret said, "was that I must not live my life, think my thoughts, publish my magazine. I must live her life as dad had done." Margaret of course refused and of course her mother withdrew all financial support and returned to Indianapolis, but Margaret's sister Jean stayed on. She joined the magazine's staff which was comprised of Margaret and her unpaid companion Harriet Dean, a recent graduate of Vassar.

Subscriptions continued to rise. However, Margaret's essays about the virtues of anarchism caused a large decline in advertising. Characteristically, Margaret fought back. She said: "I donated a page to every firm that should have advertised and didn't—a full page with a box in the center, stating why that particular concern should have recognized us." The magazine's former advertisers were neither cowed nor amused.

Living became increasingly hand to mouth. At this time her sister Lois, "bored," Margaret said, "with her husband's self-importance," showed up along with her two sons, Tom and Arthur. Lois had divorced her husband eighteen months after the birth of her youngest son, Arthur (later named "Fritz") and now looked to support herself and her children by taking a position with the *Little Review.* Of course she was welcome, but a salary was out of the question.

To make ends meet the four women—Margaret, Harriet, Jean and Lois and her two boys—embarked on a circuitous path that first took them to a cottage in Lake Bluff, a village thirty miles from Chicago. There, they got through the winter but by spring found they could not pay rent and eat, too. Margaret had one of her brainstorms—camp out on Chicago's North Shore and live rent-free!

People often accused Margaret of being unreal. But she said: "What have I been so unreal about? I have never been able to accept two great laws of humanity—that you're always being suppressed if you're inspired and always being pushed into a corner if you're exceptional. I won't be cornered and I won't stay suppressed."

By May she had talked the others into pitching tents on an unpopulated beach. Notwithstanding its peril and precariousness, it was a glorious time. As Margaret recounted it:

> I was often up at sunrise. The first gesture of the day was to rush into a tent [they had taken to sleeping under the stars],

change from pajamas to bathing suit, plunge into a cold lake, run on the beach. Then a fire of brushwood, a breakfast of coffee, bacon, fruit, an egg (if we were lucky). Then the ritual of the first morning cigarette, and then the ritual of dressing. At this point in the *Little Review's* fortunes I possessed one blouse, one hat and one blue tailored suit. The blouse could be made to serve two days. Then I washed it—by moonlight or by sunrise....We accepted the rain as an adventure and splashed along the shore line. The storms were sometimes so violent, the blackness so overwhelming, that only in the flashes of lightning could we see to what depth we were wading in the lake. I would squeeze a few buckets of water from my suit, pat it gently into shape, hang it on a cord in my tent and go downtown the next morning looking immaculate." Then she adds with a characteristic flourish—"I remember these storms usually happened late at night, giving us an excuse for midnight swimming." As wonderful as Margaret found these experiences, Lois soon tired of camp life and married for a second time, taking Tom and Arthur with her. With winter setting in, Harriet had had enough and left. Margaret and Jean packed up and moved into conventional quarters in November.

In February 1916 into Margaret's life walked a woman who instantly captivated her. Margaret had started the *Little Review* to publish the world's best conversation and in Jane Heap she found "the world's best talker." Trying to describe what she meant, Margaret explained: "It isn't a question of words, facility, style. It isn't a question of erudition. It isn't even a question of truth. (Who knows whether what she says is true?) It is entirely a question of ideas. No one can find such interesting things to say on any subject. I have often thought I should like to give my life over to talk-racing, with my money on Jane. No one else would ever win—you can't win against magic. What it is exactly—this making of ideas—I don't know. Jane herself doesn't know. 'Things become known to me,' she says."

She and Jane soon developed an intense relationship of polarity; Margaret living from the emotional center, Jane the mental. They cut an unusual sight on Chicago's boulevards, Margaret so beautiful and chic in tailored clothes and Jane, very mannish in appearance, a certain Mongolian cast to her face. One man called Jane "the first full-blown Lesbian case I ever saw." That wasn't what Margaret saw. "My Jane," she said, had "handsome features, strongly cut, rather like those of Oscar Wilde in his only beautiful photograph."

In Jane, Margaret saw an artist without pretensions who was *not* out to change the world or convince others of her opinions— "I hate propaganda," she had told Margaret, when offered the co-editorship of the *Little Review.* Nevertheless, Margaret's ardor and incessant arguments eventually wore her down. Or perhaps, and more likely, Margaret said, Jane could think of nothing better to do. Margaret loved to go to parties and salons and get into her version of conversation in which she said that she was "the buzz" and Jane was "the sting." For her part, Jane said that "Margaret carries me about under her arm like a fighting cock ... and throws me into every ring she sees. And she sees nothing but rings." Many thought that Jane liked the challenge but Margaret said that Jane "never had the sardonic pleasure in it that was often attributed to her. She regarded the pricking of the bubbles of self-illusion—helping people to distinguish between wish-fulfillment and reality—as essential to the race."

Jane, on the rebound from an affair, needed something new. And what could be more new than Margaret and the *Little Review.* Jane was blessed with an exceedingly sharp intellect that could penetrate to the essence of a situation or person. She was a natural complement to Margaret's intuition and enthusiasm. Jane challenged and pushed Margaret to define her feelings and insights. She told her—"Martie, you should know more." Jane not only brought more focus to the *Little Review* but gave it a strong and contemporary graphic quality. Most important, they both, said Margaret, were in "total agreement about what is, and what wasn't, Art." Jane came to express this in a formula: "To express the emotions of life is to live. To express the life of emotions is to make art."

That spring the California millionairess Aline Barnesdale— whom Margaret jokingly called "Nineteen Millions"—invited

Margaret to visit her in her home in Mill Valley, Marin County, just north of San Francisco. Despite Margaret's knowing Nineteen Millions had no liking for Jane, Margaret invited Jane to come along. They boarded the Canadian Pacific with just five dollars between them and several baskets of food. Discovering that two had arrived on her doorstep rather than one, Nineteen Millions, red-faced and angry, refused to honor her invitation. Margaret, loving Marin's great natural beauty of mountain, bay and ancient redwood forests, intended to stay. Fortuitously, she received a check for a small inheritance from her grandmother's estate and rented a studio on the side of Mount Tamalpais. Here, as Margaret said, Jane and she "could talk, undisturbed, for five months.... My mind was inflamed by Jane's ideas because of her uncanny knowledge of the human composition, her unfailing clairvoyance about human motivation. This was what I had been waiting for, searching for, all my life."

Margaret said Jane had a sense for looking beyond the surface into the essence of people and things. It often got mixed with her own personal biases but often it was on target. In Jane Heap she said that she had seen no more highly organized mental-emotional equipment anywhere. "I had chosen her mind as representative of what I called the creative mind. I wanted the *Little Review* to reflect this point of view above any other."

But Margaret found that Jane had little interest in writing and she had to go to all ends to convince her. Said Margaret: "The process of encouraging Jane to put down on paper the things she said consisted, first, of reiterating the impossibility of such a feat; second, of regretting the lack of money which prevented us from installing a dictaphone; third, of assuring her I could take down her conversation in long hand; fourth, of convincing her that she needn't turn self-conscious about it; fifth, that—well, that everything would be wonderful."

Their long California summer interlude was, for the most part, idyllic. Margaret was able to get a loan of a Mason and Hamlin piano and also for five dollars to buy a horse which she rode through the redwoods of nearby Muir Woods. They attended local anarchist meetings, talked into the wee hours in their paja-mas, had fudge breakfasts and, as Margaret put it, had "intellec-tual combats." Although Margaret claimed to have been born with "a gentle nature, a flexible character and an organism as equilibrated as it is judged hysterical," she loved and, it might be said, lived for the verbal battle. "I had never been able to under-stand why people so dislike to be challenged," she explained. "For me challenge has always been the great impulse, the only libera-tion." Jane, more in command of herself and her argument, gen-erally gave much more than she got. Eventually their talk explored what Margaret called "the psychology of combat." Jane taught her new ways of defending herself, how to use words and gauge an audience.

"I assimilated it," said Margaret. "And I have almost never been able to use it." But, Margaret explained, she had an altogether dif-ferent reason for talking. It wasn't to convince others or to win an argument but to evoke her own ideas. When Jane said her tech-nique was too infantile, Margaret told her "my object in talking is neither to learn nor to convey but to enter into new emotional states, since I can't produce ideas unless they are forced out of me by an emotional explosion, I have gone on all my life being infantile."

In California the famous issue of the *Little Review* with all sixty-four pages *completely empty,* save for two pages of Jane's drawings, was produced. The reason, explained Margaret, was that since no art was being produced, the editors would publish only blank pages.

Wherever she went, Margaret—beautiful, outspoken, outgo-ing and sometimes outrageous—easily magnetized both men and women. Jane, possessive and jealous, had had to suffer through Harriet Dean at the *Little Review,* then Emma Goldman and here in California, Nineteen Millions. Margaret said it was in Califor-nia that the darker side of Jane's nature became all too self-evi-dent. Jane brooded, sulked, pouted, and had a need to dominate and torment. As Jane kept a revolver in her trunk, her bouts of jealousy and threats of suicide could never be taken as mere talk.

That fall the women returned to Chicago. Margaret began a correspondence with Ezra Pound in London and she sent him a copy of the *Little Review*, asking for his opinion. Pound supplied polite encouragement and suggested they eliminate typographical "horrors" by not printing until the galleys were proofed, a chore Margaret had blithely ignored. Pound put the word out around London about the magazine and sent in subscriptions. Finally he wrote to suggest that he become the foreign editor of the *Little Review*. He said he wanted "an official organ ... a place where I and T. S. Eliot can appear once a month (or once an 'issue') and where James Joyce can appear when he likes, and where Wyndham Lewis can appear if he comes back from the war." Margaret and Jane gladly agreed. The accord made, Pound, a poet with a rare nose for the mercantile and self-promotion, then asked that he and his friends be allotted two pages of editorial per issue. In exchange, though he could offer no money, he knew an anonymous patron (John Quinn, a lawyer with strong political connections and a Joyce enthusiast) who would pay contributors, and Margaret and Jane could keep all money from the new subscriptions that would be generated. And so the magazine was remade in the triadic force of Margaret, Jane and Ezra. It was to prove to be a primordial ferment that made the *Little Review* like no other of its kind, before or since. Soon the magazine was publishing not only Pound but Ernest Hemingway, T. S. Eliot, Wyndham Lewis, John Rodker, Ford Maddox Ford and, of course, James Joyce.

Margaret, feeling that the magazine had reached its limit in Chicago, began to think of moving it to New York. With 1916 ending, Margaret felt, "It was time to touch the greatest city of America. It would then be time for Europe. The only way to make the L.R. [*Little Review*] the international organ I had planned was to publish it from New York where our position would be more commanding. We hadn't yet met all the interesting people in the world."

Preparation for leaving Chicago put Jane, said Margaret, in "days of a coma of regret and indecision." But Margaret pressed ahead and in 1917 the women boarded the train for New York. Once ensconced in a hotel, Jane—who had refused to look out the taxi window—took immediately to bed. Finally, Jane revived and the women found a basement studio for twenty-five dollars a month which lay just at the perimeter of Greenwich Village at 31 West 14th. Later, they moved to 24 West 16th where they found a four room apartment and Margaret again got the loan of a piano. To conserve the little money they had, the women avoided bars and restaurants, cut each other's hair, cooked, sewed, made their own clothing, and continually did without. Their apartment soon became a notable and lively literary salon where writers, poets and painters could read and discuss their work. Margaret always attempted to stir the waters to get some decent conversation going.

A shock came when all four thousand copies of an issue of the *Little Review* were burned for obscenity by the United States Post Office. Their publication of James Joyce's *Ulysses* would only inflame the government. Ezra Pound had spoken of his admiration for James Joyce and one morning a package from Joyce arrived. Margaret said she "opened the package, read the beginning pages and came upon the passage speaking of the *ineluctable modality of being* ...." Then Margaret said, "As I read *signatures of all things I am here to read*, I felt like crying. I called out to Jane who was in the next room, 'This is too beautiful. We must publish it right away.' Jane read it and was terribly moved."

A few days later someone asked Margaret—"But what you mean? Do you understand it?"

"I didn't think of what it means," said Margaret. "'Ineluctable modality' were two words not in my vocabulary; and I don't know what 'seaspawn' and 'seawrack' are. All I know is Joyce has produced a paragraph of great prose—in other words, Art."

The following year, in March 1918, the *Little Review* began to publish James Joyce's *Ulysses*. It ran monthly for three years, twenty-three parts appearing, and for alleged obscenity four times the United States Post Office, said Margaret, "turned the magazine to ashes. It was like a burning at the stake as far as I was concerned. The care we had taken to preserve Joyce's text intact; the worry over the bills that accumulated when we had no advance funds; the technique I used on printer, bookbinders, paper houses—tears, prayers, hysterics or rages—to make them push ahead without a guarantee of money; the addressing, wrapping, stamping, mailing; the excitement of anticipating the world's response to the literary masterpiece of our generation ... and then a notice from the Post Office: *Burned.*"

Margaret was always "chronically intense," she said. Perhaps in need of romantic stimulation, she began an affair, a small fling, that year with a Chicago friend's young niece, Gladys Tilden, who was in New York pursuing an acting career. Though Margaret professed to not be in love with Gladys, Jane's sulking was so intense that Margaret wrote to Jane's former lover, Florence Reynolds. Older than both Margaret and Jane and a large contributor to the magazine, both women addressed her as "Mother."

"What is the matter with me?" Margaret asked. "I feel a bondage that I'm impelled to break even if it entails an ultimate loss, the sacrifice of something I wouldn't and shouldn't be without. I can see no perfect plan of adjusting it all—restoring one's personal freedom (perhaps I should say one's impersonal freedom—the very breathing of air that is not poisoned by 'meaning')—but when we discussed a plan of separate living that seemed to allow of all this and the sharing of interest as well, it developed later that it was one of the things that distressed her."

In 1918, Margaret and Jane met Djuna Barnes. Though only twenty-six years old, Djuna was already a well-known journalist and an aspiring writer. She took a very direct approach to journalism. For example, she submitted herself first to be force-fed and then wrote "How It Feels to Be Forcibly Fed." But journalism only paid the bills. Her great desire was to be a writer. Margaret and Jane recognized her talent and soon the *Little Review* published her "A Night Among the Horses," the first of what would be many stories and poems.

For the first year or so of Djuna's relationship with Margaret and Jane, all went well. Each had talent, was well-read and in the

31

thick of literary life. Djuna and Margaret, Jane said, were very much alike in appearance. Both were tall, stylish redheads, though Margaret, always very aware of the power of appearance, had dyed her hair blond. Djuna's beauty and intelligence rivaled, if not exceeded, Margaret's.

Djuna, high-strung, bold-voiced, sharp-tongued, was also very private concerning herself and her past. After ecstasy, conversation was Margaret's greatest love. She liked wide open, no-holds barred conversations that went deep and exposed much. Djuna, though known, even feared, for her acerbic wit, came to exasperate Margaret. "Djuna would never talk," complained Margaret, "she would never allow herself to be talked to. She said it was because she was reserved about herself. She wasn't, in fact, reserved—she was unenlightened.... It embarrassed her to approach impersonal talk about the personal element. It embarrassed us to attempt a relationship with anyone who was not on speaking terms with her own psyche. Her mind had no abstract facets."

Jane and Djuna, attracted to one another, soon began a romance. This, of course did not measurably improve the conversation between Djuna and Margaret. A friend of Jane's described a meeting in a restaurant between Djuna and Margaret:

"Djuna took me over to a table where a mousy girl, Margaret Anderson, was dining with some friends. Djuna began hissing, 'I hate you, I hate you, I hate you' over and over again. The tan mouse smiled sweetly but there was an electric spark in her smile and they had an ominously quiet, violent fight before Djuna stalked out with that long stride of hers."

In any event, Jane said that she and Djuna broke up. Djuna said of Jane—"Deep personal madness." To which Margaret replied—"Deep personal knowledge—a supreme sanity."

In October 1920, the Society for the Suppression of Vice served papers on a bookstore for selling the *Little Review* to a minor. The Society took Margaret and Jane to court over their printing of *Ulysses*. John Quinn, the lawyer who helped support the *Little Review,* agreed to defend Margaret and Jane. Like many men before him Quinn found Margaret "a damned attractive young woman, one of the handsomest I have ever seen, very high-spirited, very courageous and very fine." He was less impressed with Jane who he termed "a typical Washington "." Though Quinn made a formidable defense, the women were fined one hundred dollars and fingerprinted as criminals. Before placing a finger on the ink pad, Margaret rose up to her full height and declared to the clerk that she would not stain her hands with their filthy ink until she was given "a cake of very good soap, a bottle of very good Eau de Cologne, and a very clean towel." The clerk dutifully complied. Margaret ceremoniously extended her fingers and left the courtroom laughing.

In the early 1920s wild stories of expatriate Americans on Paris' Left Bank had filtered across the ocean and in 1921 *McCall's* magazine sent Djuna to report on site. Her reputation as a journalist and serious writer preceded her. Only twenty-eight, she had already published more than a hundred articles, forty-five short stories, and some twenty-five short plays. She took a flat on the Left Bank along the Boulevard Saint-Germain close to the Brasserie Lipp, the Coupole bar and the Café des Deux Magots where the American crowd hung out as well as the Dôme and the Rotonde in Montparnasse. In New York she had met the astringent poet Robert McAlmon who was now a key figure in expatriate circles. A friend of Hemingway, Ezra Pound, William Carlos Williams and Joyce, McAlmon was once near penniless. Now he was well off after a divorce from the daughter of a wealthy English shipping magnate. He used the money from his divorce settlement to publish his own writing and the poems and prose of his friends. He knew everyone and introduced Djuna around. Djuna interviewed many of the avant garde, including Joyce. He had a high regard for her and gave her a bound and personally inscribed copy of the proof sheets of *Ulysses*.

The constant uncertainty and struggle for money, the conservative establishment's literary assaults on the *Little Review* in the *New York Times* and other newspapers finally began to eat deep. Said Margaret: "By 1922 I knew that I had had enough of one type of struggle. For a number of years life had had the aspect of a polar expedition—all life serving only to maintain life. It was time to change such an existence. It was time to bring the *Little Review* to an end." But Jane wanted to continue. Her interest and energy dwindling, Margaret groused but persevered.

In 1923 an unexpected event put more weight on her dwindling energies than Margaret could withstand. Margaret's sister Lois had a nervous breakdown and was hospitalized. With Margaret's mother, her father, now with her sister—a type of nervousness seemed to run in her family. "Lois is really me—only less so," said Margaret. Both were very intelligent and sensitive but, as Margaret saw it, never allowed to develop. "The only training we three received when we were young," recounted Margaret, "was to conceal, control, or destroy our particular brand of sensitivity. We were never taught to develop it—or how—or for what purpose. We weren't even told or taught to *exercise* it.... I had *at least* the physical constitution of a horse and could dominate my wounded sensibility *at least* until I got to the place where I could direct my own life, in my own ridiculous but pleasing way—to the point *at least* of acquiring those conditions necessary for the expenditure of that sensibility."

No one knew when Lois' state would be improved enough for her to return home. With the stepfather, a Chicago attorney, either unable or unwilling to care for his stepsons, Fritz and Tom, Margaret agreed to take them in. The oddness in those days of two lesbians raising two young boys, the extreme differences in temperament and age, and all the attendant tensions and uncertainty involving the boys' mother—it was not a situation conducive to harmony. (Years later Fritz wrote: "To this day, I am not at all sure why Margaret and Jane took on this responsibility. It was a strange form of 'planned parenthood' for two women neither of whom, it seemed to me, would have wished to have children of their own, and a mixed blessing from any point of view.")

While Margaret met her sisterly obligation by taking the boys, it was Jane who had to raise them. Margaret had always been clear about marriage, husbands and children—she wanted no part of them.

The boys arrived in New York feeling unloved—"like pieces of unwanted luggage for which storage space was needed," as Fritz later recounted. Raising Tom apparently was no problem for Jane but she and Fritz waged relentless battles. Usually psychological, their fights sometimes spilled over into the physical. One day, for example, Jane became so frustrated with Fritz's intransigence that she pulled a board from a crate—with the nails still in it, unfortunately—and hit him with it. Wrote Fritz of the board incident: "Jane lost that one (or I won it, depending on how you look at it) because although the nails went all the way into my back and I was bleeding, I did not break down, cry or otherwise participate in the scene. Jane was more contrite, fell to her knees, hugged me and begged my forgiveness. I think that was the first time that my born 'rage to live' turned into active hatred. I told her that I would not only not forgive her—'It was not my province' was one of the things I said—but I told her that I would get even. I regret, in the long run, to have to admit that I did. On the same compulsive, unconscious, dreary level."

The two boys were very different in temperament and size. Tom, older and bigger, liked to fight while Fritz, younger, smaller, and more intellectual, did not. It was Jane's idea that to end the constant bickering and rivalry they should intentionally fight one another. Wrote Fritz: "Jane [psychologically] fastened on an unconscious drama that satisfied her—and perhaps Tom's—needs. We were ordered to have a fight, dressed only in shorts, to see who could beat whom up. I—in a rage—explained that it was no solution to fight physically and that I wouldn't. This seemed to please both Tom and Jane and the result was that I was beaten up. Jane finally stopped the 'fight' when I was bleeding badly, led me to the bathroom where I could bleed into the bathtub and when the bleeding stopped, ordered me to clean the bathtub."

It didn't help that Lois' boys came into the women's lives when they did. The physical attraction Margaret and Jane had felt for each other had waned, and the unending struggle to keep the *Little Review* alive had continued to sap Margaret's energy. On both counts—ending their love affair and the magazine—Margaret found Jane's resistance "staggering." Always subject to nervousness, Margaret had always managed to hold her "nerves in control." Now her subconscious erupted full force. Like Lois, she had a nervous breakdown. Fortunately, Margaret was as practical as she was aesthetic, and it was only a number of months until she was well again. But it was a signal—Margaret's old life was ending and a new one beginning.

Cover of the *Little Review* special issue devoted to Frank Stella

STELLA NUM

A typical issue of the *Little Review* featured avant-garde writers, some of whom would become cultural icons

AUTUMN **1924**

LITTLE REVIEW

WINTER **1925**

AN INTERNATIONAL JOURNAL OF ART AND LETTERS

A REVIEW OF

JUAN **GRIS**

NUMBER

PAINTING. SCULPTURE. DESIGN. ARCHITECTURE. PROSE. POETRY. MUSIC. DANCE. DRAMA, NOTES ON THE THEATRE. MUSIC-HALL. CINEMA. CIRCUS. SPORTS. BOOKS. AND ON THE TRIUMPHS. EXPERIMENTS. CRIMES OF THE MODERN ART WORLD

75 CENTS

$3.00 YEARLY

COLLABORATING IN THIS NUMBER—
E. HEMINGWAY—JEAN TOOMER—R. McALMON—G. STEIN—GEORGE ANTHEIL—P. de MASSOT—R. CREVEL—PICABIA—RIBEMONT·DESSAIGNES—N.ASCH—D.RICHARDSON—F.LÉGER—PAUL ELUARD—PRAMPOLINI—ETC.

The editors of
the *Little Review*

Jane Heap

Margaret Anderson

Solita Solano

Georgette Leblanc

Djuna Barnes in Paris

New York, Paris & the Prieuré

NEW YORK. 1923. MARGARET HAD A NERVOUS BREAKDOWN. IT WAS THE LOWEST POINT IN HER LIFE. THE NINE YEARS OF fighting to keep the *Little Review* alive had taken their toll.... The fights with Jane, the jealousies, and now having to take in Lois' kids, she was forced to be what she insisted she would never be— a mother! It was too much. She saw nothing but darkness and gave in to a severe depression.

Then four strangers entered Margaret's life, one after another. Their impact was so great that if one's life was seen as an octave, these four strangers would radically change the trajectory of her life's octave. Within months, she would give up the *Little Review,* end her romantic relationship with Jane, and find both her life's teacher and the second great love of her life.

In December 1923, William Butler Yeats came to New York at the invitation of John Quinn, the lawyer who had defended Margaret and Jane in the *Ulysses* trial. A magnificent poet and an early contributor to the *Little Review,* the tall, bespectacled Irishman and magician—he was a member of the Golden Dawn, a magical society—gave readings and attended parties, meeting the American literati of the day. Margaret's long-smoldering desire to go to Europe was rekindled after hearing Yeats' stories of James Joyce, Ezra Pound and other artistic rebels on the European scene. Then came the second stranger—A. R. Orage, who told of an ancient esoteric teaching of self-development and conscience and the powerful teacher who had brought it. And then appeared the third stranger, the teacher himself—George Ivanovitch Gurdjieff.

She had never heard of Gurdjieff or his ideas until in the early 1920s she had read P. D. Ouspensky's *Tertium Organum*—a book she believed written by "a great mind." Ouspensky was a Russian student of Gurdjieff's who now lived in England. The first time she heard someone knowledgeably speak about Gurdjieff and his ideas was in January 1923, when fifty-one-year-old Alfred Richard Orage was sent to New York by Gurdjieff. Orage, a renowned English literary critic and the former editor of the highly esteemed *New Age*, a London literary and political magazine, had given up his career to follow Gurdjieff.

Orage had come to proselytize for his teacher and was lecturing in bookstores such as the Sunwise Turn, speaking of the ancient teaching of the Fourth Way and Gurdjieff's Institute for the Harmonious Development of Man by which he hoped to propagate the teaching. Both Margaret and Jane attended Orage's talks as did many of the city's intelligentsia, including novelists Jean Toomer and Zona Gale, critics Gorham Munson, John O'Hara Cosgrave and Schuyler Jackson, and *New Yorker* writer Muriel Draper.

Of Orage, Margaret said: "He was tall and easy, but quick and sure—the most persuasive man I have ever known. He sat down and began to tell, simply, why he had come." Afterward, the women went with Orage to Childs Restaurant and peppered him with questions. "By midnight," said Margaret, "we had learned that this doctrine would not fulfill our hopes, it would exceed them."

In late January Gurdjieff himself arrived from France with a troupe of students. The first demonstration was at Lesley Hall on 83rd Street just west of Broadway. The program chiefly consisted of an introduction by Orage followed by group and solo dances from Central Asia, piano music played by Thomas de Hartmann, a noted Russian composer, sets of obligatory exercises and demonstrations of various kinds of magic and tricks.

In Gurdjieff, Margaret divined—

> a messenger between two worlds, a dark man with an oriental face, whose life seemed to reside in his eyes. He had a presence impossible to describe because I had never encountered another with which to compare it. In other words, as one would immediately recognize Einstein as a 'great man,' we immediately recognized Gurdjieff as the kind of man we had never seen—a seer, a prophet, a messiah?... What philosophers have taught as 'wisdom,' what scholars have taught in texts and tracts, what mystics have taught through ecstatic revelation, Gurdjieff would teach as a science—an exact science of man and human behavior—a supreme science of God, world, man—based on sources outside the scope, reach, knowledge or conception of modern scientists and psychologists.

She said Jean Toomer, who had studied the Alexander Technique, a method of physical integration, had been equally taken with Gurdjieff. When he first saw Gurdjieff, Toomer had said: "I saw this man in motion, a unit in motion. He was completely of one piece. From the crown of his head down the back of the head, down the neck, down the back and down the legs, there was a remarkable line. Shall I called it a gathered line? It suggested coordination, integration, knitness, power.... I was fascinated by the way the man walked. As his feet touched the floor there seemed to be no weight on them at all—a glide, a stride, a weightless walk."

Another friend of Margaret's was the critic and editor Gorham Munson. He had written to a friend of Gurdjieff's coming:

> The sensation in New York for the past month has been the visit of Gurdjieff, Orage, and a troupe of pupils from Fontainebleau. They came unheralded, give out no addresses, assign no purpose for their visit, and put on quite suddenly demonstrations for invited audiences. It is the very devil to find out when and where they are demonstrating, and it is the very devil to get admitted. At last, however, Lisa [Munson's wife] and I were placed on their list. I have seen two demon-

strations and heard three lectures. The dancing is quite undreamed of. Ritual dances from the East, temple dances of esoteric cults, monastic experiences. I have never seen so much complexity, contradiction, and detailed variety held together in an unaccountable unity. It is a dance of design (of complicated geometry) rather than of motion. Strictly impersonal. Also there are demonstrations of tricks, semi-tricks, possibly thought-transference, and these have been concentration tests. Gurdjieff is the most powerful man I have ever seen: God or Satan himself—almost. Everyone is talking—literati, society, little girls—amazing rumors spread.

The fourth stranger to enter Margaret's life was Georgette Leblanc. No sooner had Margaret been introduced to Georgette than she became entranced. Of their first meeting she wrote: "Ah, I said [to myself] when I first saw her marvelous mystic face: this is the land I have been seeking; I left home long ago to discover it— a new continent, an unearthly place, the great world of art." Margaret, seventeen years younger, gave Georgette new inspiration and *élan vital*. Soon, she was accompanying Georgette on the piano during recitals.

In Georgette, Margaret had discovered, "My basic happiness was founded on this fact—this unmatchable fact: that one sometimes finds a human being with whom one can have a true and limitless human communication. The words for this blessing are 'love' or 'understanding.'" Georgette was someone about whom Margaret at once felt—"There is something perfect in her soul."

Margaret told Georgette of her interest in Gurdjieff and his teaching, and that she wanted to visit his Institute for the Harmonious Development of Man in France. Georgette was curious, having attended a performance of his troupe. As Margaret got on well with Monique Serrure, Georgette's friend, plans were soon made for Margaret to return with them to France. Margaret's old love Gladys Tilden had a friend, Louise Davidson, who, hearing about the upcoming voyage, quickly enlisted as Georgette's theatrical manager.

Jane had always chafed at Margaret's affairs but—Georgette! "Mart," she cried, "how could you!" She refused to accept *"The miracle of Georgette,"* as Jane put it, mimicking Margaret. Old jealousies sprang to the fore. It did not help that Margaret—with Georgette's encouragement—wanted not only to end her affair with Jane, but also to divest herself of the *Little Review.* Jane should take over the editorship of the magazine, Margaret thought. As Margaret reported the conversation:

> "I am definitely giving up the *Little Review*," I told Jane.
> "You can't give it up. You started it."
> "Are you mad? I started it—I can give it up."
> "You have no sense of responsibility."
> "Self-preservation is the first responsibility."
> "You certainly can't give it up."
> "I certainly can give it up. I'll give it to you."

Jane's jealousy reared its head. Adopting the attitude of the self-righteous victim she refused to say good morning to Margaret, was curt in all her answers and otherwise was withdrawn. Accustomed to this "Jane," Margaret ignored it all. She made plans to leave for France with Georgette, Monique and Louise. Finances would be no problem—an American millionaire, an ardent admirer of Georgette's, had promised to provide funds and the necessary allowance.

Once Margaret firmly decided she was going to Europe, Jane ended her pout. She decided to go, too, and to take Tom and Fritz with her. She and the boys sailed one week after Margaret and her new French friends. Jane had a number of reasons for going. She was still emotionally involved with Margaret. But she, too, wanted to visit Gurdjieff's institute and also to meet the artists and writers of Paris. Another reason may have been her interest in one of the dancers Gurdjieff had brought, Olgivanna Ivanovna Hinzenberg. A willowy beauty from an aristocratic Montenegrin family, the twenty-six-year-old Olgivanna was one of Gurdjieff's most gifted dancers. According to Jane, she and Olgivanna had "played" in New York and Jane looked forward to seeing her again.

In June 1924, Margaret, Georgette, Monique, and Louise sailed for France. Docking at Le Havre, the women immediately went by car to Paris, taking the high road out of the dull commercial city. They soon found themselves in the farm and château country of Normandy. Far below they could see the Seine winding its way toward Paris through the beautiful landscape. Suddenly, there at the edge of the river, Margaret saw "rising from the rocks the most fabulous fairy castle."

After some prodding, Georgette said it was a view she had seen often. Margaret's fairy castle was the fortress-château of Tancarville. Built in the eleventh century above the River Seine on the outskirts of Saint-Romains de Colbus, it had a long and prestigious history, having been a fortress under William the Conqueror and a refuge of Richard the Lion Hearted. Margaret wanted to know who lived there now. Georgette finally confessed that her sister and brother-in-law, a mystery writer, lived there. Seeing Margaret's wonderment, Georgette added, "Château life has never interested me."

In Paris the women found that many of the literary types regarded Gurdjieff with suspicion and warned them against going to the Prieuré. Much of the talk in the cafés, bars and salons still swirled around the death of the New Zealand short story writer, Katherine Mansfield. At the behest of her friend A. R. Orage, she had gone to the Prieuré to meet Gurdjieff. Impressed, she asked to stay. Though it was clear to Gurdjieff that she was dying of tuberculosis, he nevertheless agreed. She arrived at the Prieuré in November 1922 and participated in what activities she could. Within two and a half months she died. Her husband, John Middleton Murray, blamed Gurdjieff. Though the accusation was preposterous, it didn't stop the rumors and speculation.

Among the many writers and artists the women met in Paris was Ezra Pound. The thirty-nine-year-old poet greeted the women in a high voice filled with nervousness and self-consciousness, dressed in a large velvet beret and a flowing tie reminiscent of the Latin Quarter artists of the 1830s. His hair and beard were carrot colored, his face young-looking but having a ghostly pallor, his eyes strange and bird-like. The impression of the *Little Review*'s foreign editor on Margaret was such that she said "I felt I had been sitting through a human experiment in a behaviorist laboratory.... It gave me somehow the sensation of watching a large baby perform its repertoire of physical antics gravely, diffidently, without human responsibility for the performance."

Pound, who fashioned himself as the fulcrum of Parisian artistic life, invited James Joyce and his wife-to-be Nora to meet the women. Though Joyce had a bawdy side, with women he was formal, staid and dignified, never calling a woman by her first name. Margaret found him very much like her father as a young man, gentle, kindly, with a smile suggesting deprecating humor and a quality of personal aristocracy. With intimates like the American poet-publisher Robert McAlmon he caroused and delighted in discussion—staying out into the early morning hours and often having to be literally carried home. With others Joyce was quite diffident, preferring to speak little. On this occasion he did tell several stories, one about himself and Marcel Proust. Some friends, he recounted, had arranged a dinner so that the two authors might talk. After the initial greetings, Proust said, "I regret that I don't know Mr. Joyce's work." To which Joyce replied, "I have never read Mr. Proust." And so ended their conversation.

With Nora the women easily fell into rapport. Her sense of drama, Irish mockery, and personal challenge to Joyce they found delightful. Of Nora, Margaret said: "She is one of those women man loves forever, and hopes one day to take effectively by the throat." Perhaps unwittingly she was echoing something of what Jane and many others felt about *her*.

Following Pound and Joyce, the women went to the rue de Fleurus in Montparnasse to visit Gertrude Stein and her companion Alice B. Toklas. Rotund and formidable, Miss Stein gave a hearty welcome in her mannish but velvety voice and ushered them into the living room, its walls lined with Picassos, Braques, Juan Gris, and some Cézannes. A commanding personality, self-confident with a deep laugh, Gertrude seated herself, as was her custom, in a large chair, higher than the others, in the middle of the room. She was used to presiding over the Parisian literary scene and believed that since Shakespeare, only she, and perhaps

Henry James, had done anything to develop the English language. "The Jews," she once said, and not in jest, "have produced only three originative geniuses: Christ, Spinoza, and myself."

With views as uncompromising as Margaret's and a temperament as narcissistic, if not more so, it was not long before the two clashed. Gertrude, wealthy from inheritance, was soon chiding Margaret for not paying *Little Review* contributors. Retorted Margaret, always ready to cross swords—"It's not a question of right but of duty. No one else will publish them." As the women tested one another, Gertrude noticed that whenever Margaret made some comment she considered especially sincere, she placed her left hand, ungloved and fingers outspread, on her heart. Upon her right hand, which Margaret thought not as pretty, she always wore a white glove. This hand gesture and image convinced Gertrude that her rival was an "ecstatic." Said Alice B. Toklas of Margaret, "She puts her hand on her heart because she is afraid it will jump away from her."

Interestingly, Jane and Gertrude got on well. Later Jane would write to Mother, "How I love her—we had such charming hours together." She became Gertrude's self-appointed literary agent, bringing her writing to the attention of T. S. Eliot who was then at the English quarterly *The Criterion,* as well as becoming heavily involved in trying to sell Gertrude's *The Making of Americans* to an American publisher (McAlmon had already printed it in Paris).

Of Gertrude, Margaret would later say:

> I dislike immensely Gertrude's type of egoism; her awesome self-enamouration shows itself either as a comfortable, chuckling kind (which isn't too unsympathetic), or as a grotesque, arrogant kind as when she announced on meeting a Frenchwoman for the first time, "I am a genius, one of the greatest in the world today"—which seemed to me slightly insane. The Frenchwoman said, "She frightened me." I was also put off by an atmosphere of commercialism that I felt emanating around Gertrude like an aura. It made me uncomfortable, as if I were in a place I didn't belong.

The women went on to meet the cream of Parisian-based artists, musicians, sculptors, and writers, and intellectuals. Among the writers they met was an early contributor to the *Little Review,* Ernest Hemingway. Hemingway was then living in a small apartment on the Left Bank with his wife Hadley and their baby. Hemingway—or "Hem" as his friends called him—Margaret found to be quite other than his macho public persona. He was softhearted, simple, and obsessed with being in love. He fell madly in love with Margaret who thought him "gooey" and rebuffed him. She recounted how he would "come to the Sélect Café every morning and push through the terrace chairs like a prowling animal with a wound." Jane thought Hemingway's animal prototype was a rabbit—"white and pink face, soft brown eyes that look at you without blinking. As for his love for boxing and bull-fighting—all that is thrashing up the ground with his hind legs."

The women met a great many intellectuals also but there was no rapport. As Margaret would say some years later, "Georgette was to formulate what she considered the difference between us and intellectuals. We live for emotions, she said, they live for events. In our relations with people we wait upon the development of personal atmosphere; they don't wait, they crouch."

The women were invited to the Friday afternoon salon of Natalie Clifford Barney for talk, dancing and lemonade. Years before, Barney had inherited some $3.5 million from her father and had leased a three-hundred-year-old house at 20 rue Jacob where she had lived in style since 1909. The most famous and flamboyant lesbian in Paris, perhaps in all of Europe, Barney was a champion of sexual freedom and a leader and benefactor of all things lesbian.

An unabashed sexual huntress, Barney's love life was legend. Known as an Amazon who loved to conquer, she would later figure in two novels. One was Radclyffe Hall's *The Well of Loneliness,* where she is depicted as "Valerie Seymour." The other was Djuna Barnes' *Ladies Almanack,* which included a biography of Barney as "Evangeline Musset," "as fine a Wench as ever wet Bed." Djuna's other satirical portraits of the regulars at Barney's salon were Janet Flanner, Solita Solano, Dolly Wilde, Romaine Brooks, Radclyffe Hall, Una Troubridge and Mina Loy, the only heterosexual. Other women who also attended Barney's salon were Colette, Gertrude

Stein, Alice B. Toklas, Thelma Wood, Nancy Cunard, Noel Murphy, Sylvia Beach, Adrienne Monnier, Hilda Doolittle known as H. D., Bryher (Winifred Ellerman), and Berenice Abbott. Male guests included André Gide, Jean Cocteau, Paul Valéry, Ezra Pound, Rainer Maria Rilke, and William Carlos Williams.

Most likely it was at Barney's salon that Jane Heap ran into Djuna Barnes. Djuna, now living in Paris permanently, had been in an intense affair with a tall, lanky, handsome twenty-year-old American silverpoint artist and sculptor, Thelma Wood. Djuna had met Thelma in Paris in 1921, almost penniless, and had taken her in. Wood drank heavily, regularly dressed in men's clothes and chased women. Even Djuna's beauty, talent, and intelligence, uncommon by any standard, were not enough to keep Wood faithful. A succession of affairs, most notably with playwright and poet Edna St. Vincent Millay, left Djuna in tears. No doubt Djuna was glad to see Jane who, of course, lost no time in telling Margaret she was "overjoyed" to have got together again with Djuna. To Margaret, who now had eyes only for Georgette, it was old news.

What did arouse Margaret's ire was Jane's outright betrayal. Before sailing for France, Jane had told Georgette's American suitor that Georgette and Margaret were lovers. Now word came saying that he was withdrawing his promised financial support. But the women, especially Margaret, were used to making do; the important thing was they were in Paris.

Besides the literary salons of Barney and Stein, the women of course took in Parisian night life. A must was the Jockey, a cabaret on the rue Campagne where, as Bob McAlmon said, "almost anybody of the writing, painting, musical, gigoloing, whoring, pimping or drinking world was apt to turn up.... The so-called 'bohemian' or art world having so few intolerances about morals, or the way people make their living." The Jockey, the Bricktop and the Stryx were all among *the* places to meet. Conversation was always in currency and though Jane more than held her own, not everyone appreciated her as Margaret did. McAlmon, in particular, spoke of her "breezy, traveling-salesman-of-the-world tosh which was impossible to recall later."

The women's real destination, of course, lay not with the people and night life of Paris but some forty miles southeast at Fontaine-bleau-en-Avon. It was here behind a high stone wall with heavy iron gates, fountains and long avenues of lime, maple, chestnut and conifer trees set in a park of forty-five acres that Gurdjieff had founded his Institute for the Harmonious Development of Man. It was here that some sixty men and women had assembled to study the teaching. With the constant admonition to remember and observe themselves, the students were put to long and hard physical work felling trees, digging ditches, doing farm work, gardening, housework, laundry, and cooking meals. After dinner Gurdjieff might give a talk on, say, "Essence and Personality"; or Thomas de Hartmann, one of his oldest St. Petersburg students and a famous Russian conductor, would play on the piano a selection of the unusual music that Gurdjieff had brought; or there would be prac-tice of sacred dances and body movements which required great attention. Saturday evenings there would be communal Turkish baths first for men and then the women followed by a feast and rit-ual toasting of the idiots. Referred to as The Science of Idiotism, Gurdjieff maintained that this was an initiate ritual that had been practiced for 4,500 years and expressed the secrets of the inner life of Man. It was never to be practiced apart from the sacramental meal and always with alcohol, never wine. There are 21 different idiots with Gurdjieff being number 18; 19 and 20 are Sacred Indi-viduals performing functions in the whole Megalocosmos; and 21 is the Unique Idiot, our God.

After hearing the toasts to the various Idiots at one meal, at the next Gurdjieff asked students to pick their Idiot. Gurdjieff said it was impossible not to be an Idiot, as everyone was one. (The Greek root meaning of the word is "I make my own.") They were to choose from the first twelve Idiots. These ranged from the Ordinary Idiot to Super, Arch, Hopeless, Compassionate, Squirming, Square, Round, Zigzag, Enlightened, Doubting and Swaggering. Each had its particular designation. The movement of the Idiots was not forward but backward from the Idiot they chose to Ordinary Idiot. The reason was that only in the recognition of one's nothingness could there be true development toward consciousness and conscience. Otherwise, all forward movement was certain to be stopped by a "wrong crystallization"; that is, a fusion of a particular level of consciousness on the basis of false personality. If such a crystallization is not dissolved before a given Idiot is reached, it may become insurmountable. This is because this very defect, or defects, was a definite factor in the original ascent. Interestingly, the limitation of a wrong crystallization is not realized until the results that such a crystallization produces have been observed.

Only through work on oneself—the correct remembering and observing of oneself—does one automatically descend to Ordinary Idiot. Once the level of Ordinary Idiot has been recognized and reached, the ascension is also automatic. Every two or three years a new Idiot is reached—Super becomes Arch, Arch becomes Hopeless, Hopeless becomes Compassionate, and so on.

The ritual itself was simple. At the beginning of the meal, the Director proposed a toast, "To the health of all Ordinary Idiots." If a person was present who had chosen or been designated as an Ordinary Idiot, the Director added, "And to your health also," saying the name of the person. Letting a few minutes go by, the Director then proposed a second toast, "To the health of all Super Idiots," and so on.

It was still June when Margaret, Georgette, Monique, Louise, and Jane, with Tom and Fritz in tow, arrived at the railway station at Avon and made their way down the hill to the Prieuré. There their arrival was noted and they were given small cell-like bedrooms. Jane wrote to Mother [Florence Reynolds] that "Mart [Margaret] was too funny, sailing about in her grand clothes and guest manners. The peace is too lovely—lovely château, old furniture and many fountains... Olgivanna was in the kitchen—and couldn't play with me... resented Martie and is too much under the Institute rules to be herself... all changed from New York."

Jane wrote to Mother in the middle of July saying that soon after they arrived on "Tuesday, July 8th at seven o'clock in the evening a gendarme came to the Institute to say that Gurdjieff had been found unconscious and smashed up in his car in the middle of the Fontainebleau forest. Gurdjieff spent two days in the hospital and then was brought back to the château. He had a brain concussion and was in a coma until Sunday, five days after the accident. Though revived, he remained in his room for another week or so."

A few days later Margaret wrote to Mother. She did not mention the accident, perhaps because she knew Jane already had. She told Mother she found the Prieuré "charming." Life there reminded Margaret of her college days with "the ridiculous atmosphere of students all rather frightened and ill at ease (at least the English and American ones) and the latter overjoyed like little kids who plan to 'cut classes' and break all the laws possible. Gurdjieff is too sweet for words—seemed to me infinitely touching, wistful, etc." She reported that everyone worked very hard, entirely dedicated to their jobs to the exclusion of all else, and then at the end of the week have a feast of some sort, like roasting sheep in the woods.

The women had heard soon after their arrival that P. D. Ouspensky, Gurdjieff's earliest St. Petersburg student who had written *Tertium Organum* and was said to be writing a book on the teaching with Gurdjieff's approval, had the previous January broken with Gurdjieff. They were surprised then to find him one evening sitting dutifully at the dinner table at Gurdjieff's left. Margaret was not impressed. "[He] acted like a small boy, laughing more than he meant to, saying what he meant not to, flushing with the Armagnac forced upon him during Gurdjieff's Toasts to the Idiots. Though Ouspensky must have taken part in this ceremony a hundred times, I always felt that he had never discovered its significance; that he knew ideas but he didn't know people."

Jane wrote to Mother that the atmosphere at the Prieuré was "hushed and sad" because of Gurdjieff's sudden accident. Margaret had met Olgivanna and thought she was good-looking but was "outraged because she had to work so hard" to get her attention. Jane continued to try to attract Olgivanna but without success. She thought Olgivanna was acting "very strange." Finally, Olgivanna told her she was "afraid to bring life into [the] Institute." Rebuffed, she wrote to Mother that "I am playing with Lady Rothermere," a wealthy Englishwoman who had financed Ouspensky's move from Constantinople to London and was contributing to Gurdjieff's teaching. Dining in the same Russian restaurant one evening, Jane wrote to Mother—"You should see Lady Rothermere tear off a little flirtation with me—throwing cigarettes across the room to me...my emanations were high they tell me and Lady Rothermere thought they were for her."

Fritz and Tom loved the Prieuré and wanted to live there. Margaret and Georgette rented a farmhouse at Passy, about two miles away, from which they commuted to the Prieuré, absorbing the atmosphere there, participating in the daily work and chores, attending the movements, and listening to readings in the salon. Georgette had left after her first weekend complaining volubly about how anyone could stay there with that "unpleasant charlatan." But her displeasure passed and she returned. While Margaret found Gurdjieff's teaching tough going, Jane was immediately taken up in it. Said Margaret:

"Jane knew more about life and art than other people did. The things that 'became known' to her were the most important things anyone ever discussed in my hearing until the day we went to Gurdjieff; and from then on Jane talked more profoundly about his knowledge than anyone else ever did—even, to me, Ouspensky."

Though Gurdjieff was not available for personal communication or instruction his teaching emanated through some of his pupils. Margaret spoke of one woman (most likely Madame de Salzmann) who "in her outer manifestations personified what they had all tried to attain—a holding-in rather than a going-out. She was a genial kind of person but she always made you conscious of a silence in her. She didn't tell you what she 'thought' about anything." Her behavior both perplexed and exasperated Margaret who still evaluated people by their expressiveness. "I decided that she didn't think," Margaret said, "or that she was inarticulate." However as time passed Margaret noticed that the vagueness of her talk changed when she was questioned—she felt the power in this woman's answers which "offered no more than it called for." She came to appreciate that the "woman didn't thrust herself at you, it was as if she realized that one has very little self to thrust. She gave you no more stories of her inner life, she seemed to know that no one has any inner life worth mentioning."

One day, a friend of Margaret's and Jane's from New York, a *Little Review* contributor, visited. She was interested in information. Rebuffed again and again, she finally asked—"Can't someone put this Fourth Way teaching of Gurdjieff's in a phrase?" Continuing to insist, Jane told her: "It's a method to keep your past from becoming your future." Margaret, for her part, of course engaged in endless discussions. She had one all-night struggle with a group of people over the question of "esoteric science and religion."

In the early dawn, the first rays of light streaking through their room, Jane summed up the night's conversation: "You people [the religious] are talking of an emotional experience—religion. You say we make a god of the mind because we are talking of something that is experienced on three planes. Your emotional experience can be compared to a dog's joy in greeting his master. Because a dog has only two planes of experience. I'm not minimizing the dog's experience, but your statements reduce all humanity to animals."

Other than Jane, none of the new American students, with the possible exception of the novelist Jean Toomer, had so quickly grasped the fundamental premises of the teaching—that man was asleep, that he could not do—and the fine delineations inherent in its scale of ideas. Jane was still caught in her impulses and her beliefs but, through making repeated and serious efforts at the teaching's two practices, self-remembering and self-observation, she was beginning to see *where* and *how* she was caught.

A. R. Orage had come from New York to the Prieuré and brought with him his new lover, Jessie Dwight, a young woman almost half his age, very pampered and immature. Gurdjieff disapproved, warning Orage that she was "a native," a person with no spiritual potential. But Orage, in the throes of his chief weakness—his eye for the ladies—resisted as did, of course, his young love. There were many arguments between Orage and Jesse and much ambivalence, but Orage believed that somehow it would all work out, that he could have both Gurdjieff and his love affair, too.

Whatever his personal dilemma, Orage had a sure grasp of the fundamentals of the teaching and was both considerate and articulate in helping others. He had heard that Margaret was becoming "famous" for her identification with her emotions and she could neither see what they were nor how she manifested them. One day Orage approached her while she was pulling up weeds in the vegetable garden and in his genial but pointed manner asked:

"Why are you always arguing about right and wrong."

"Because I'm going to convince people," she said.

"But you know you can't."

"No, I don't. I believe that if I can present these ideas intelligently enough—.

"Good heavens," he said, "you don't really believe that people are ever convinced of anything by listening to ideas?"

"Of course I do," she said. "What other way is there?"

"There are only three ways of influencing people," he said—"magnetization, competition, example."

Suddenly Margaret saw that her idea of trying to rationally, logically, convince people in reality convinced them of nothing. She might continue her habitual arguments but she hoped never with the belief that she formerly had.

Because Margaret had a great love of nature, she took many walks through the nearby forests of Fontainebleau mulling over what Orage had told her. One day on a path she met Orage and told him—"Oh, I love the earth."

"Don't talk like that," he answered. "Some men love the earth, as a father loves child, or the child, the father—you're only in love with it."

Margaret held Orage in high esteem and the two had many such exchanges and talks. On one occasion Orage told her: "Imagination as we use it is simply an excess of desire over ability." At another time, Orage said to Margaret:

> Merely to convey thought is not an art but a craft, if not a trade. Over and above the desire to communicate thought, there is for the artist as writer the desire to make it prevail in the minds of others; in short, art is a means of power. To express himself is not enough: he wishes to impress himself. Readers feel towards him the repulsion as well as the attraction of the snake for the bird. Power they instinctively feel is there, and they are afraid of it. Style is only the voice adopted by great writers to make their power more attractive. Style is power made gracious. We must write as if Homer and Demosthenes were to be our judges, as if our lives depended upon their approval.... All perfection is the fruit of sacrifice. Art is perfect when it seems to be nature.

Her love for music was as great as, perhaps even greater than, her love of nature. Music was often a topic of conversation. Orage, having heard her play the piano in the salon of the Prieuré, once asked what the object was.

"It is the logical way to recapture continuously," she said, "that state of ecstasy without which life is not worth living."

"That is not an object," Orage pointed out. "If you say you are playing the piano to make money or to give concert tours you have named objects."

He paused, a strong stillness enveloping them, and then said quietly:

"Act—don't be acted upon."

Act—don't be acted upon—the words ignited and lived in Margaret, became active sources of thought. She began to review all her life in terms of objectives. What she saw was that "I saw no objects, I saw only states. I saw myself committing many actions, but always after having been acted upon; and always to achieve one of three states—liberty, ecstasy, or peace."

When she spoke with Orage again he reformulated the idea in an unforgettable metaphor—"Remember," he declared, "you're a pianist, not a piano."

The metaphor so strongly resonated that she came to realize she had not created the *Little Review* so much as it had been created through her. It had been created in reaction as a vehicle in which to manifest her reactions. She had only been an instrument. When Gurdjieff said "Man cannot do," he had meant it. He had meant exactly that—as long as people had not objectified themselves, had not actualized themselves in terms of being present to and remembering and observing themselves, they were playthings, everything just happened to them. She began to see that, indeed, "everyone was doing it—the artist above all. The artist organism is preeminently the acted-upon organism."

Looking at life from this perspective—acting in life and not reacting—she concluded that "the quality of every life is determined exclusively by its position in relation to acting or being acted upon. I have had the drastic experience of realizing that my thirty years of fighting have been not actions but reactions." In a word, the *Little Review,* regardless of its merits, was simply another manifestation of her sleep. *She* hadn't done anything. As Gurdjieff had said to Margaret, "You rest in dream?"

That August, when Gurdjieff had recovered somewhat from his auto accident, he assembled everyone present and told them that now, twenty-one months after the Institute had opened its doors, he was closing them. His mission was to establish the teaching he had brought, the Fourth Way, in the West and the aim of the Institute was to train what he called "helper-instructors" to help in disseminating the teaching. Despite the high level of people he had attracted, he saw that people's egoism made this impossible in a short time. Instead, he changed horses entirely, and decided to propagate the teaching by writing a three-volume work entitled *All and Everything.* Though Gurdjieff had officially closed the Institute, Margaret, Jane, Georgette, Monique, and Louise, and most of the Americans were allowed to stay on.

That October another issue of the *Little Review* had to be published and so Jane left for New York, leaving Fritz and Tom at the Prieuré. Once back, she sought to adopt them. This brought the boys' father back into the picture after what Fritz later termed "a complete absence of ten years." Their father opposed the adoption. The boys were brought back to New York and were soon caught in the middle of a battle between him and Jane. Although he eventually withdrew, the turmoil left scars.

Lois, the boys' mother, continued to check in and out of sanitariums. Margaret saw little hope for her sister ever regaining her footing. "Why do I say Lois can do nothing with her life today that will spare her the necessity of going insane each year?" she asked. "I'll answer this by describing what that life would be for me, and you can imagine that it's just about as bad for her."

Margaret's answer was to heap all the blame on Lois' new husband:

> If I were forced to live in the same house or the same room—or even see all the time—a human creature with whom I was deliriously in love—I couldn't stand it even for a week. If that creature were someone *who hadn't even my respect,* what would I do? Develop gray hairs, become viciously *ditragnée,* disagreeable to the degree of danger, insane—or commit a murder. And if that man breathed too loudly in the next room and in a rhythm that I couldn't stand, if he snored and talked and laughed and blew his nose and didn't powder his face and had too large hands and 'smelled man' and ate sloppily and scratched his head and creaked his chair and bought clothes that weren't properly cut—and never failed to present the commonplace reaction—and if he were of an intact bourgeois, and pleased with it, and incapable of going beyond ABC in his wit or his thinking, and unaware of everything that might constitute a moment of human intelligence, and—well it's enough. And if I know that public opinion would classify him after all, as better than most husbands—this bigoted, selfish, naive, boring, infantile creature with whom I had to spend my life!—this man with a nervous organism so different from

mine that any decent science of life would tell us never to bring our vibrations into contact with each other!—this man so *ravi* [enraptured] with his offspring (the reproduction of his glorified self) that it would send any spectator to violet vomiting!—this man with all the typical (god!) good humors and bad humors, gaieties, glooms, moods, broodings, tempers, complaints, illnesses.... And when I reflect that it was this *creature* (who had filed my nerves down to the raw—he and his crying, tyrannical, brutish child)—this creature who had tied my hands completely, made it impossible for me *to come or go* without *sacrificing one thing or another essential to my life*— made it impossible to keep my two children with me (the ones that I adore and who are capable of giving me something, and I them, under conditions half normal at least)—that it was this creature who held my break-down as my own fault entirely, and imposed the law that if I didn't accept *his* solution of our lives he would leave me, without money, to drift... well, I say with conviction that a room in a sanitarium or a prison cell would look very restful to me.

Jane and not Margaret was the one primarily involved with raising Lois' boys, Fritz and Tom. Through it all Jane and Tom seemed to have gotten on pretty well, but Jane and Fritz—both grounded in an enormous self-will—continued to butt heads. "It was highly volatile and explosive," said Fritz. "There was, at times, a great deal of emotion, of love, between us, but the very emotionality of the relationship frightened me." Fritz's obstinacy and independence were a constant trial for Jane and she frequently punished him.

In the spring of 1925 Jane returned to the Prieuré. She brought the boys with her. Fritz had already adopted Gurdjieff as a father-figure. He now had one aim in life and that was to be like Gurdjieff, who he saw as a "strong, honest, direct, uncomplicated—and entirely 'no-nonsense' individual." And Gurdjieff saw promise in him. As he would tell Fritz years later, he came to the Prieuré a "wounded animal" ... but—and this was significant—"When you come Prieuré first time you not yet spoiled, have not learn to lie to self. Already even then you can maybe lie to mother or father, but not to self. So you fortunate." When it was decided that the boys should stay on at the Prieuré when Jane returned to New York in the fall. Fritz was overjoyed. Tom was doing well at the Prieuré and so was Fritz, though Jane always thought of him as "maimed."

Jane had spent much of the summer with Margaret and Georgette and had a wonderful time, though she noticed Margaret's continuing difficulty with accepting Gurdjieff's teaching. Though Gurdjieff was no longer teaching, she went as often as she could to the Prieuré, but the conversations with students there usually turned into arguments. What she agreed with, Margaret staunchly agreed with, and what she didn't, she just as staunchly resisted. "She is rather tragic to me sometimes," Jane wrote to Mother. In a conversation about the Institute it seemed to Jane that Margaret "was fighting for life."

Leaving the boys at the Prieuré, Jane returned to New York in the fall of 1925. Orage, recognizing her editing skills, enlisted her to help with chapters of the manuscript that Gurdjieff began sending to him to edit. Whether she attended one of Orage's groups is unclear, but it is certain that Gurdjieff's ideas about the difference between objective and subjective art—the one is conscious, the other not, the art being a product of being acted upon—began to penetrate and slowly change the way Jane perceived the art the *Little Review* was publishing. Suddenly, though the impressions had gathered and been digested over a long period, she began to see art from Gurdjieff's point of view. No doubt her work helping Orage with the translation of Gurdjieff's *All and Everything,* itself a work of objective art, was of immeasurable value. Seeing the vast and irreconcilable difference between objective and subjective art, her dream world in which the *Little Review* was the centerpiece collapsed. She began to live with the dawning recognition of the magazine's utter irrelevance.

Once Fritz and Tom began living at the Prieuré, Margaret played little, if any, part in their lives. As she had once given them up to Jane, she now gave them up to Gurdjieff. Consequently, they again felt abandoned, unwanted, with all the attendant confusion, guilt and rage, but Margaret was either unaware or did not care.[1]

Gurdjieff had taken Fritz under his wing, making him his attendant and giving him private lessons in the teaching once a week. Things went well but after a time Fritz, egotistical and as strong-willed, began to get into trouble. In time, his rebellion even extended to Gurdjieff. Like many adults, Fritz came to be in "galoshes"—had a split mind—over Gurdjieff. What he didn't know was that this was a state that Gurdjieff consciously induced in his students, evoking and putting them between a "yes" and a "no" in themselves, so they could see how the mind actually worked and, in looking deeper, come to experience an awareness that was beyond the ordinary mind. It was always a painfully disillusioning experience, quite open to projection.

Margaret, Georgette, and Monique had continued to live at the Passy farmhouse through the following year. They visited the Prieuré, but all of Gurdjieff's time was given to writing the *First Series* of *All and Everything* and to maintaining his business enterprises in Paris in order to support the château. He had no time left for teaching. After a number of moves in 1926, the women finally ended up living at Georgette's sister's Château de Tancarville in Normandy.

Though quite rich, the chatelaine and her husband lived frugally, keeping the ten rooms of the château dimly lit and poorly heated. Margaret was used to making every place she lived hers by completely redecorating, but there she was forbidden to touch anything. Her bedroom overlooked the Seine and had a canopied bed, a dressing room and antechamber, all done in the Empire style with drapery of gray and yellow silk, a tall mirror, lace covering the marble mantelpiece, and on the night table a small kerosene lamp with a pink shade.

Here the three women boarded at the château intermittently, moving out for short stays in modest Paris hotels when they could no longer abide the avarice and stilted habits of Georgette's sister and her

---

1. When the boys had first come to live with her and Jane in New York, Margaret had been unable to cope. Apparently, she had no mothering instinct, or perhaps it had been swallowed by her narcissism.

husband. Georgette was able to convince her sister to let them use several other properties they owned such as Le Palais des Muses, a thirty-room château in Neuilly-sur-Seine in which Louis XIV had once stayed. There was also a château-pavillon in the forest of Saint-Germain called La Muette, or La Folie d'Artois. And also an abandoned lighthouse near the Tancarville château which she rented to the women for fifty francs a month. There, Margaret began to write *My Thirty Years War,* the first of her three-volume memoirs, whose title was originally *The Autobiography of a Resisting Nature.* Georgette's memoir, an act of exorcism, was entitled *Maeterlinck and I.* "Each day I feel," she recounted, "that I leave myself a little more, the better to go towards my encounter with myself."

Though the women lived at the lighthouse, they traveled a good deal with Georgette's concert tours of Europe, with Margaret continuing to accompany her on the piano. Then, a concert series unexpectedly canceled, Georgette went off to Cannes to recuperate "with some rich idiot," as Margaret put it. Margaret despaired.

On February 19, 1927, that all changed when Margaret met Solita Solano. Besides her beauty, independence and interest in literature, Margaret had never met any woman since Jane with as sharp an intelligence. The two began an affair at once. When Georgette, having returned from Cannes, heard Margaret's exclamations about her new friend, she listened patiently but did not consider Solita a serious challenge. That quickly changed when Georgette met Solita. Having previously lost Maeterlinck through jealousy, she made the best of the situation, saying nothing, giving Margaret all the freedom she wanted, trusting that their relationship would endure.

Solita brought Margaret to the Hôtel Bonaparte and introduced her to Janet. She liked Margaret but thought her too emotional. Janet found Margaret's profile "delicious, her hair was blond and wavy, her laughter a soprano ripple, her gait undulating beneath her snug *tailleur* [suit]." And though later the two women would rarely agree on anything, Margaret was on her good behavior and did not indulge her need for "conversation."

Later, Solita introduced Georgette to Janet, who felt about her pretty much as Jane had. She couldn't stand her. All of Margaret's "rhapsody," Janet said, about "Georgette's ethereal nature, her psychological and spiritual perfections, gave her the seeming character of an archangel" and were more or less real. But Janet believed that what Margaret called Georgette's "heavenly superiorities" more rationally could have been explained by her "exquisite French manners, full of consideration for and courtesy toward all the people surrounding her." Being an actress, Georgette tended to behave in a theatrical manner, which Janet found only less disconcerting than her singing which made her want "to jump into the Seine." As Janet told Solita after meeting the women, "I loved you and Margaret and disliked dear Georgette."

Margaret was not so spellbound with Georgette that she did not come to see her vanities. As she said, "She had many vanities, but no *amour-propre* [self-love]; she was self-absorbed, but never selfish; she was naive, but not childish—she was childlike; she had an anxiety-complex, but with a manner that redeemed it; she had the electricity of tempter, but she used it abstractly, not personally: she often lacked judgment, but always constructively; and she had an ego that never behaved egotistically. Perhaps I could assemble her qualities under one major tendency: personal distinction, aristocracy of nature—in other words that greatest, to me, of all human attributes: an unspoiled heart."

At the end of 1928, just before Christmas, a letter arrived at the Prieuré for Fritz. The postmark was from Chicago. It was from his mother, Lois. Five years had passed since he had seen her. She invited him to return to Chicago, assuring him that Bill, his stepfather, had agreed that the boys would be "supported, educated, and welcome." Fritz's decision was instantaneous. He felt he had had enough of Gurdjieff and the Prieuré. At about the same time, Jane wrote to Tom and Fritz saying that she would be in Paris over the holidays and inviting them to spend Christmas there with her.

Having Christmas together in Paris, Jane said that she and Fritz were able to bury the past and reconcile. Unfortunately, this lasted only to the moment when Fritz told her of his decision to return to his mother. Once again, he and Jane locked horns. She reminded him that as she had adopted him he was in her custody and could only return to Chicago with her consent. Her subsequent visits to the Prieuré and many letters from New York, as well as lectures and advice from older students at the Prieuré, all marshaled by Jane, Fritz said, "only served to increase my determination to leave at any cost."

C. S. Nott, who had first met Jane Heap in 1924 in New York, said she "had the most stimulating and penetrating mind of any American woman I have ever met, and like all people with strong positive vibrations her negative ones were equally strong. She could be quite ruthless and regardless of near friend or old foe when she wanted something. She had a strong masculine side; as she said to me, 'I'm not really a woman.'"

Whether the problem with Fritz was the final straw or not, Jane finally decided to live in Europe permanently and to give up the *Little Review*. Its publication had been an increasing burden since Margaret's departure and the magazine's frequency had fallen from a monthly to a quarterly to now an annual. She decided to put out one last issue and to enlist Margaret's help.

Predictably, when Jane found that Margaret was now in a serious relationship with Solita as well as Georgette, old jealousies sprang up. A truce of sorts developed and Margaret finally became involved. Eventually, Solita and Janet Flanner were also enlisted to help with the issue, inasmuch as it was being compiled in their hotel. From the start, Margaret felt the final number should be something very different from all that had been previously published. Her idea was to "ask the artists of the world what they were thinking and feeling about their lives and work."

> Will you give us an interview?
> We are bringing out a final number of the *Little Review*.
> We should like a "round-up" of all the men of this period—

men of the first rank in the arts—who have appeared in our pages, together with those of equal rank in other departments of life who have our interest and admiration.

Here is a chance to tell the truth about yourself as no interviewer, critic, or historian could do.

1. What should you most like to do, to know, to be? (In case you are not satisfied.)

2. Why wouldn't you change places with any other human being?

3. What do you look forward to?

4. What do you fear most from the future?

5. What has been the happiest moment of your life? The unhappiest? (If you care to tell.)

6. What do you consider your weakest characteristics? Your strongest? What do you like most about yourself? Dislike most?

7. What things do you really like? Dislike? (Nature, people, ideas, objects, etc. Answer in a phrase or a page, as you will.)

8. What is your attitude toward art today?

9. What is your world view? (Are you a reasonable being in a reasonable scheme?)

10. Why do you go on living?

Many replied, including Sherwood Anderson, Brancusi, Jean Cocteau, Nancy Cunard, T. S. Eliot, Janet Flanner, Ford Madox Ford, Emma Goldman, Ezra Pound, Ernest Hemingway, Mina Loy, Aldous Huxley, Wyndham Lewis, James Joyce, Gorham Munson, Bertrand Russell, Gertrude Stein, Joseph Stella, and William Carlos Williams.

From Orage:

I doubt whether you will get any sincere answers to these questions. After all, the stuff of the answers is the stuff of which "literature" is the disguise—and as your questions are mainly literary, they will naturally preserve their private capital. I wouldn't answer the questions in public myself for anything. Why? The public doesn't deserve my confession. And couldn't make me any equivalent return. In a small group, sworn to secrecy and eternal friendship, these mental confessions would be salutary and, in fact, necessary—

but where, even, is such a group? It can scarcely exist outside a monastery isolated for life. I shall be interested to see what, if any, replies you receive.

As for ... [sic], why do such answers surprise you? It's characteristic of world-reformers that they take themselves for granted. Under the pretense that they are too trivial subjects for question, they really mean that they are above it. These ass-gods of reform!

Anyhow, best of wishes.

A. R. Orage

From Gertrude Stein:

Good luck to your last number. I would much rather have written about Jane because I do appreciate Jane but since this is what you want here are my answers.

1. But I am.
2. Because I am I.
3. More of the same.
4. Anything.
5. Birthday.
6. 1 Weakness. 2 Nothing. 3 Everything. 4 Almost anything.
7. 1 What I like. 2 Hardly anything.
8. I like to look at it.
9. Not very likely or often.
10. I am.

From Djuna Barnes:

I am sorry but the list of questions does not interest me to answer. Nor have I that respect for the public.

Georgette wrote:

1. My life.
Myself.
Conscious.
2. Yes, I would change with that person who has realized himself the most completely.
3. A few moments of reality.

4. To lose what I love. To die before having been a little satisfied with myself.

5. The moment which destroyed what I believed to be my life. That interval in which I passed from infancy into the *méchanique humaine*.

6. a) I lack impatience, intolerance, anger, rancor.

b) Pity, bounty, gentleness, patience, indulgence, and inadaptability.

c) My wish to hear truths and to perfect myself, my scorn of public opinion, my indifference to material things.

d) What do I really hate? The phantom which, in infancy, I set up in my place.

7. To live, understand, and know. To laugh, sing, play, listen to good and bad music.

Society, calumny, vanity, irreducible opinions, futile conversation, what is known as "character"!

8. One of man's most interesting illusions.

9. I am a being I am trying to understand, in a scheme I do not understand.

10. To live more, and better.

And from Solita:

1. c) [sic] A conscious, developed human being. a) Function fully in the physical, emotional and mental systems. b) Myself.

2. Because my ego would forbid such a change.

3. My development.

4. Death.

5. Finding what I wanted in love. Believing I had lost it.

6. Weakest characteristics: Stupidity, indifference, lack of imagination, immaturity, tolerance. Strongest characteristics: courage, will-power, fidelity, respect for order, selfishness (unmaterial), intolerance, tenacity, sensibility. Like most about myself my strong characteristics and perfect health. Dislike most my weakest characteristics, my physical details and my handwriting.

7. I like new ideas, love, science, travelling, work, the sun, a few human beings, a very few examples of the arts, perfume, wine, airplanes, Spanish dancing, France, the Orient, the tropics, chess, cigarettes, kittens, the sea, illusions, Christmas trees, chic women, money, monocles, excitement, privacy, good

manners, volcanos, deserts. I dislike the stupidity and vileness of all human relations, educational systems, pomposity, stories (dirty *or* clean), vagueness, what passes for art, clichés, injustice, reality (except laboratory data), not knowing anything, unattractive people, provincial life, masculinity, the cold, actors, and singers, reproaches, the theatre, novels, restraints, old age, banal conversation, games, mountains, poverty and cigars.

8. It's pleasant but unimportant.

9. Which one?

10. I have enjoyed it at times. I may again.

The last issue of the *Little Review* was most noted for Jane's farewell editorial "Lost: A Renaissance." The *Little Review,* she wrote, had been a part of the revolution in the arts begun before the First World War. Unlike magazines that had an intellectual program, the magazine "had the corresponding emotions; and consequently an energy that nothing has been able to turn aside... except itself." The magazine was to have been a forum for modern day artists who might equal or succeed the artists of the past. The experience was otherwise. "I do not believe," Jane wrote, "that the conditions of our life can produce men who can give us masterpieces. Masterpieces are not made from chaos. If there is confusion of life there will be confusion of art. This is in no way a criticism of the men who are working in the arts. They can only express what is here to express." The magazine had published twenty-three new systems of art representing nineteen countries and none had survived. The only work they had published which approached being a masterpiece was James Joyce's *Ulysses.*

> But it is too personal, too tortured, too special a document to be a masterpiece in the true sense of the word. It is an intense and elaborate expression of Mr. Joyce's dislike of this time. Self-expression is not enough; experiment is not enough; the recording of special moments or cases is not enough. All of the arts have broken faith or lost connection with their origin and function. They have ceased to be concerned with the legitimate and permanent material of art. [And as such] The actual situation of art today is not a very

69

important or adult concern (Art is not the highest aim of man); it is interesting only as a pronounced symptom of an ailing and aimless society.

And so the dream was sacrificed. Jane had understood what Gurdjieff taught, proving her understanding in the fire of acting upon it. She had loved the *Little Review*—it had given her an identity, power and fame. And she had the courage to kill her own dream in order to begin to live the teaching. It was a tremendous act and it would open the doors for her to take her place as a teacher of the Fourth Way.

Jane and Georgette now got a chance to know each other better. Said Margaret: "No greater contrast can be imagined than that between the natures, characters, temperaments, personalities and behaviour of my first two great friends. In the beginning it seemed impossible that any bond could be established between them. But it wasn't long before Georgette found a key to communication. As she explained later to an enemy of Jane's:

> When I am face to face with Jane, for me it is as if she were two persons. I don't address myself to her human side, I see facing me only an astonishing mind, so astonishing that its superiority can separate it totally from the human being that she is. I have the impression that this separation is not total for you. You think of the other side—of the person you know—as much as you think of the person you are listening to. It is this that creates a latent discord between you.

Said Margaret of Georgette and Jane: "Of course they finally became the greatest of friends. No one could resist being a friend of Georgette's after hearing her talk seriously."

It was during this period that Jane found a new love, the English couturier Elspeth Champcommunal, the chief designer at Worth. Elspeth saw the state of Margaret's clothes. Living as frugally as possible, Margaret bought very little so the clothes she had, except for a pair of Parisian workman's overalls, were mostly threadbare. Elspeth gave her a new wardrobe.

Meanwhile, the argument between Jane and Fritz had continued. In the fall of 1929 Gurdjieff's advice was sought. Jane took Fritz to the Café de la Paix, Gurdjieff's Paris "office," to see him. Jane used every argument at her command including the boy's lack of understanding that in leaving the Prieuré, and in effect, Gurdjieff, he was giving up, as he would come to say later, "the greatest opportunity for knowledge and education that I would ever have."

Gurdjieff said little other than to ask Fritz if he had listened to Jane and had considered the whole situation. Fritz replied that he had and that his decision remained unchanged. Upon returning to the Prieuré, Gurdjieff again questioned him. Fritz would later write that Gurdjieff asked him if he "had considered and evaluated my relationships to my mother, to Jane, and to himself and the school [the Institute] conscientiously, and if, having done so, I still wanted to go back to America." When Fritz remained resolute, Gurdjieff agreed and Jane immediately capitulated.

Soon, Jane came to the Prieuré with tickets, passport, and legal papers and Fritz packed to leave. Gurdjieff was going to Paris so he would not be there when Fritz left and so, before driving his Citroën out the gate, Gurdjieff beckoned to him. He shook his hand and with a sad smile asked—"So you decide to go?"

Fritz was only able to nod his head. Gurdjieff put his arm around him and leaned over and kissed his cheek. "Must not be sad," he said. "Sometime maybe you will come back; remember that in life anything can happen."

At that moment the boy realized that despite his misunderstandings with Gurdjieff, his affection for him remained undiminished. "I realized, although not immediately," Fritz later wrote, "that if he had at any time put the question of my departure on a personal, emotional level—the end of my personal association with him—I probably would not have left. He did not; as I have said, he always seemed to me to play fair."

At the dock Jane gave Fritz a copy of the document which broke the adoption. She told him—

"You may be shocked when you read this, but try to realize my position and remember that it was very difficult to break the adoption without some reason that would be legally valid."

Reading it, Fritz gathered that he had been "expelled" from the Gurdjieff school because he was "morally unfit." Though shocked, he assumed that it had to be worded that way for legal reasons.

In October fifteen-year-old Fritz Peters crossed the Atlantic on the *Leviathan;* during the crossing the Wall Street Crash occurred. No one met him when he landed in New York and, after some difficulties, when he got to Chicago he found his way to his parent's home, a large and luxurious apartment overlooking Lake Michigan. Bill, his stepfather and an attorney, at once mixed the boy a drink and offered him a cigarette, both of which Fritz accepted. He told Fritz that his mother was again in the hospital but should return and reminded him that they had a seven-year-old daughter, Linda, who lived with them. After observing that he did not know many boys his age who drank and smoked, Bill confronted Fritz with the adoption document. The two wrangled and the stepfather produced a long letter from Jane which went into greater depth about the meaning of the document, saying that Fritz was "some sort of sexually depraved delinquent given, principally, to the practice of corrupting other, smaller, children."

For three hours, his stepfather grilled him, attempting to elicit an affirmation or denial of what Jane wrote. Fritz parried, telling him in effect that if he admitted to the allegations, he would believe him; and if he denied them, "he would always wonder if I were telling the truth or not." Further, as Fritz had no way of proving his innocence, he would say nothing. "I would leave it up to him—not to decide which one of us, Jane or myself, had been telling the truth—but simply to decide whether or not Jane had been honest."

His mother returned the next day. Soon Lois and the stepfather received letters from mutual friends of Jane and who had heard from Jane about Fritz's growing delinquency. (Jane's actions in all this was a puzzle which still remains.) They did not want to see him. Thus, Fritz returned home at the cost of being branded an outcast, a role that would be his for the rest of his life.

G. I. Gurdjieff as he appeared in the 1920s

The Château du Prieuré in 1989

Café de la Paix,
sidewalk tables on the
Boulevard de Capucines

A dining room in
the Café de la Paix

74

Solita Solano

Noel Murphy and Janet Flanner

Nancy Cunard

Georgette Leblanc

Margaret Anderson at Château Tancarville

Château Tancarville

Creation of the Rope

PARIS. APRIL 1931. TWO WOMEN FROM SAN FRANCISCO, ALICE ROHRER, A WEALTHY MILLINER, AND HER COMPANION KATHRYN Hulme, a writer, had just arrived. Before touring Europe, they hoped to sell their car. They had heard that some American women writers living in Paris might be interested. A meeting was arranged with the writers at the Café Flore on the Boulevard St-Germain, a well-known expatriate habitat often frequented by Picasso and his crowd. When Alice and Kathryn drove up to the café, what they saw were three American women all dressed in black tailored suits and white satin scarves folded Ascot style, sitting in a row at a front table behind three pairs of white gloves and three martinis. Kathryn thought—"The three Fates! It was like seeing in triplicate the sophisticated chic that only years in Paris could produce."

The three well-tailored women in black introduced themselves as Solita Solano, Janet Flanner and their friend Djuna Barnes. Kathryn was especially excited to see Djuna as *transition*, a small literary magazine, had just published a short story of hers, in the same issue where Djuna's new novel *Ryder* was reviewed. After drinks and chatting, Kathryn offered to show Solita how to drive the car. At the end of the lesson, Solita thanked her, saying, "I don't often have a chance to act in the physical center. I'm always in the other two."

"The other two what?" asked Kathryn, perplexed.

"Centers of course ... emotional, mental. Man is a three-centered being. You don't have to live in just one, like a beggar, as someone said."

To Kathryn what Solita—this "nervous high-strung creature who speaks shorthand in gasps [and] looked capable of any degree of original thinking—was talking about she had no idea, but nevertheless it made an impression.

The car sold, Alice and Kathryn went off on their tour around Europe.

Alice Rohrer was a self-made woman, an immensely successful milliner—"Madame X" as she was called—whose hat designs were the choice of San Francisco's chic society. "Madame X" was in fact a country girl from the Cumberland Mountains, one of five daughters. Her early life was such that she had run away from the family farm in her teens and apprenticed to a millinery wholesaler in Baltimore. Smart and ambitious, Alice had taught herself the business, by careful and painstaking observation working her way up from apprentice to blocker to trimmer to fitter and, finally, to master designer. At some point Alice married what she called a "good little man" and was soon divorced.

Moving to San Francisco, she opened a shop and began designing hats. Artistic, self-assured, with a sharp business acumen, Alice's designs were such a success that within a few years she was employing thirty women. Blessed with a Fragonard face, Alice's deep-set dark eyes were framed by a swept-back coiffure, highlighted at the temples with silver streakings. This, together with her very thin figure, gave her an enchanting elegance and ethereal quality.

Kathryn was still in search of herself when she met Alice in 1927. After several years at the University of California at Berkeley, Kathryn had quit to go to New York to become a writer. Five years later, in 1926, she married an old college friend. Divorced a year later, Kathryn returned to live with her mother in San Francisco. The divorce hurt, especially since her parents had divorced, but she now accepted that a relationship with a man was not to be.[1] She was twenty-seven when she met Alice, who was born January 6 and was ten to fifteen years older.

They made a good enough match that one day Alice, wanting to visit France and North Africa, suggested to Kathryn that she accompany her as a driver and friend, with Alice taking care of all expenses. In early May 1928, the two women set off on the first of their many travels together.

Months after meeting "the Three Fates," Kathryn and Alice returned to Paris and called Solita. Meeting again at the Café Flore, the conversation eventually turned back to when Solita spoke about man as a three-centered being. Sensing genuine interest, Solita told Kathryn and Alice about Gurdjieff and the esoteric teaching he had brought. They wanted to know where to find him. He was no longer teaching, Solita said, but she knew a woman student of his who was authorized to teach—Jane Heap. "It's the only important thing in Paris," added Solita.

Solita took them to Montparnasse to meet Jane. Jane's magnetism and presentation of the ideas made a tremendous impression on both Kathryn and Alice. Jane described the teaching that Gurdjieff had brought as a "method of effort—conscious effort, not mechanical, automatic effort.... Man," Jane told them, "is the highest possible development of the self-evolving form. Nature can do no more. All further development requires conscious effort."

Said Kathryn: "I had never before heard anything like Gurdjieff's formulation of man's dilemma—man the 'unawakened,' the 'man-machine' imprisoned in the habit patterns of his likes and dislikes, his vanities and fears, his greed and envies. I had never before heard that there was something one could do about this dilemma."

After a month of attending Jane's weekly meetings, one afternoon Kathryn, Alice, and Solita were having a drink in the Ritz Bar when Alice said she had decided to return to California and

---

1. Growing up there had been a problem with gender identity. Either because Kathryn was a tomboy or her father had wanted a boy, he had called her "Tom" and had had her hair cut like a boy's. Unsettled and fearing him, she bit the nails of her right hand down to the nubs while in high school.

sell her shop so that she might pursue *"our* Gurdjieff studies" without distraction. Kathryn was about to protest but Solita stopped her —she had heard the intonation in Alice's voice.

While Alice was away, Margaret Anderson and Georgette Leblanc appeared at one of the meetings. Kathryn saw Margaret as "a Valkyrie, a warrior in search of a challenge. Our sessions sparkled when she was there.... she knew how to load the questions she fired at Jane, how to bait her to reveal more than perhaps was intended for beginners." Kathryn saw Georgette as a "Tanagra figurine" with her statuesque beauty, blond hair and the aliveness of her large green eyes.

After years of hand-to-mouth, the first volume of Margaret's memoirs, *My Thirty Years War,* was published in 1931. Margaret's book received a great deal of praise. The review that Margaret liked best was Sherwood Anderson's in *The New Republic:*

> So you too, Margaret Anderson, have written a book ... *My Thirty Years War.*
>
> But Margaret, you are yourself a character in a book. You are not real. No one ever thought you were real. You are, have always been, something that comes into other lives. You are not a woman. You are not a man. You know little enough of the rest of us. What do we know of you?
>
> Well, I dare say you eat, you sleep. I know that you wear clothes, gorgeously lovely clothes. Words flow from you. There are some two hundred and seventy–four pages of words gathered here in this book you have put out for us to read. Speaking for one man, I read it Margaret, with extreme delight....
> And so last night I read your book, not wanting to sleep, wanting to hear your voice again, wanting to feel again your beautiful belief in unreality. O thou unreal creature.
>
> Did you know, Margaret, that I loved you, that a thousand men, a thousand women have loved you... You inspired love and devotion. You weren't after anything. You never did push yourself forward. You didn't have to. You had but to walk through the streets, though a hotel lobby. Whenever you went men's eyes followed you, women's eyes followed you. Women were not jealous of you. Men did not look at you with greasy eyes.

You were not like the rest of us, struggling down there in the Chicago mud, going constantly, falteringly, in and out of our unreal world. You were unreal. You were a character in a play. You were a novel or a painting come to life.... You have brought back other days and they were good days. You made them good days while you stayed with us.

Anderson's review captured the archetypal, magical quality that Margaret emanated and that set her and the *Little Review* apart. Margaret had gotten a good advance and royalties were projected to be sizable. With the money she bought a Citroën and Georgette convinced her to lease from her sister and brother-in-law a run-down château called La Muette, just west of Paris, where Louis XIV first met Marie-Antoinette. Though they had just moved in that Christmas day, Georgette staged a musical soirée. She invited Kathryn, Solita, Louise, the Italian playwright Luigi Pirandello, composer Darius Milhaud, American pianist Allen Tanner, and Elspeth Champcommunal, the English couturier, and Jane's new love. Jane was to attend but was hospitalized with diabetes.

In February 1932 Alice returned to France having concluded her business in America. Kathryn went to le Havre to meet her. They drove back to Paris in Alice's gleaming new Packard convertible roadster. Having heard that Gurdjieff sometimes frequented the Café de la Paix, Alice insisted upon going straight there. Drinks were ordered—a sherry for Alice, a cognac for Kathryn—and they chatted and relaxed amid the café's sumptuous decor of gold Corinthian pilasters that upheld ceilings frescoed with clouds and cherubs.

Looking about the café, Alice wondered aloud—"However could Mr. Gurdjieff concentrate in a place like this?"

Just then Kathryn was looking at a man on the green velour banquette opposite them industriously writing in a notebook.

"Some can," answered Kathryn. "That one for instance. I don't believe he has looked up since we came...."

At that moment, searching for a word, the man lifted his head. The skull was large, dome-like and shaven. The black eyes were large, very intense. The handlebar mustaches were curled up at the ends. It matched the face Kathryn had heard about at Jane Heap's.

"But that must be Gurdjieff!" exclaimed Kathryn.

But already Alice had shot out of her seat, calling— "Come … we'll go right over and speak to him."

It was Gurdjieff.

Alice did most of the talking and when he learned she had a car, he invited the women to follow him to the Prieuré.

Following him was a nightmare. Said Kathryn:

> He drove like a wild man, cutting in and out of traffic without hand signals or even space to accommodate his car in the lanes he suddenly switched to … until he was in them, safe by a hair.… In the breathing spaces at red lights, I sometimes saw him off to the right or the left, black fur cap set at a jaunty angle, puffing tranquilly on a cigarette. He always got away first on the green light even (so it seemed) when he was one or two cars behind the starting line.

They had dinner at the château and Gurdjieff invited the women to stay the night. By the time they arose the following day he had left. A bit perplexed, they drove back to Paris. Kathryn and Alice often went to the Café de la Paix hoping to see him but they never did. However, over a year later on a visit to New York, the women unexpectedly saw him at Child's restaurant on Fifth Avenue sitting with a group of American pupils, but were too shy to talk to him.

The Monday night meetings continued at Jane Heap's apartment. The task of telling one's life story had been completed and now the meetings refocused on efforts to remember and observe.

On a personal level—while the lives of the other women had settled down—Solita's was more and more chaotic. In her relationship with Janet, she managed the money, collected items for Janet's "Letter from Paris," and edited it—and then on weekends she would be left alone as Janet went off to see Noel Murphy in Orgeval. Also, her relationship with Margaret, now in its seventh year, had begun to cool. Margaret had become involved in a secret and passionate correspondence with the English actress Josephine Plows-Day, known as

"Tippy." At sixty-four years old, she was sixteen years Margaret's senior. Margaret had met the actress in New York through Gladys Tilden, the actress's niece and one of Margaret's former loves. Margaret liked a challenge, the dramatic, the creative—ecstasy.

One day Solita discovered their letters. In a rage of jealousy, her ideal of "absolute freedom" forgotten, Solita could not help herself. She wrote Tippy informing her that Margaret was a lesbian. Though Tippy· must have known, the outraged actress—a devoted member of Frank Buchman's Oxford Group, the predecessor of "Moral Re-Armament"—immediately wrote back informing Solita that "On this Crucifixion Day, I want you to know that I long for you to be redeemed and made clear ... die to your sin." A few days later, Margaret also received the same advice. Betrayed by Solita as she had been by Jane, Margaret's wrath was devastating—she is even thought to have hit Solita—and their relationship ended.

Distraught, having lost Margaret—and guilty about having not only betrayed her lover but her own credo of "absolute freedom"—Solita found herself alone in the most absolute psychological sense. She was without connection to anyone. Brought to the brink, she acted:

> In the autumn of 1934 in a crisis of misery, I suddenly knew that I had long been waiting to go to him [Gurdjieff] and that he was expecting me. I sought him out and sat before him, silent.... He was then living in the Grand Hôtel, over the Café de la Paix—his "office," while waiting for a flat to be found. The Prieuré group had dispersed, there were no followers or pupils near him except Elizabeth Gordon who sometimes came to the Café.

Now Solita was more receptive. She had studied the ideas of the teaching and verified what she could in terms of her own observation. Having worked on herself—impartially seen and absorbed her manifestations, having objectified to a degree her life story and what had shaped it, she was no longer as ruled by her sensibilities. The rough surface that Gurdjieff presented, his deliberate "stepping on corns" no longer obscured the unique quality of being he radiated. Now when he spoke to her of the teaching, Solita had the material necessary to both relate and apply what Gurdjieff said to her own life.

If the intervening seven years since Solita had first met Gurdjieff had been hard for her, so, too, had they been difficult for him. His mission had been to establish the teaching in the West and, though he had persevered, he had encountered one obstacle after another. First the car crash in 1924 with the resulting closure of the Prieuré. Then three arduous years of writing the *First Series* of *All and Everything* and upon finishing it, realizing it was unreadable and had to be rewritten. That same year, Orage—the student most capable of helping to establish the teaching—had ignored Gurdjieff's warning and married Jessie Dwight, and quickly. Orage settled into family life, becoming a father and—given his young wife's resistance to his involvement with Gurdjieff—put himself in galoshes, i.e., had a split mind, over Gurdjieff. Hoping to reenlist Orage, in January 1930 Gurdjieff visited him in New York, but met with no success. Gurdjieff returned in November and delivered a terrific shock to Orage, hoping it would shake him out of his slavery to his chief feature—a weakness for women—but Orage sloughed it off. In May 1931, Orage—maintaining that he had not "the absolute faith" he imagined was required of him— left Gurdjieff.

Lack of funds forced Gurdjieff to close the Prieuré in May 1932. In 1933, no longer able to keep up the mortgage payments on the Prieuré, he lost it completely. In 1934 he published a pamphlet *The Herald of Coming Good.* It was so completely misunderstood all copies had to be recalled. In November Orage unexpectedly died, thus ending any hopes Gurdjieff had for stepping down the teaching through him—and there was no pupil of Gurdjieff's who could take Orage's place. He did complete the *Third Series* of *All and Everything* in April 1935—although some believe he simply stopped writing.

So when Gurdjieff and Solita met that autumn day at the Café de la Paix, both had arrived at the nadir of their lives; hers subjective, his objective. Given his traditional viewpoint regarding what he called "the third sex," he must have had serious concerns about accepting her as a student. But, as he would later say to her, Kathryn and Louise (Alice was away)—"You very dirty ... but have something very good—many people not got—very special." Moving quickly—or perhaps this was already planned—Gurdjieff told Jane Heap to end her Montparnasse group and go to London to lead groups there. Jane told Kathryn, Solita and Louise of her new assignment and the end of their group. There would be no new group. Gurdjieff, she declared emphatically, would never teach again. She refused to tell them of his whereabouts. On October 18th she left for London.

Was this a test of their seriousness? their resolve? The women refused to accept what Jane told them. They would find Gurdjieff themselves. They took turns standing watch outside the Café de la Paix. Finally, on Saturday, October 19th, Kathryn saw him and without hesitation approached his table. After some talk, Gurdjieff asked if she would like to be a "candidate for shearing." She nodded. Gurdjieff gathered up his notebooks and told her to follow him to his hotel room next door at the Grand Hôtel.

The room was small and filled with books and his manuscript. A man was busily typing. Gurdjieff took some twenty pages of the manuscript and told her to read it. He poured glasses of vodka and the three sat eating from a piece of smoked sturgeon, a block of white goat's milk cheese and some jarred herring. There was also some bread. At the end of the meal, he invited Kathryn to dinner that evening at l'Ecrevisse, or "Madame Crawfish," in Montmartre, a restaurant he was said to own or have a share in. He called it his "crayfish club" and told her he took people there and "sheared" them. He told Kathryn she could bring one friend. She brought two, Solita and Louise. He welcomed them all. The next day he met the three women at the Café de la Paix. He regarded them individually and then as a group, saying, "You very much changed—if before worth one hundred dollars, now worth thousand." They then returned to l'Écrevisse for dinner. As in the days at the Prieuré, he began toasting to the Idiots. He invited the *patron* and the cook to toast, and the waiter as well. Pouring everyone's shot glasses full of his favorite Armagnac, Château de Larresingle, he raised his glass, his bald cranium shining in the candlelight, his dark eyes glistening with delight, and proclaimed—

"To the health of all ordinary idiots."

In one swallow he downed the glass.

He saw that Louise was unsure about drinking.

"Never mind idiot doctors, drink," he said, "good for you."

Looking at Solita, he said, "Drink, drink."

She readily emptied her glass.

"No, no." he advised. "Woman must drink only half glass of toasting. All she wants, but in half glasses. Now you not drink next toast."

A bit of conversation followed, and at the appropriate time he again poured the glasses, this time toasting—

"To the health of all super idiots."

Each evening the women found themselves alone with Gurdjieff. After dinner they would go to Kathryn's room at the Hôtel Bonaparte where Gurdjieff listened as the women read aloud the opening chapters of his *First Series,* entitled, *An Objectively Impartial Criticism of the Life of Man or, Beelzebub's Tales to His Grandson.*

Monday evening at dinner with Gurdjieff, the proprietor himself hurried forward to show Gurdjieff to his table, already set with service for four. The proprietor kissed his fingertips and described the excellence of the *écrevisses* he had found that morning in Les Halles.

Though Gurdjieff had just had all his upper teeth pulled and a new plate installed, the waiter set before him a huge platter of crimson 'river lobsters' steaming in a thin reddish sauce. "Oie, oie!" Gurdjieff cried and ladled it like a soup into the dishes the waiter held. Then he forked a heap of crayfish onto each dish. Gurdjieff then opened the bottle of Château de Larresingle and poured it into the six glasses he had ordered set before him—four for himself and party, one each for the patron and the waiter—and then lifted his glass, instructing the women to drink only half on the first toast and the proprietor and waiter to drink all, and gave the first of his famous ritual toasts—*"A la santé de tous les idiots ordinaires."* [To the health of all ordinary idiots.]

Kathryn, not remembering the sequence of Idiots, drew Gurdjieff's ire. Louise gave the correct idiot, however, and Gurdjieff, dark eyes glistening, declared, "I am astonished." Only Solita knew the correct sequence. As a precaution, she had written the sequence down the night before and memorized it.

Before the dinner ended, Gurdjieff mentioned that he planned to start a new group. They would be its nucleus, he said.

The women were overjoyed.

"You very dirty," Gurdjieff told the three women, then added, "...but have something very good—many people not got—very special."

Solita began to cry.

"Must not cry."

"But I must."

"Must—but must not."

At dinner's end, Gurdjieff and the three women returned to the Bonaparte and read in Kathryn's room, number six, Jean Cocteau's old room, until midnight. Janet Flanner and Solita had rooms on the top floor and at one point Janet came down. Solita introduced her, saying—"Old friend, we live here ten years."

Gurdjieff regarded Janet.

"Oh," he said, "sometimes such friendship very bad, great hate comes out, then love, then more hate."[2]

Such a direct "tramping on corns" did not endear Gurdjieff to Janet and thereafter she and Solita often wrangled over what Janet saw as Solita's "devotion" to Gurdjieff.

A few nights later, the women read aloud in Kathryn's room until 2 A.M. The following morning they met him in the Café de la Paix and took the train to Fontainebleau, reading aloud from his manuscript the entire way. They went to his brother Dimitri's little house. Gurdjieff showed them a machine he had invented.

"It looked like a radio," Solita said. "Beside it is a rod that emits moans, music, buzzing or shrieks according to what has approached; its tone changing for each person's vibrations."

The following evening Solita walked alone with him from the restaurant to the hotel for another reading. Just weeks away from her forty-seventh birthday, Solita told him—"I'm too old to begin this work—it's too late."

"Never too late," Gurdjieff said, "but now twice as hard."

They walked a bit further and he asked—"You wonder why I so good to you?"

"Yes. Why?"

"I not tell you yet."

Almost to the Bonaparte, he asked—"Is it bad for you that I am good to you?"

"No, I am sure not."

"I think so too."

The next evening at dinner thunderbolts flew. Solita had asked a mental question.

"Now you know your illness," Gurdjieff said sternly, "your sickness. It is curiosity—American curiosity. Always you want to know more and more without understanding what already I have said to you. For that you will die *merde!*"

Solita's eyes began to tear.

In a softer voice, Gurdjieff asked, "You angry?"

2. It would seem from Gurdjieff's first comments about Janet Flanner, as well as Solita's later comments, that Janet is a denying source in regard to Gurdjieff and the Work that Solita must overcome if she is to develop. This is quite often the case in relationships. One wants the Work and the other denies it, feels threatened by the other's interest in it, and so works to undermine. A struggle ensues which tests the valuation and resolve of the seeker. As there is usually a sexual aspect involved in such relationships, the struggle is not only on the intellectual and emotional levels but instinctive as well. If the denying partner does not become neutral, the relationship must be ended. One partner has outgrown the other, new wine cannot be put in old bottles, as it is said. With Janet, while she insisted on having other relationships, she could never let Solita go. Solita was not strong enough to break away herself, even when she later wants to start a new life with another woman. This situation ultimately may have led to a confusion in regard to Gurdjieff on Solita's part.

"No ... it's true what you say."

Regarding Louise, he told her, "You are psychic weak."

To Kathryn: "You are like cow who comes home at night and stares at new painted barn door. Not know home because just was painted."

Again to Solita: "I have thought of seven things about you and one I tell. You have eye of suffering wolf. Only eye, very special thing. I have seen wolf, female wolf, attacked by pack, hungry, tired, bitten; in agony she turn look on me, like look in your eye."

Before leaving he told Solita that she was a slave to functions— "Tonight you were bitten by your flea. You be careful not to catch more fleas or you cannot sleep in your bed."

On Sunday, Gurdjieff telephoned, telling the women to meet him at the Coupole. He shopped for their lunch, bought caviar, vodka, Russian cold foods. Then they carried it all back to Kathryn's room for lunch. Afterward, the women read for hours. That evening they met him at the Écrevisse. He spent 300 francs for dinner and two bottles of Armagnac. He scolded Solita, Kathryn and Louise for treating Louise's dog "Tuppy" like a human being.

Then he spoke about emanation of all bodies.

"We emanate. This is an active function; a dirty process, as dirty as making *merde*. But sometimes there can be something else but dirt in emanations."

Solita sat expectantly waiting to hear what the "something else" was.

"No," he said, looking at her. "That I not tell."

He paused, Solita still hanging breathless in midair—"Many more things like this I know," he said, "but can never tell."

He went on to speak about everything having emanations— "We each one surrounded by atmosphere of our emanations. We each have atmosphere around us all the time—dog also, also bottle, also earth." He spoke of one way to accumulate our emanations so that they are not lost. "There are seven ways," he said, not saying what the others were. "To do this," he said, speaking of the exercise he gave—"you must remember yourself."

Just before October's end, an older woman, conservatively dressed and wearing a hat which she never took off, came to Kathryn's room for the reading. She sat quietly and listened attentively throughout the reading. At the end Gurdjieff greeted her, exclaiming—"M*ees* Gordon, welcome!"

He told everyone that Miss Gordon had been with him since the Prieuré's opening in November 1922. Then, turning back to her ,he said: "M*ees* Gordon, it's now or never. You don't have much time left. You must do something special now."

Miss Gordon sat with a long face, determined not to react.

"If you do not," continued Gurdjieff, twisting his mustaches, "*merde* you have been, *merde* you are and *merde* you will perish, like dog."

Miss Gordon's face flushed.

Told of the emanation exercise, Miss Gordon tries it and asks at the next meeting, "Where, Mr. Gurdjieff, should center of gravity be for this—in mind?—in leg?" She explained that there came a stoppage when she tried.

He told her the stop came because, "You have too much mind on it—*must* have *attention*. Attention is the working together of the association of thought with association of feeling. Memory working together with sense makes attention."

He said it was important to do the exercise with this attention. "Can make mistake at beginning and that can be dangerous, then you have only psychopathic attention—a mental center attention—not totality of memory-sense attention."

Gurdjieff turned to the rest of the women and said in another voice—"M*ees* Gordon will be like Mother Superior for you and you must treat her as such."

On November 1st, Gurdjieff telephoned at 6 P.M. to say he would come at 9:30 for another reading. Night after night the women had read and this night they were all were so tired they could barely sit in their chairs. Nevertheless, at midnight, now the usual quitting time, Gurdjieff motioned that the reading should continue. Kathryn read mostly, as she was the best reader. The women, especially Solita, tried to not yawn and to sit upright in their seats. Gurdjieff sat with one leg folded beneath him as always, watching each woman intently. At one point, the subtle but powerful substance he generated became apparent. The room became charged with energy and the women revived. When the reading ended at 3 A.M., five and a half hours after it had begun, no one was tired.

The next evening at dinner Gurdjieff said to Solita: "I think on you today. This evening is for you—you are hero of evening. I bring special chapter for you."

He handed her Chapter 16, "The Relative Understanding of Time."

Four days later, Gurdjieff had the women read without a break for six and a half hours, from 8:30 P.M. to 3 A.M. Gurdjieff said he planned to continue to write for two months, finish his last book [the *Third Series*], and then start classes. After that they could never see him alone, only from a distance. He said that how they were with him now was "an accident." They read from the *Second Series* [*Meetings with Remarkable Men*]. During the reading, he told them, "I can pronounce 400 consonants for your 36. Sound-producing organs in man are more important than his eyes. Americans worst nation for sound-producing."

Days later Solita sat with him at the Café de La Paix. He told her, "I make special program now for you. You badly organized—too much here, too little there, one place empty, good physical, fourth center wrong. I give initiate exercise for which you must take vow. On what you choose take vow? What is most important for you?"

"My eyes, Mr. Gurdjieff."

"Then let be so. Would you believe could exist such type man who would give eyes before his arms or legs? Yet is so."

Then he gave her the special program she was to follow.

One evening Gurdjieff, who had always been careful to take the chapters of the manuscript they had read with him, inexplicably, left them behind. Had he forgotten? Was it intentional? They didn't know. But the real question was: *what were they going to do?* Without his permission, they decided to make 'pirate' copies. Solita dictated and Kathryn typed while Louise stood look-out on the small balcony. Solita sent copies to Margaret and Georgette in

Vernet, in northern France, and Kathryn sent copies to Alice in New York.

After dinner Gurdjieff and the women would often go to the Café de la Paix for coffee and sit outside under the stars. One evening, studying the faces of the people who passed by their table, he pointed out that beneath the outer mask, or persona, each person wore, there was an inner animal, one that typified each person's inner natures. Their "inner animal" each person had always to contend with. But one also had to remain friends with it. For without the help of this inner animal, one couldn't achieve the aim of the teaching—the creation of a soul.

Gurdjieff asked if they would like to know their inner animals. The women hesitated. Gurdjieff said he would begin with Louise, Her inner animal was a sardine ... a sardine at that moment it leaves the water to die on the sand. While it had energy, it kept throwing itself about in somersaults and afterward, when its energy was spent, it only kept "quivering, gasping and flipping its tail." Later, he added "wart" to her inner animal—"Sardine-wart." Wart meant carbuncle.

Regarding Solita, he said—"Kanari."

"Canary?" cried Solita. "Oh, Mr. Gurdjieff ... *not* a canary!"

Eyeing Kathryn—"She is Kroko*deel.*"

Perplexed, Kathryn asked what he meant. He gave an analogy. While he didn't like crocodile meat and never ate it, "crocodile I like," he said, "I can send ahead of me to swallow enemy, can be *useful* to me. *Now* you understand?"

Alice returned from America, and on November 20th gave a dinner at the Écrevisse and invited Miss Gordon. Though Gurdjieff had appointed her the group's secretary, often he openly pointed out her weaknesses. Quick flushes and small livid angers followed his remonstrations but she quickly collected herself. She was quite devoted to him and understood, from her experience at the Prieuré, his method of teaching. She was also protective of her position.

This evening she asked Solita suspiciously—"Have you been seeing Mr. Gurdjieff?"

"Yes—every day, sometimes twice a day," said Solita.

Miss Gordon, her face turning red, shouted, "That's a lie!"

Solita didn't answer.

Alice said, "Yes—today we've been with him since noon."

Gurdjieff called Alice "Th*een* One." Regarding her, he said— "Now you not look on me like cow, but like *boa constrictor*—not like empty snake, but full one. You not have poison, you swallow whole. Like crocodile."

Having established that, Gurdjieff now poured glasses of Armagnac and began the ritual of toasting to the Idiots. As he proposed each toast, he identified each women's Idiot. Louise was a Hopeless; Solita, a Compassionate; Alice, a Squirming; and Kathryn, a Square.

Gurdjieff had moved from the Grand Hôtel to a new flat on the rue Labie behind the Étoile, just inside the old fortifications of Paris and, beginning November 24th, the women went there for lunch every day. With all its windows shuttered and only lit by one small salon lamp, the flat looked like a cave. As the women arrived, Gurdjieff greeted them from his small kitchen where he stood in short sleeves, baggy trousers and carpet slippers, his red fez cocked at an angle, its tassel moving to and fro as he cooked—exotic delicacies.

The meal prepared, he took his place at the head of the table. Solita, who set the table, waited on him. There were long silences followed by ritual toasting to the Idiots. He would teach, exhort, attack or mollify as required. Afterward, the women filed into one room for the reading while Gurdjieff, in another, interviewed each women singly about the exercises. Kathryn, whom he called "kitchen boy," generally washed the dishes. "I like such kitchen boy, he not make me nervous," he said. On leaving, everyone put fifteen francs in the kitchen box to pay for the meal.

One day Solita had lunch alone with him. He gave her the Good and Evil chapter to read [Chapter 45, "In the Opinion of Beelzebub, Man's Understanding of Justice Is for Him in the Objective Sense an Accursed Image"]. He told her to read it first to herself, then to the others, then to read it again alone.

The next day after the reading of the chapter, Gurdjieff declared that while men had never seen angels in the world, they always thought they had seen devils. The more *good* men thought they were, the more devils they could see—such men saw devils where a really good man did not. Self-calming, he said, is the only devil in us.

Later, he and Solita alone, he told her: "I know you give me all your heart. Soon you must decide if all give up in world."

He began to explain to her a new exercise. Suddenly he stopped, saying:

> The way you receive my instruction is with very bad expression. People who are watching us would think I am telling you something quite else. There are spies for me everywhere. You must always keep your inner world for yourself alone. This is a serious matter for you. There is no correspondence between your exterior and your interior. Lucky for you I can read your interior or I would not be able to judge you. Often you have not corresponding expression of your inner life. The world cannot always judge you correctly. Sometimes when even a good effort at understanding you make, you have quite idiotic expression. But I see because I have knowledge of these things. You must always watch yourself, always remember yourself. You are a bad case of lop-sided. Always you have been for mind and nothing you find for understanding, because that is quite another thing and for that you must have teacher— but not in your idiot American sense.

He sat in silence for a period of time. Solita said nothing, afraid he wouldn't give her the exercise. Finally he explained it, saying she must do it three hours a day. "If ever you tell this," he warned, "terrible punishment for one who tell will happen. Don't know how or why this happens, but always is so, like a law."

Later, he said, "And remember yourself before the world," adding, "They must nothing see."

"Why have I no correspondence, Mr. Gurdjieff?"

"Heredity and bad education. Now you not try to think. You must catch up to your thinking, your mentation will come later when I have given you data for understanding."

The next day Gurdjieff left Paris for a few days. This allowed the women to catch up on their work and get some sleep. Solita began to read all the alchemists, and found that Xenophon defined the "I" as the compound result of consciousness, subconsciousness, and instinct. It sounded simpler than Gurdjieff's definition of the "I" as "a-relatively-transferable-arising-depending-on-the-quality-of-the-functioning-thought-feeling-and-organic-automatism."

On January 7, 1936, Solita found herself alone with him at the Café de La Paix. She looked as though she had been crying. He asked why.

"Afraid to tell you—you will say again I am psychopathic," she said.

"No, no, tell me."

"Today is the anniversary of my mother's death and I always have guilt and remorse about her."

"How long ago she die?" he asked.

"Fourteen years."

"Then not psychopathic," he answered. "Very good thing. Mother very important—you get fire from mother. But not think about her only once a year—but think often."

Solita took her mother's picture from her purse and handed it to him. He studied it, gave it back to her, saying, "Mother is mother."

"Small thing is like big thing when it ends badly," remarked Solita.

"There is tapeworm—and another worm."

On January 13th, his birthday, all the women gathered at his apartment. He sat on his big divan cross-legged, the women sitting before him like a class. His manner for the first time was that of a teacher. He talked continuously for an hour and a half. The subject was "man's search for a soul."

"You have heard my horse and cart representation," he began. "I will make another to represent man. This one in his search for a soul. Man in his history has always believed he had a soul and sought for it. This is the aim of all religions. If in ordinary life I were asked if man has a soul, I would say no, because in general, man has not. Before man can have a soul, he must have an 'I.' Only when he achieves an 'I' can he develop a soul."

Gurdjieff continued with a long talk about what was necessary to develop oneself in preparation for making a soul, saying that nature would help a young person to make the effort that would be demanded. "After a certain age," he said, "this effort is very difficult and often impossible. If each of you decide to continue to work with me, you must now be ready to give up all outside life—no engagements, no cinemas. You must always be ready to be here with me at all times, at any moment I call for you."

Gurdjieff then told Miss Gordon, Solita, Kathryn, Louise and Alice to form into a special, mutually supporting work group. Speaking allegorically, he said that they were going on a journey together under his guidance. It would be like climbing a high mountain. For safety, each of the members must be roped together, each one thinking of the others, all helping one another "as hand washes hand." He said that "If two people have lived a common aim together, they will always have a feeling of brotherly love, whether they love or hate each other, and nothing in family love can equal this feeling."

Afterward, the women went to the Café Flore to talk and have coffee. Miss Gordon said the experience with him that day was incredible—in twelve years, she said, he had never spoken as directly to anyone. Discussing how he had metaphorically "roped" them together, the women decided to call their group "the Rope."[3]

3. The way in which Gurdjieff works with the women of the Rope is quite different. Miss Gordon, of course, is a veteran of the Prieuré and is entirely committed to him. It would seem that Solita, Kathryn and Georgette opened to him immediately, while Margaret fights him, plays games and hides. One gets the sense that Alice, too, was not entirely open with him. Of Louise, not enough is said to form an opinion.

Said Kathryn: "We knew, I believe, even from the first day what that invisible bond portended. It was a Rope up which, with the aid of a master's hand, we might be able to inch ourselves from the caves of illusory being we inhabited. Or, it was a Rope from which, with sloth and lip service, we could very well hang ourselves....It was stronger than any bond I had ever felt before—for any man, woman or charity child who had ever crossed my zigzag path on earth."

At lunch the third week of January he told the women: "There are three kinds of onanism. The Greeks called them onanism, Platoism and Socratism.... Each center has its own onanism. Man lost his tail because of titillation in three centers."

A few days later he told Solita, "Imagination has always been your weakness and your enemy. Must now take quotation marks off the imagination, forget it and hate it. And you must see what your old friends are like. No one who liked you before must like you now—must hate you. Your friends all are special *merde*. Seeing their *merde-ness* will help you see your own."

He said that there is a place within that stores emanations. When enough accumulate, they will crystalize and then one has force. To accumulate, muscles should be "weak."

Solita said it was difficult for her to be aware of her body as a whole, as it seemed her center of gravity was in the solar plexus and so she was more aware of emanation from that part.

He said it was "very important to know body as a whole for this work, very important." He said that feeling has two centers—solar plexus feeling and spine brain.

Miss Gordon asked, "How can one know which is sense brain and which is feeling brain?"

"Can know," he answered, "that when come to those stops—maybe you have no spinal brain working at task—and you can know that by the absence of feeling in the spinal cord."

At the end of January, after dinner Solita casually brought out her puff and powdered her nose. Gurdjieff scolded her—"I am Oriental and man. Never can I see woman making prostitute thing without my insides turning over. Never has woman sat my presence and painted face. I see you make now six times and each time if I had had knife in my hand, I wish send it through your heart. This seven times and finish. At Prieuré no woman even dare smoke before me. This idiot fashion put paint on face exist only New York and in territory around Place Opéra. Only prostitute make in other places. If you wish make this thing, you must in water-closet go as if to make *merde,* and not make *merde* in my salon. What your father and your brother say to you ten years ago if you paint face in their presence? Me, I am Gurdjieff, and compared to me you are *merde* nonentity."

Then he made a ceremony of apologizing to Solita and the women. He said, "Now Kanari hate me, she hate me for two days."

At the end of February, Noel Murphy, Janet Flanner's love, went to the café with Solita to see Gurdjieff. Tall and self-assured, Noel came right to the point.

"Why do I have headaches all the time?" she asked.

He looked at her through his glasses. Finally, he answered, "Liver. Come lunch."

At lunch he told Noel, "You are combination camel and sparrow. I not understand why Kanari call you friend. I know very well psyche Kanari. Also I have made special study of camel properties during forty years. Never can two such animals be friends— is not basis of friend. Now I look to see if you are male camel or female camel. I not know yet. But I know even what kind of *merde* you make. You ever see camel *merde?* Small hard rounds, no scientist ever understand why *merde* like that. But I know. I also study strange sex organ female camel have."

Noel turned red and white, but didn't react.

Before lunch ended she mentioned she was going to the Opéra that night.

"No, not go, such music only titillation."

"What's that?"

"Masturbation," he told her.

Noel, not understanding how he meant the term replied, "Oh, I don't mind that, do you?"

Gurdjieff looked at her a long time and did not reply.

There were readings before and after dinner. Gurdjieff talked about the proper mixing of food and showed them a scale of seven notes in spices—brought out seven bags from the store room and named them do, re, mi, and so on. Solita was told this scale was very bad for all but her.

Gurdjieff later said to Solita, "After you do exercise, necessary you rest twice as long as you have done exercise. Be passive afterward."

Solita asked if that meant sitting still or could she do her work on the typewriter. He laughed.

"Oh, yes. You passive then. You well asleep then."

He said that one can never stop associations, as these are automatic. So let associations flow but be active. "With other part of mind," he said, "you work at task, and this is active. Pretty soon you find you have beginnings of new kind of brain—a new one for this new kind of mentation—and that other one becomes entirely passive."

Meeting another day for lunch, he asked Kathryn, "How feel?"

"Oh, wonderful, body gladness," she answered, "I get up in the morning and sing."

"Well, I often hear of crocodile tears," Gurdjieff replied, "but never before of crocodile song. And you, Kanari?"

"Stronger, but sad all the time."

He was delighted. "I have been expecting that from you; is as I thought. This is remorse of conscience and only the beginning. You will be much more sad later, as should be for your *merde* life you have lived."

He said to Solita, "You must now live in suffering between two worlds, the two worlds of man. You must die in first, be resurrected in second and only then live in both."

"If only I had something solid to build on. Cannot even explain inner state."

Said Gurdjieff: "Yes, no words for these things. But say anything you wish and I will understand from intonation." Later, Gurdjieff said to her, "I have made first stone foundation. You can be objectively happy now. Look at those people there in street. You have something they not have. Later I will put second gravity stone. Then third, up to seven. You need no longer say you will try. That is over and now you have only to do and do. Later I can tell you what I must not yet tell. Man has two mentations and you know what kind I wish for you. Only now is being-data being crystallized in you. In past everything rolled off like water from back of goose. All went in and out again."

Later he said, "High sex combined with laziness of organism." And "Even God cannot tell where will find what lost."

Kathryn spoke about the task he had given her of not smoking to see what new flow of associations resulted.

"This can be thing for power," he replied. "I tell you one very important thing to say—each time when longing come. Say, 'I wish result of this my suffering to be my own, for Being.' This saying can maybe take force from animal and give to Being. Can do this for any denial of something that is a *slavery.*"

By May 1936, the meals had become a prolonged midday dinner. Afterward there was a long break. Then the women would sometimes return for a late evening supper which could last to near midnight and sometimes beyond, especially when there were visitors. Margaret and Georgette—to whom Solita had regularly been sending reports of the meetings with Gurdjieff—left Vernet and returned to Paris near the end of May and immediately joined the Rope for daily meals.

Georgette's great lyric beauty had not survived the rigors of time and three grave illnesses, but at sixty-seven years old she was even more alive to the search for her true self. Death she had struggled with many times and she had told herself—"If I am to live, I swear to myself to go further than before ... I do not give myself the right to come out of danger in the same state in which I entered it." Though she tired easily now and slept irregularly, she gave herself wholeheartedly to Gurdjieff and his teaching, attending all the luncheons and voraciously reading the typescript of *All and Everything.* Gurdjieff said she was still young, it was her liver that was sick. All the organs were blocked.

Gurdjieff soon made Margaret and Georgette part of what he called "Knachtschmidt and Company." It was a name he always said with a smile. In old Russian this referred to, he said, groups of shoeless and shabbily clad peasants who came together at the end of the day's work to "make something."

At lunch one day during the toasting to the Idiots, Gurdjieff asked Margaret to choose her idiot.

"Zigzag," she said.

"You cannot be zigzag," he told her.

"But," said Margaret, "that is my condition now."

"Condition? Your condition has nothing to do with inner world. You defile zigzag. Wish go too high. Zigzag is high idiot, goes this way, that way, struggles against *merde* he knows he is. Is as if you, a deacon, put on archbishop's robes."

Alice arrived for dinner in a very nervous state—she had seen an autobus crush a boy on a bicycle.

Said Gurdjieff, "All things happen around you in life, but you now are obliged to be able to take from each. Save such feelings you have for when something happens to a near one."

"I remembered the time I was struck and dragged by an automobile."

"That is worse," he replied. "That is egotism. Egotism for present is dirty thing. Egotism for future is property of man."

On June 5th there was a big strike in Paris. Gurdjieff instructed the women to buy candles, bread, and find water. "Then have all that is necessary. I accustomed to revolutions, for me is simple thing, all life have had."

Nodding toward Margaret who sat on his left, "From first gravity guest on my left there comes a terrible vibration."

"But you know why, Mr. Gurdjieff," said Margaret.

"I not know."

"But you can imagine."

"Excuse, I cannot imagine. You can imagine, but I cannot. I am old man. Thirty years ago I could imagine, even was time I imagine I was God—or your Uncle Sam."

Later, speaking about tapeworms, he said: "When tapeworm is satisfied it have beautiful smile like bird of paradise. When angry and wants something, he makes so—angry face, angry noise. Kanari, you ever see tapeworm?"

"Only in bottle, Mr. Gurdjieff."

"Ah, then not see psyche of tapeworm if dead in bottle. Like medical student who see skeleton and then thinks he knows about life."

On June 9th at the Café de la Paix Gurdjieff told Margaret that her inner animal was a Tibetan yak, a cousin of the European cow.

"But in your case," he added, "you not look on door of new painted barn like cow which concerns itself only with question, 'Is that my home, or is it not?' You think like business man about quality of paint, how much cost, if will last, how react in rain—forget self completely."

"But Mr. Gurdjieff," Margaret replied, "cows are placid, I don't wish to be a cow."

"Cows not always placid; sometimes yak, this Tibetan cow, go berserk. People run inside house, shut door. Something take the psyche of this cow and entire being is wild—try break through wall—could even kill her children."

Gurdjieff filled his glass again. He noticed that Kathryn's was empty and Margaret's half full. "Here," he said, "is example of strange thing in nature. Krokodeel is small man, should drink small. She [Margaret] is big man and should drink big, but they do just opposite. In my opinion earth-man not have such un-logic."

Gurdjieff said to Solita, "You need not laugh—sometimes when I look at you I see in your face an exact Rebecca. You know story Rebecca?"

"At the well," answered Kathryn.

"Water," said Solita

"These Old Testament stories," noted Gurdjieff, "can be more important than all the words of Jesus Christ."

Said Solita: "We don't even know Bible and yet we come here to learn from you."

Answered Gurdjieff: "Yes, you should all have shame. I study Bible when I was twelve years old. Little boy, I sit in corner and with one eye I look from window where other boys play and one day my grandmother see me with attention going out window and she did a thing I never forget to this day. She had long beautiful pipe which she always smoke. This pipe she take and throw at me, not at my head but at shoulder here. I can feel it yet. Pipe all broken and was beautiful pipe. This make terrible impression on me and I understand how much she wish I study Bible. And then I study. I very afraid my grandmother. In village she was the oldest person and had most authority. She had one thousand times more authority than all your kings. She could say to people, 'My grandson not study Bible—kill him.' And they would kill me."

"But you don't hate her for it now?" said Solita.

Gurdjieff said, with great feeling, "No, I love her for it."

Said Kathryn: "Sometimes second gravity thing seems more important than first gravity thing."

"You see that? You understand that?"

He said that attention depends on the "degree of the gradation of the state of 'being,'" which the ancients spoke of as the strength of embrace of attention. Ancient science defines attention as "the degree of blending for sameness between the impulses of observation and constation by the processes of one totality with the processes in other totalities."

The next day at lunch Gurdjieff, toasting to Margaret, said: "May God help you transform into some other animal. As you are now, any wolf can take. I pity. I wish esteemed animal sit with me at my table. When I used to hunt for yak, never shot at skull, impossible to kill like that, must aim at heart to kill. Also can kill by aiming at Mary Jane, the soft part."

Later Margaret mentioned something, using the word "charm."

"Charm?" questioned Gurdjieff. "What is? No, you not tell. I know what is. I know by inner feeling. Is prostitute word. You not use such word. Only man in quotation marks uses such word. When real man hear, he squirm inside. Moreover I could tell you hundred just such words—all dirty words, make real man feel dirty when he hears. If you wish be friends with me, you not use such word."

Several days later at lunch, speaking to Louise, he saw Margaret staring at him.

"Why you look on me?" he demanded.

"Because I see something in your face, Mr. Gurdjieff. I like to study it."

"Excuse, you not see anything my face. For study me, you are too young. Three thousand years in your America, then maybe can study me. Study Sardine. In her I make association, I make changes. Her psyche you can study, you are not able to do more. Study her where I make changes come."

Margaret protested, "But I see you do the same thing in four different ways."

"Could be 104. But is not the same thing. I never do same thing."

Solita said, "Sometimes I feel I look on you like dog on master, wait for you to throw stick or order me to sit up."

"No, Kanari, not dog. No dog ever occupies himself with abstract questions."

At lunch he used the word "canning" and Kathryn thought he said "cunning."

"No," he said, "canning. *Canning* and *cunning* have same root and in ancient times meant the same thing. I speak of real cunning, not the dirty meaning of the word. The highest aim of man is to be cunning. The magus is cunning. The magus is the highest that man can approach to God, because only he can be impartial and fulfill obligation to God. In old times the magus was always made chief because he had cunning. Other magus could do either white or black magic but the magus who had cunning and canning could do both white and black and was chief of the initiates. Man with real cunning is man without quotation marks. Angel can do only one thing. Devil can do all."

Since May when Georgette and Margaret had arrived, Gurdjieff had worked with Georgette to improve her health. By mid-July the pain in her body had abated, energy had returned and, for the first time in twenty years, she slept through the night. "Physically," she said, "I am living a springtime in this cold month of July. I feel charged like a dynamo." During a luncheon Gurdjieff told the others—"She was candidate for death, she is already candidate for life." Then he looked at Georgette, mischief laughing in his eyes, and said, "I only said to her, 'Read the book, madam, read the book.'"

Alice and Kathryn reminded him they were sailing in August for America.

"I will fix in you," he told them, "what I have made already so it will not be lost. I will give you a program for living so you can know how to live in inner life. You must remember when you feel bad you must not lose yourself with mind. Some days you feel bad, then with swing of pendulum, you feel good. On your worst day, prepare for best day. This is the law. What is important is that you never lose self. Let mind be big sister to take care of little sister who is now in the house. Your nature is the little sister."

At the end of the first week of July, Gurdjieff took a four day excursion to Vichy. The Rope came along. At the Park Café, what he called his "summer office," Miss Gordon said: "I cannot believe, Mr. Gurdjieff, that we sit here with you like this. I think about that chapter—'Reflexes of Truth'—when a great man was being met for the first time, how difficult to see him. And now here we sit."

"Yes, all is different since accident. Then I die, in truth all die. Everything began then from new. I was born that year, 1924. I am now twelve-years old boy, not yet responsible age. I can remember how I was then—all thought, feeling. I was heavy, too heavy. Now everything is mixed with light."

He spoke at length of Madame de Hartmann, and the care she had always taken with him when they traveled. "She is first friend of my inner life, such thought she had for me."

Miss Gordon was very touched by this long story.

Seeing this, he said to Kathryn: "You know when Mees Gordon was born, small devils, not big ones, but still devils—stand around and prepare her in totality for me. From her, not from your Rockefeller, my future depend. Small devils make, arrange her whole life, not for her, but for me."

Miss Gordon wept. This way of thanking was too much for her.

Gurdjieff nodded toward her, not looking and said, "You know, if she were not drunk, she would cry now."

From virtually her first luncheon with Gurdjieff, Margaret had resisted and fought. He attacked her attitude consistently and openly. She fumed and fretted. Her state was one in which everything was hated. Even her beloved Paris repulsed her. "Walking [to Gurdjieff's apartment]," she complained, "through the noxious gases of the exhaust fumes of automobiles, my throat burning, my ears crackling with the loudspeaker city, my head fainting with fury, my heart failing, my eyes trying to see what they saw but, instead, distant hills... well, it was too much." What was really bothering her were the luncheons. She found them bewildering and, worse, boring. All the interest in food—Gurdjieff insisting that the women know what was being eaten and why—was taken to a level she never imagined, nor wanted to. Worse, was the conversation. It was so meager that Margaret said: "[I] felt called upon to do more than my share in developing the few remarks that were made." Somehow, no matter what she said, it fell flat, went no place. What was going on? Were it not for Georgette, Margaret might have left.

Gurdjieff was known for purposely "stepping on corns," pointing out the weak spots, falsity, any kind of subterfuge. Margaret was like a fighter who was losing badly but would not go down. Gurdjieff came at her from one side, then another, by turns confusing her, challenging her, ignoring her, trying to crack her shell, to break through to what was real in her.

At a luncheon he said, making an allusion to Margaret and Solita, "Funny picture how yak tries to be nightingale."

Later, he remarked:

"Yakina cannot understand as much as Kanari because she has fat behind. And when she makes *merde,* yak kills all small animals. Can you imagine what would be if yak could fly? When Kanari makes, not serious thing—even on head could only be wetness. Yes, it would be terrible if yak had wings."

Looking at Margaret, he asked, "You like?"

Margaret made no reply.

Goading her still more—"Think what picture that makes. You like such picture?"

"*Like* is not big enough word," Margaret replied. "No, I *not* like, Mr. Gurdjieff."

"But you understand more than usual?"

"Yes."

Having received an affirmation, Gurdjieff immediately switched to another level, saying: "Then you must like. This is first time in life you ever heard such, never any other place can you hear what you now heard. So you must like."

During lunch Gurdjieff said to Margaret: "Which you wish help you now? God or devil? Devil this time? Ah, then will have roses, roses for millions of years, until so hate smell of roses would rather have *merde* to smell. Now I wish drink alone this toast with Th*een* One, because tomorrow we talk. Not one drop for you, Kanari, you are representative of art and not understand commercial thing. Even if you gave all, it would mean nothing, because it is your nature not to understand such values. But when she and I talk tomorrow, only she will understand, because she have factors for this and much data. When I need money, you representing art give all, give 9,000 francs and think it is great thing because it is all. But she knows it is only *merde* and small thing, not even to speak about. For example, remember how I tell about man who take home food for dog? A *commerçant* [business] person never do this, but representative art would take, even if he had no dog, he would say he had, and take for his own breakfast."

At a later luncheon while toasting to the Compassionate Idiot—Solita—he looked at Margaret.

"Now you formulate," he told her. "Let devil help."

Margaret hesitated.

"Tell, tell. You must tell your good wishing for Kanari's health."

"But I already said it—in my mind," Margaret said.

"Is cheap thing in your mind. Many things can happen in your mind that we not know about. You must make effort. Show your wishing with your whole presence, with you in it."

Margaret began, "May devil help—"

But Gurdjieff broke her off: "Too late now."

"Better late than never," she said gamely.

"Now you are two times cheap," said Gurdjieff.

At a following luncheon Solita had asked a question and Gurdjieff suddenly said: "Look, Kanari, they take habit expecting you will be put in galoshes for such questions. From one side is good, you can make practice. Slip in and out of galoshes easily, never stay long in, never long out. But when Yakina will go in galoshes, she will stay forever. And if Kanari is in when Yakina fall on top, you can imagine poor Kanari. Must go into toe, worst place for stink."

Margaret spoke up: "I wish take risk, Mr. Gurdjieff. I wish to ask a question."

He nodded.

"We wish to know what is the interior animal of Crocodile."

"Is baby. Interior naive like baby. Not like M*ees* Keep [Jane Heap]. Her baby is much older. Kroco*deel's* is only two and a half years. Partly I blame Th*een* One. She always wish to be mother. There is a saying, by the way: 'If you call yourself a mushroom, then into mushroom basket you must.'"

"And what is my interior animal, Mr. Gurdjieff?" asked Margaret.

He made no reply. He had already given it—tapeworm—and Margaret had forgotten.

On July 30th at lunch Gurdjieff regarded Solita.

"Look, she have oily face," he said, "she wishes I fill glass. Come, drink, drink. It will relieve my aching left corn if you will drink."

"No," answered Solita, "even for corn I will not drink. For what purpose was my suffering last week if today I drink more than necessary?"

"Come, come, give glass."

She continued to refuse. He took her hand.

"I wish you to be able to drink like ordinary man," he said. "Drink like man who not like to drink. Wish or not wish, drink as those who drink around you drink, for company and not be slave."

He noticed Margaret smiling—"You spoil with smile what I make just now with Kanari. In truth you have not data to be friend for anyone. Now I would never choose you for friend. A moment before, a moment later, would not have been so bad, but at exact moment you smile, as if you had said, 'Ha, ha, ha.'"

Then he said to Margaret: "You say you hate yourself or you love yourself, but you say it only with your outside. Some day you will say it with your inside. Such thing will happen when I die. All man must die early or late, even I. I have no special (dispensation)."

Several days later at luncheon Margaret spoke up, saying that her "shell" had cracked at last.

"You must know your self-love before you can kill it," said Gurdjieff, indicating that she only thought her shell had cracked.

Margaret said that she knew it now.

"And your vanity?" asked Gurdjieff.

"Nearly the same, are they not?"

"Is sister. Still not enough to know them. Must now have something independent."

Gurdjieff looked at Georgette Leblanc and said, "Pity you not understand."

Said Georgette, fondly, "Yakina will explain later."

"She explain? How could she understand? Perhaps three months after—never she understand till three months. Now look—she angry."

Later, concerning the wolf and sheep in us confided to our care, Gurdjieff said: "Wolf satisfied? No, full."

Solita asked, "Is the difference between satisfied and full, a psychic difference?"

"No, objective. Only such a condition is a guarantee for wholeness of sheep. Life must always be such—and every day. Not only outer life but chiefly inner life. If so live your life, you will be intelligent. Can only be intelligent when self-sufficient—enough for all in yourself."

"Then," said Solita, "I must be intelligent, for every day I spend in this struggle. But even when sheep is safe, wolf is always looking around—so I'm not intelligent."

"No. Only candidate for."

Said Kathryn: "I remember what you said—always fix your eyes on the point beyond—and take that direction."

"Yes, but necessary take account every day of even this, or else that direction will become only a point fixed in mind—a habit of thinking."

Later, "Now I hope I have not offended your Scotchness, Mees Gordon."

"No, can't any more offend my Scotchness."

"But you I can offend—angry make."

"Yes," admitted Miss Gordon, "can angry make."

"Of course. From same source is Scotchness and offendedness. Same root have in psyche. You, Kanari, more than another, understand when I tell allegorically. You have smell."

Alice asked, "Is my animal really boa constrictor?" She said she knows boa is outside animal, but she wishes to know interior. He had told her earlier that her interior animal was a tapeworm.

"Yes. It was easy for me to put serpent in her because she already had by heredity a capacity for great swallowing. Now what suffering she will have. Because I put the serpent in her, she will always wish to swallow. And sometimes there will be nothing to swallow and so she will double suffer."

He toasted Sardine: "May both sources help you to make something for you that is your own. Even if only small thing."

Later, "Sardine, you have small brain. Kanari have big brain, for such animal, a very big brain. And is cunning brain. Sometimes is as clever as—dog."

When he heard Solita was going to the Hôpital de St. Louis to study: "Nerves are pipes—like those for electricity and radio. Remember this when you study. For earning money your articles, only four hours must work if intelligent—only donkey work eight hours. But study is different—forty-four hours a day study because is bank for future."

Gurdjieff at lunch the next day said, "Today I constate one thing about Sardine-Wart. Before she was dead—only reason not stink was that one small part still alive. Today I see other parts begin resurrect and I begin to take interest. She is still hopeless but another kind. Now is for us newly arrived baby."

He turned from the stove and looked at the three women sitting in his kitchen and said: "I nervous and angry now because in my kitchen sit three parasites who destroy the good of nature. They swallow pieces which I need for tonight and I have not possibility for buying more. They drink my blood."

"Dangerous parasites if they drink your blood," said Solita.

"No, blood can be cheap thing compared what I tell. You speak of blood, not even know from what blood proceed. They do worse than take my blood, worse than if take three liters, because for me to be angry or nervous costs more than three liters of my blood."

Solita was taken with the formulation of "from what blood proceed" but worked with herself not to ask.

"Kanari, I see that some impulse proceed in you. Now she look on me like dog on stick, not dare speak."

"Yes, I will speak," she answered, "because the words you use just now, 'impulse proceed' might be telepathy. I wondered if blood proceeds from different impulse than other organs."

"Blood is only result—not important. There is many another thing in man." He went on to speak of active elements.

Solita asked—"Can active elements change bones? Since I have come to you, even bones in hands are changed. Everyone has noticed I no longer have the same hands."

"Yes, of course. Can change even tail in man. Active element makes everything. Even the kind of breath you have depend from active elements.... Now my tapeworm sing—not 'Marseillaise' or 'Internationale.' He would only sing 'God Save King,' never would he be Communist—only monarchist or republican. Tapeworm of man is lazy and spoiled. He not have, like man, possibil-

111

ity of denying himself or wishing to suffer and make sacrifice for future."

Later he spoke in a disapproving tone of people who were either hot or cold.

Miss Gordon spoke up, "But you have said, 'Go the whole hog.'"

"That is not for people like you—you cannot go the whole hog."

The next day at the Café de la Paix, Alice and Kathryn gave him some money.

Said Kathryn, "Here is one pair of group who have strange property—one has cunning, the other canning and when they work together they have good result."

"You speak in joke but what you say is good thing. Both cunning and canning are necessary in all things. This is why there are two magics. Black magic is cunning—often also is cunning and canness—you understand the difference? Black magic is ideal for being. Cunning and can-ness is like conscious and unconscious, or like two words used in Bible for meaning two kinds of evil, voluntary and involuntary sin. You, Kroco*deel,* have cunning, I see possibility for developing big thing. And Th*een* One have very great canning possibility. What you have now you think is big thing, but compared to how you can be, is like baby made but not born."

Later, "Now I tell one most important thing, one lawable thing. If something you must do—some work or task—you must plan ahead of time, you can never do at the time, but if make exact plan before you must do, then is as if have aim and all prepares for this."

Solita, amazed, sat staring at him after some formulation.

"Look!" he cried, "What state she be in. There is old expression for describing such state. With one eye on heaven and one eye on earth and in place between exchange opinion. How is up there, down here, what can be, what will be. But when tired, she not look on sky or earth, but look on *merde.*"

"Oh, no!" cried Solita, protesting.

"In general I tell. Is such law. This expression from centrum come."

Near the end of July, Gurdjieff declared a three month break that would begin in August when Kathryn and Alice left for the

States. Before they left he told Kathryn, "Keep the fire burning. One thing you must know: nervousness has a momentum. Mind cannot stop nervousness. It must go on until momentum finished. Important remember this—when you see our darling [Alice] nervous, let be—soon will pass."

On August 2nd Gurdjieff, along with the rest of the Knachtschmidts, went to the Gare St. Lazare to see them off. Jane Heap, in Paris on a visit from London, also came. Gurdjieff brought a string bag of Persian melons for Kathryn and Alice to eat on their voyage. When the boat train for Le Havre pulled slowly away, Gurdjieff gave a blessing, raising his right hand, thrice toward each woman.

Near the end of August, Gurdjieff and Solita, Gabo and Valya, Gurdjieff's nephew, took a trip to Vichy. They started at one o'clock from the Café de la Paix, the car packed with luggage and a sack of watermelons. Gabo and Valya were in the back seat, Solita in the front beside Gurdjieff. At Fontainebleau they stopped at his brother Dimitri's house for lunch. There they left Gabo, who was replaced by Dimitri and Nicolai, Elizabeth Stjoernval's teenage son. The night was stormy. It did not deter Gurdjieff from driving the roads through the forests at 115 kilometers per hour [70 miles per hour], the towns at 90 [55 miles per hour], all the while with Solita working the windshield wipers, finding the right roads, and lighting his cigarettes. Although they stopped on the road four times, they made Vichy before ten o'clock—in less than five hours.

At Vichy there were no rooms at his favorite hotel, so they waited by the curb while Dimitri gloomily looked for replacements. After visiting 18 hotels (Vichy had 5,000), he found accommodations. The group finally had dinner at 11 P.M. Gurdjieff had caught cold in his left arm. For four days it maddened him. Also the next day at lunch, he got food poisoning and was ill for two days.

The real drama, however, began the second day. He told everyone where to meet him but every time there was no meeting. Reasons were manifold. He either gave the wrong name, the wrong hour, or his watch had stopped—anything. Those who had met him would be sent to search for the missing. Hours and hours passed in this way. Once he walked by a table where Solita sat waiting for him. She was reading and did not see him. Later, when she told him she had been there, he said, "Even I look on each face." At dinner he would lead them to a table, often very grumpy, Solita behind him, Valya carrying watermelons in newspapers, Nicolai with Armagnac in newspaper, and Dimitri in the rear, with indigestion, muttering, *"Jamais un peu de repos."* [Never a bit of rest.]

Sunday Gurdjieff told Solita to meet him in the café by the river. She waited for two hours before Valya and Nicolai found her and led her to the café in the middle of the park. Explained Gurdjieff when she protested—"But there *is* water—can see if stand up."

Monday they went to the baths, then at noon drove far into the countryside to have a picnic. All they had was watermelon and Armagnac, so stops were made for other provisions. At Clermond-Ferrand he picked up a Russian nurse and her little boy. They sat on the three men's laps in the back seat. The heat was intense but Gurdjieff kept all the windows closed because of his arm and cough.

For an hour, they looked for the ideal picnic place. Having passed up some lovely spots, Gurdjieff finally chose a steep hill where they picnicked, carefully sitting atop pointed rocks, clutching the food to keep it from rolling downhill, and struggling to keep their balance. The men tore the chicken apart with their hands, wiping their hands on their trousers. There was only one glass for all. In ten minutes, Gurdjieff declared the picnic over and they piled back into the car and drove on to a lake.

Said Dimitri, "Just think, to eat a piece of bread we must come 70 kilometers and spend a thousand francs."

In the car Solita talked to seventeen year old Nicolai.

Gurdjieff, angry, said: "M*ees*, you not see all the places I pass because you talk."

"I talk to Nicolai about his future."

"You had better think about your own future, M*ees*." He said to look at the mountain before them. "Only now you can see after eating. Never can man see anything when he is hungry—only a bit here, a bit there."

They then drove another hour to look at a lake for ten minutes.

By September, Georgette's condition had improved to where she was entirely without pain and was able to lie fully stretched out on her bed, not half-reclining as she had previously had to do. "Evidently," she wrote in her diary, "the brain is not our sole organ of control—other organs also register what takes place in us, and perhaps more accurately than the brain does; I have the impression of a wheel turning within me, motored by a renewed bloodstream and by my conscious will to receive the help given me."

As the months had gone on, Margaret had made stronger and stronger efforts to state her convictions and, also, she said she was willing to be convinced, "if only my arguments could be met and destroyed." This not being indulged, everyday she felt a new rebellion. She once had seen a film of a child who was a black sheep. The child told the teacher that he could do what he wanted as long as the child could be the boss. The teacher agreed and the child's life took on direction and inspiration. "I have always felt," said Margaret, "like this kind of child. I felt it now stronger than ever." Margaret withdrew into muteness; one that was "fierce and also futile." It lasted for a year or so, and she began to despair. This was followed by her entry into silence. "I no longer wished to speak. I knew by this time that I had nothing to say, that if I had lived from birth until the present moment without having spoken one word, the result would have been the same; I could simply have made gestures to show that my cup was not full but always running over. I no longer wanted to speak because I never knew what would come out."

Margaret said "I tried to stop living as if in emulation of Rachmaninoff's 'Second Piano Concerto.' I entered what I now call the D period—depression, discouragement, disgust (of self), despair, decrepitude, destruction.... Life now became a desert." Finally, she began to see. "Our imaginations had been the excess of desire over ability. Our intelligence had been merely a justification of this excess. Our intense emotions had amounted to the pleasure of having emotions. Our art had been a hope of repeating those emotions forever. Our 'rich' personalities had been an obstacle to understanding these facts. We who had been born outside the dull, the routine, the conflicting; we the convinced, the convincing; we the inspired, the inspiring—what had we been all our lives? Almost nothing at all.... Georgette as usual had a picture of our plight. 'We have spent out lives walking under parasols,' she said."

When Miss Gordon returned from London, Gurdjieff told her, "Now you are home again. Only here do you all feel at home in true sense."

Looking at Louise, he said she had selected the "best pieces" of everything on the table and offered them to everyone, not remembering there would be evening guests.

"You choose and give as if they are your own and not my pieces. Even under you go, looking for best pieces. Parasite, nonentity and by the way *merde!*"

In mid-October Gurdjieff met with Solita privately. Her seriousness regarding the teaching and her sincerity toward Gurdjieff had never waned but only increased. Her infatuation with Margaret and her jealousy of Janet and Noel were behind her. In Gurdjieff, she had found something of another order entirely. Knowing of her interest in science, he told her to review all her science studies, then apply it to the teaching.

On October 30th, Solita's birthday, he said, "This day of your borning." About Americans, he said, "They not yet spoiled. Nice burros. Future is donkey, yet at same time might be something else. Not yet crystallized into turkey who have no future. Now this is your day. You may have what you like—only of course not question."

Speaking of having a "fulling wholeness," Gurdjieff asked: "Which you like best, dinner or music?"

Said Miss Gordon, "Is different thing."

"No, is all same thing. Different octave but from same scale composed. I hope someday you will understand the unity of the law of *Heptaparaparshinokh*—everywhere the same.

Someone mentioned "our five senses."

"Five senses?" said Gurdjieff. "How you tell—senses? Firstly, is not sense. Secondly, you have more than five. Sense means sensation. You have not word in English for what I mean—feeling-with-sensation. Kanari, what would be word?"

"I don't know."

"But try—say what word you think."

"Would 'contact' have your meaning?"

"No. With eyes I see you and you see me. But unless I wish, you not have contact with me. *Svolosh*[4] language, your English."

That evening he invited Solita alone to dinner at a restaurant. When she arrived she found the table set with a clean table cloth, caviar and a birthday cake. While she was eating, her toast came so unexpectedly soon that she tried to swallow quickly.

"Never defile Armagnac."

"But I haven't yet drunk—I'm waiting to swallow."

"No, you waiting only for me to drink."

"Not true—yes, both true."

"Always in galoshes at your toast."

"Perhaps," said Solita, "I am candidate for round?"

"What is round but candidate for square? What is square but candidate for round?"

Later, he told her, "Your name mean *Alone,* already I know it, existed in Egypt. I know all names from there. One man there was called Holy *Merde* and from name he swaggered—because meaning was he had fulfilled such transformation with honor, used all active elements according to law. There was ceremony in Egypt for name's day, not for borning day. Day of physical birth is only of domestic interest. Real day was day you were given some great person's name."

At the end of the celebration, he told her that now he would go to the Café de la Paix. "Before I lived with someone—woman—now I live alone. Live with angel would mean nothing to me—because I live with devils."

---

4. *Svolosh* is Russian for garbage pail.

Said Solita, referring to Janet Flanner, "And I live with some-one who is always angry."

"Always angry, always laugh, always with lovingness, not make different. All is empty thing."

One day at lunch he said, "This is most important day for you. In twenty-four hours from now when you have assimilated this medicine, you will be responsible for all your acts, conscious and unconscious. You take position of responsibility. A record is not kept for each soul, as people believe, but only for responsible souls. There is a law of sinning and you are now subject to this law. If not fulfill all your obligations, you will pay. For every satisfaction, so much dissatisfaction—the Angel Gabriel's books must balance."

At the beginning of November Georgette went to Gurdjieff's flat. She knocked and he opened the door. He stood in the door-way, the light from the little salon illuminating him fully. She told him—"I am completely well, I am in a new body."

He stepped back and leaned against the wall.

"Then, for the first time," she said, "he let me see what he really is. It was as if he had torn off the masks behind which he is obliged to hide himself. His face was stamped with a charity that embraced the whole world. Transfixed, standing before him, I saw him with all my strength and I experienced a gratitude so deep, so sad, that he felt a need to calm me. With an unforgettable look, he said, 'God helps me.'"

That same day Kathryn and Alice returned to Paris. Hurrying to Gurdjieff's apartment, they found him preparing a pheasant dinner.

"At the sight of us," said Kathryn, "a slow smile spread over his dark face, growing in radiance like a gathering of suns as he sur-veyed us. Then he opened his arms straight out like a bear's and we rushed into his welcoming embrace that was wide enough to hold the two of us at once—'Th*een* One!... Kroko*deel!*'"

On November 5th Margaret came for lunch. She had not been there since August. At the toast for Squirming Idiot, he said to her, "You are official arch [Idiot], but now also squirming. Like when take fish from water and put on earth. For this I have formulation:

Two chairs. You can never sit in same chair as when first come here, but you have possibility of next chair. Is now or never."

Someone asked which of the Idiots is the worst.

"Walrus," he said. "Yakina, do you know which is walrus?"

"Yes, like Miss Heap."

"Yes, walrus, this walrus sit, look around. In him are all idiots, like in man. Everything like man he have, even brain. And so it goes, down to tail part. All parts in him idiot, all idiots in him—except, of course, unique."

Margaret explained that the reason she had not come sooner was because she had to finish her book.

"Such *merde* your book, all you write," said Gurdjieff. "I pity you. You are turkey."

Soon, Gurdjieff gave the group a new series of exercises which required a complex and sustained inner attention beyond anything that had before been attempted. He asked them to take a pledge before beginning each new exercise that "we would not use this for the self, but for all humanity"—what Gurdjieff expressed as "good-wishing-for-all."

For Kathryn this opened up an entirely new perspective. "This 'good-wishing-for-all' vow," she said, "so deeply moving in intent, had a tremendous effect upon me. For the first time in my life, I felt that I was truly doing something for humanity as I strove to make my own molecule of it more perfect. The meaning of this Work, which at first had seemed quite egotistical and self-centered, suddenly blossomed out like a tree of life encompassing in its myriad branchings the entire human family.... It was my first experiencing of the Mystical Body of Christ of which I knew nothing then."

On December 5th , he gave the women chaplets to use.

One day at lunch, special potatoes—curried, spiced, and running with butter—were brought in.

"*Mees* Gordon, I think never in England you see such potato."

Miss Gordon, falling into the trap, answered, "Never—and cooked in so much butter!"

"Look, already she begin to be worried concerning how much cost butter. You know, for such potatoes like this, must be boiled in butter. But still not clean. You know potato difficult to make clean, so first butter must be poured off, then again must be boiled in butter. But still not clean."

"Then three times boiled," said Miss Gordon.

"Yes, three times boiled in butter."

"I knew there must be three," replied Miss Gordon, bemused.

"Excuse... there is fourth time in this preparation. Fourth time potato is baked in butter."

"Oh. Now must go to seven?" asked Miss Gordon.

"Of course. Or three or seven. This case, seven."

Solita said, "Now once we come to toast and I not in galoshes, Mr. Gurdjieff."

"You chronically in galoshes."

A little later he said that only one half of him was massaged and the masseur now waits to do the other side. "If not do, then I be lop-sided"—he wilted on one side—"lopside, you know have one end. Is not like stick which have two end. If man is lopsided, then eveything he receives is lopsided; if is on bad side then all receives is bad, if on good side then this not harmful thing. Is why man can sometimes be happy."

That Christmas the group spent with Gurdjieff. First, Kathryn drove him to the Café de La Paix for breakfast. Alice met them there. At one point she spoke of the five Dionne quintuplets, saying that the scientists had allowed them to spend this Christmas with their family and that they planned to study them.

"Study," Gurdjieff mocked. "How study when scientists come from the same barrel? Such nonentity, all of it. With such thing as five from the same birth, there can be nothing to study. Five take what was meant for one. No individuality can be there.... Now man begins to breed like mice. Never before in history was such thing as this—four, five at a time. Twins even were a rare thing. Soon now, five will not be notable. People will speak only about six, then of seven. Nobody sees what this means ... quantity destroying quality."

Later, Margaret and Georgette joined the group and they all dined together. Gurdjieff also celebrated Christmas according to the Russian Orthodox calendar, on New Year's eve. He made it into both a Russian Fair and a surprise party. All the Rope were invited as well as his friends from St. Petersburg, the psychiatrist Dr. Stjoernval, and the barrister Rachmilievitch, as well as the chauffeur and his family, the apartment house manager, all the nieces and nephews and Gabo, his Russian aide-de-camp and kitchen helper—about forty or fifty people in all.

The Rope had made up forty hatboxes full of gifts. Only eighteen adults at a time could be accommodated in the salon where an immense Christmas tree stood decorated with colored lights, small Russian dolls and ornaments of rare glass. Everyone else was crowded into the bedrooms, kitchen, dining room and hallway.

Gurdjieff appeared and began to distribute the hatboxes. Everyone in the Rope believed that they would be given to others, so they were all surprised when Gurdjieff exclaimed with a full smile—

"For our dear esteemed, Our Reverence, M*ees* Gordon."

This was followed by a hatbox for Alice—"For our dear delicious Th*een* One."

For Solita—"For our dear singing Kanari!"

For Kathryn—"For our dear and terrible Krokod*eel*!"

Margaret's and Louise's boxes were presented with the same flourish and then, giving his mustache an appropriate twirl, he said to Georgette—"For our dear esteemed so-so-so, so-so-so Madame!"

In February 1937, Gurdjieff and the Rope took a trip to the Riviera; it was their last with him as a group. One evening they went to the Hôtel Splendide for dinner. Their table looked out on the mountains. Gurdjieff said:

"Yakina, you must be happy here near mountain. Yak have one specific, very original. Is heavy animal, too much have inside, yet always go where is most difficult, like goat. Choose to go where is stones, where no other animal would wish to, except goat who is light and for which going is natural. But yak will turn from smooth path and choose steep high place with stones. Also another very original thing have."

Kathryn put in, hopefully: "Mama-papa business?"

121

"No. *Merde* business. Then yak very original movement make, not like any other animal. If you could watch you could learn much about the human psyche." He paused, then said, "Look, Kroko*deel* ponder about mama-papa business. This also she makes very different. But here you would not understand about Yakina, for she is too far from you."

Gurdjieff had not had anything to drink in many days but then began.

"Look, I am already drunk, yet take only small amount. But all in body wait to take. I even assimilate more than is."

There were a number of Americans eating dinner at the hotel. He said, "Americans drink water just before they eat. I have seen. Now the body takes many hours to make liquids necessary for digesting, and water they drink sucks out and sends on these special liquids and when food arrives there is nothing for transforming. They eat only to make *merde*. Also they eat butter which coats stomach so what must pass through walls cannot pass. Also chocolate makes coating. This is only for travel, to stop feeling of hunger."

Gurdjieff went on to say, "Every thinking man—and by man I also mean woman—must be occupied only by this interest—to develop a soul." And, "It is as important to compose a dish in its correctly-blended elements as a composition of music or the colors in painting. Harmony in scale. Must have much knowledge to be a good cook. A culinary doctor."

A Russian priest passed by. Gurdjieff stopped him and they talked. Then he translated for the Rope. "God is old man; sand run out and he cannot stop it, moreover any devil can take."

The priest looked shocked—eyes popping, mouth pursed, tossing back his curls—and quickly left.

"Eat, Kanari," he said, "potato not make fat. Necessary eat potato, he have starch."

Solita told him that starch makes fat.

"Excuse, not if you know with what to combinate. Starch is very important, one of seven divine things for man. Without it he could not even breathe. And now man use such divine thing for collar for pimp and petticoat for prostitute. Starch gives everything—body heat, material, even God thing."

At the beginning of March, at Gurdjieff's apartment Kathryn helped peel a bushel of potatoes. He squeezed them, hot, in his hands, added four pounds of butter, then a quart of brown liquid, eighteen spices cooked together, grated boiled eggs and a bowl of chopped onions. This, he said, is the dish the king of the caravans eats—*caravanpashi*—and "you can imagine how is eaten in oasis, with cold water from well."

"Look, Th*een* One not like. Not according to her American goût [taste]."

"True both ways," Kathryn said as an aside.

"How you mean, 'both ways'? Another meaning have this word?"

"Slang word, 'goo,'" answered Kathryn, "means something without taste or substance, nothing in it you can recognize."

"Good word. Even in Bible is. You know how begin—'In beginning there was—*GOO*.' People also can be such."

Everyone roared.

"God is very far—him you can never touch. Tapeworm you can touch. He is in you. He even have his psyche, like man. He knows more than man because he have very thin (fine, sensitive) mentation."

"Even imagination?" asked Solita

"Of course. Also has more sense of reality than man. Moreover, if you know tapeworm scientifically, you can go up scale."

The conversation turned to observation. Gurdjieff asked Margaret if she had noticed a thing that had changed his face. She peered at him. He twirled a mustache which had lately been turning darker.

"You not see one change?" he inquired.

"I see nothing, except your mustache turns up."

"*No.* You have months looked on me, always you look on my eyes and not see anything else. Yet this is crying thing on my face."

"I never see color, only line."

"Excuse, man must not look on one part—is onanist thing you make to see eyes or nose only. Must total see. Man must have normal vision."

"I am not interested in mustaches," answered Margaret. "I look on a face as I do on sculpture."

"Sculpture. Now you have offended me with this word. I am objective sculptor. I see *all*—even all of you, I see—even your navel. 'Crying thing on my face.' Good expression, eh? Even your Shakespeare could not write such. He was pederast. Between every line of his poetry I can smell *pederastisme*. Such dirty life he had, not like what he write."

"You not like or you mean his life did not correspond with what he wrote?"

"No, not correspond."

He got up from the table and began to leave the room.

Alice called out: "Mr. Gurdjieff, Yakina here very excited still and wishes to ask a question."

He stopped, waiting by the door.

"Mr. Gurdjieff, you know that a change in color is not so essential as a change in line!"

"Yes, M*ees,* I agree that your American art books is written so. But still I am changed man. You know why? A week ago I had not time to waste in discussion with you. But now"—he twisted his mustache—"I have auspicious exterior and suspicious interior, so I must do everything corresponding, even titillate with you."

The next day he said, "In Russia is fish they take every day from water and beat. Then put back. This make fish angry and liver grow big. Only very rich man can eat. Some process proceed and make in fish active element, like what this chicken also have."

"Isn't that cruel," asked Miss Gordon, "is it worth tormenting the poor fish?"

"I pity your mentation. Come tonight, eat dinner, bouillon from six such chicken."

"May I also tell Yakina?" asked Solita. "She is in galoshes from last night. She knows she was 'impudent.'"

"Not *was* impudent. She *is* such. Russian expression there is: 'A hunchback can be straightened only in the tomb.'"

Margaret insisted that she was not impudent, that she had too much respect for Mr. Gurdjieff.

In the middle of March there was a conversation about fasting. Gurdjieff said that the Easter fast is fifty days.

"Forty days," stated Miss Gordon, "the Bible says Jesus fasted forty days."

"Excuse, English Bible made for old maid. I not know your Bible, from older source I know. Before Christmas is forty, then two more fasts in the year, one for planting, one for taking [harvest]. This is custom among men through the ages. I know from custom, not from your English Bible."

After a huge lunch Gurdjieff asked: "Now how will be about dinner?

Miss Gordon said she could eat nothing.

"This answer for present is English property. Tapeworm always answer for present. Man with mind must answer for future; must see how *will* be, not what *is.*"

At the next luncheon Gurdjieff toasted Alice's health, saying: "Soon you must change from squirming which is idiot I not like at my table. Always something dirty have. Squirming is only passing state for man. Is state like fish out of sea, man must not long stay or he die and be obliged to be born again. Man can stay squirming two or three months, but not for a year."

Alice refused a second helping of the fourth course with alarm. Gurdjieff: "You are egotist. Speak from head up, not speak for tapeworm. He is in your presence, you must not make angry, you must be with him indulgent. Who be kind to tapeworm, who satisfy tapeworm, tapeworm help him achieve what he wish."

He looked at Solita and said, "My dear Kanari, may God help you transformate into crow, not so much dirt have crow, which if it is small, quality have. After you are crow, we will see. I write for crow or peacock."

Turning to Kathryn he said: "Kroco*deel*, God help you transformate into elephant."

At lunch at the beginning of April, Gurdjieff said: "I hope with all my heart that there will rise in all of you feeling of humanity. American and especially English people cannot feel for even one person except self, so spoiled he is, so degenerate. Even your Negroes not so spoiled, has twice times more feeling for humanity than you Americans who hate him. Negro I like, I can be friend with, they understand tones and gestures."

There followed a long talk about the customs of the eastern countries and hospitality and "humanity-ness" and friendship. "French have no friendship for anybody. Americans have too much—a disease with them."

"China," he said, " not centrum of humanity-ness—is *merde*. Also Japan. Already spoiled. They in process of change from crow to peacock. No longer is crow, not yet peacock. *Merde* is. In America, Washington D. C. is centrum source for evil."

Kathryn, as the director of the toasts, had skipped Compassionate Idiot.

Said Gurdjieff—"For fifteen minutes she make plan about what next come, then with great swagger she tell wrong. The terribleness of it is that man—real man—must remember, if not himself, then what he does in relation his surroundings. Man must always prepare for what he do and necessary that he at all times think about what he do."

He turned to Alice and said—"Now one thing I know about you and Kroco*deel*—you unconscious animosity must have one for the other."

Earlier he had half spilled his coffee and said immediately to Alice—"Look she make black magic, *she* do this not I. She is ..."

The women say—"witch."

"Yes, she is witch. She witchness have. You can see it in her nose. Always you must look on nose to know about witchness. Also Sardine have—only not so much as Th*een* One." He said Alice did not have Harmony because, "Six parts her are empty, one part have too much, this is why her witch-ness not have Harmony."

On April 19th, Alice wore new Easter clothes to lunch.

"Look how she is *chic*. Yesterday she saw me in new suit and was jealous. Jealousy can be good thing, can be holy impulse. Man see something higher than himself, wish to be such, so make effort. Jealousy can be factor for cunning. Of course not the dirty kind, not man-woman jealousy."

Solita said the word came from the Greek *selos,* meaning zeal or eager rivalry.

"Two kinds of hopeless idiots, objective and subjective. Objective, he is *merde,* nothing never he can do. Subjective have possibility, not be *merde.* He already come into place where he himself know he is hopeless, he realize his nonentity. He possibility have not be *merde* always such as he is. Every man have moment when he can imagine what he is God."

To Alice, he said: "Now everyone imagine she can shear me; you, for example. But I make naive while you shear and at end I shear you, even of last hair, while you sit like dog in street that have lost hair. You represent yourself what you are not. You not know enough not to trust people. I wish you not be such. Here among us you can be off guard but not in world where you soon will be. Now you are in scale of nonentityness. You will go, but we not will be separated as long as with inside we same idea have. Separation not touch your inner world, because we are together there."

On April 23rd, St. George the Victor's Day, Gurdjieff gave sacks of food and money to two Russian families he knew.

Solita said, "I begin to understand what satisfaction you must have."

"Not necessary philosophize. Their emanation, vibration go out—some of total go to you. This is indirect food. Even this expression comes to me from Bible as early Christian word—indirect food. If I am not happy, I can be made so. If people around me happy, then I can be. In indirectness, mechanically, does such force show. It comes to you without your consciousness—undirect. Same word can be about sin—undirect sin, unvoluntary. So this indirect food is. Same thing also can be voluntary. You think, you make consciously."

"Already you decide to go out from average-ness. Remember when you do exercises, that mind is nothing—important only as policeman. Feeling is more near to nature."

At lunch on Easter Gurdjieff had said: "My tapeworm wish sing something higher than 'God Save King.'"

"'Hosannah?'" asked Solita.

"No, that is dirty word, only use for marriage and business you make after."

Miss Gordon said, "'Hallelujah?'"

"Is big word. Have in three things; Amen, God help us, and I am you and you are me. Very old word. Jewish take, but not is Jewish. Not even your Pope understands what it means. It includes all the scale from *merde* to God. In this high expression is everything. Now Russians feast for fifty days until Ascension Day. I glad some of you went to service Russian church, participate in such good thing, for feeling experience. All Christian church ceremonies derive from old Greek church. Once in Jerusalem I saw such ceremony as must always remember. There were nine different kinds Christians all together in one place for Christmas, even Abyssinia. This Greek ceremony open up all your feeling, you forget why is, for whom is, you forget even Christ—such knowledge they have for composing ceremony, for psychology of people."

Alice asked, "Bible also taken from Greek?"

"Of course. Everything Christian came from old Greek, then they spoil. All, all comes from Greek. Even from before time when was Bible. Your Bible is new book, composed four or five hundred years after by fisherman. And you know what understanding have fisherman."

"But before fishermen, what happened to knowledge?" asked Alice.

"Nothing happened."

"But where was it?"

"Was with initiate people, as always. They always go in one stream, it still flows today. You ask question from one stream, I answer from other, then you go back your stream with answer. Before there was nothing for man in ordinary stream, but fishermen who knew nothing, so nothing could tell but their wiseacrings. You remember the two streams I write about? Difference between two streams is the difference between interpretations of events on earth. One make elephant from fly, the other make fly from elephant. Events have two explanations—one for mankind, one for me. My stream is initiatism. You know what is in hypnotism. With that you can make water of wine for some people. For others you can make wine of water. I tell about my stream. What happen before not interest me. Remember my chapter [in *All and Everything*] on Maralpleicie—also Konuzion and poppy seeds. This is what happened before."

Miss Gordon: "But there have been messengers like you."

"Many such there are, even you have in America. For English and Americans they are something, but for me they are shit; objective sense.... You wish believe your Bible. Your Bible is one thing but mine is quite another. Nobody now believe in Christian thing—not with inner world, especially young ones. Nobody but English old maid and lesbian Americans. Your Bible is hodge-podge."

One day at lunch Kathryn said that Gurdjieff seemed to be in a kind of "hidden pitying rage about all of us." No one spoke and the first part of the lunch was eaten in silence. Alice, who had been appointed a few weeks earlier as "Cellaresse" in charge of filling and refilling everyone's glass from the Armagnac bottle for the ritual toasting, skipped by a few who had indicated she do so.

"Th*een* one," shouted Gurdjieff, "your obligation you do not fulfill. You do not see all round you, only ones near you like me, *Mees* Keep, Krokodeel. I gave you small obligation, but you do not fulfill. If you cannot do this, then all you do will be false–even hats!"

After the luncheon, Jane Heap said, "Today he is sorrowing because of us, what we've done ... we haven't been able to take enough of what he gives. We've failed him somewhere."

Alice had decided that she should return to America, presumably to look after her business interests. Kathryn would leave Gurdjieff's table as well. Kathryn was depressed at the thought of leaving but said, "I knew my place was with the Thin One, and that one of my tasks was to 'keep the fire burning' in her as well as in myself."

One day before their departure, Gurdjieff called Kathryn into his bedroom where they always went for personal talks and looking into her eyes said in the gentlest voice—"Kroco*deel*, we will not be separated as long as with inside we have the same idea. This going will not touch your inner world. Soon again we will meet."

On May 3rd Kathryn and Alice had their last lunch with Gurdjieff. He blessed both of them, his thumb tracing the sign of a small cross on their foreheads.

At the end of April, Kathryn and Alice left the group to return to America.

Margaret camping it up in her
"Annette Kellerman" pose, 1927.

131

Kathryn Hulme

Dancing With Death

PARIS. JUNE 1937. "ALMOST ALL WAS FINISHED, ME, MY WORK, ALL OF YOU," GURDJIEFF SAID. HE HAD CALLED MISS GORDON from Cannes in the middle of May, telling her that "something was" with his car and that he was taking the train.

That noon Solita, still in pajamas and typing, received a call from the lobby downstairs. It was Gurdjieff. She threw on a topcoat and hurried down the five flights. She found him pacing up and down, his arm in a sling. He said he had left the car on a steep hill, engine off, handbrake only holding, while he went to look at the view. In the car were a woman and children. Suddenly the car moved forward toward the precipice. With one gigantic bound— "Never was my brain so quick," he said—he leaped on the running board, put his arm inside and steered the car straight off the road down the hill to the only tree in sight. The car was smashed to bits, but its occupants saved. Gurdjieff was thrown into the air, turned over several times and fell on his shoulder.

The next day Solita and Miss Gordon had lunch with him.

"Such a good lunch today," said Miss Gordon.

"Yes, everything I have, except, of course, one thing. Everybody has many wants, I have only one. I need only one thing. This end of stick not correspond and even I can tell reason. Is my organic weakness of mind, I had this even when young. Is because

133

I waste my time trying to make people understand. So everything I have—except. Why I have all except is because I have knowledge. Now about this weakness that consists in trying to give understanding to people—this weakness is only this much."

He measured a quarter of an inch between his thumb and forefinger.

Said Solita quickly—"Then that means you are just that much lopsided, Mr. Gurdjieff."

"Good, good. See, Mees Gordon, how she understand."

"I'm afraid I didn't understand what Canary meant."

"Truth—English are hopeless, such sheep, donkey understanding have. Truth, pity you are English. That story about looking at sky for fifteen minutes before replying is for you and all English understanding. Reminds me of a story of a cart to which was put a horse, a goat and one tortoise. Of course all could go only as fast as tortoise. The horse very nervous. He said, 'What is this destiny which is written on my forehead?' The goat also spoke his opinion. And the tortoise who nothing understood except that every day the mountain before them seemed as far as ever, became very angry. He cursed and complained, 'Go, go, at all times we go, but stay nearly in same place.' So, Mees Gordon, never will you understand the two ends of stick. Now look her face. In one place she love me, in another she hate me. Unconsciously, of course. If it was consciously, long ago I would chickmake. Now why we sit? As for me, I have eaten justly. Now, Kanari, why you look on me? Something you notice?"

"Always notice new word."

"And you, Mees Gordon? You notice? Of course you not. 'Justly' was word."

Miss Gordon: "I didn't notice because you always use 'truth.'"

At lunch on May 18th, Gurdjieff appointed Solita as his new secretary and commissioned her to find a refrigerator for his apartment.

At the end of the third week in May, he persuaded a reluctant Solita, who remembered the last trip, to go to Vichy with him. Miss Gordon and Gabo were also invited.

"Mountains we will pass," he said, "and in such surroundings you will have material for third food."

They started off at five o'clock, Gurdjieff and Gabo in the front, Solita and Miss Gordon in the back seat between the luggage and odorous food packages piled to the roof. Once on the road to Fontainebleau, he tramped on the gas, passing by inches the cars and trucks ahead … or, when halfway past a vehicle, slowing down, the cars and trucks behind screeching brakes and blaring horns.

Solita, terrified, begged him to slow down.

He had to test the car, he explained. "Just it make one constatation. Too much money I pay for this car."

"Then stop," demanded Solita, "and let me out."

He drove a trifle more slowly to his brother's house in Fontainebleau which was empty. Solita took her luggage and got out.

"How now, Kanari?"

"I'll take the train here and meet you in Vichy." she said.

"No, no, now you sit beside me, slowly I go. Moreover, never I go more than 90." [55 miles per hour]

"No, you go 120!" [75 miles per hour]

"How you know?"

"Because I see on speedometer."

"Impossible, never more than 90. Now you sit till Montargis and if not like, there you can go and sit in train."[1]

He was better after that. They arrived at Nevers at ten. The dining room was closed, but it was opened for Gurdjieff and the group. They had a cold dinner.

"Curiosity," said Gurdjieff at one point, "is a dirty thing. That is why I am always angry for idiot questions, why philosophizing makes me nervous. In English, not exist two words for two kinds of curiosity, as in other languages. Word for other kind of curiosity is needing-to-know. For this needing-to-know you must have material. Then you will not receive something empty."

Nearing Vichy, there was a new lighting system on the road.

---

1. Driving at 75 miles per hour in the mid-1930s would likely be the top speed that a car could be driven. Given this and the road conditions of that time, Solita's concern is legitimate. However, she doesn't see that Gurdjieff is working with her—working with her nervousness and imagination—and so interprets the situation in ordinary terms.

Said Solita: "You say in your book such use of electricity is a bad thing. Yet more and more is used."

"The more they use, the greater will be the catastrophe," he said.

A black cat crossed the road.

"Why do cat's eyes shine at night?" asked Solita.

"All that family have such property."

"To make other animals afraid?" asked Miss Gordon. "Mesmerize them?"

"Yes."

"Snake also?" asked Miss Gordon.

"Yes, snake also have. And this same property man can achieve also."

In Vichy there were many Russians waiting to see Gurdjieff. The conversation was mostly in Russian. Two days later, Solita, too nervous to face the drive back in the car, told Gurdjieff that she had to go back in the train, a freelance article she was writing was overdue.

"Such story you can tell M*ees* Gordon but not to me. Joppa, you miss too much, truth."

She went back on the train. Miss Gordon said the ride back was just as wild. He raced a motorcycle and nearly crashed.

At the end of May, at dinner were his pupil Olgivanna Hinzenberg, her husband, the architect Frank Lloyd Wright, and their young daughter Iovanna.

Said Wright of the toasting to the Idiots: "Very interesting, these idiots of yours. I've invented some also."

Gurdjieff made no reply.

"Mr. Gurdjieff, you're certainly a good cook," offered Wright, trying to start a conversation. "You could earn a lot of money cooking somewhere."

"Not so much as I can earn shearing."

After dinner Gurdjieff brought out a chapter of the *Second Series* and asked who would read.

Wright immediately spoke up—"I read very well."

Gurdjieff left the room.

"Damn, I'm sleepy," whispered Wright after he had read a while. "I can't take it. Still, I don't want to hurt the old man's feelings."

He began to read again. Gurdjieff returned and sat down.

Wright stopped reading—"You know, Mr. Gurdjieff, this is interesting and it's a pity it's not well written. You know you talk English very well, too bad you can't dictate. Now if I had time you could dictate to me and I could write this for you in good English."

Gurdjieff made no reply.

Wright read a few pages and stopped again. "Now I must go and take my little daughter home," he said. "She's sleepy and so is her father."

"Yes, for her sake stop," Gurdjieff mockingly agreed. "She is young. You, of course, are old man now and life finish. But she only begin."

Wright, turning red, declared—"My life is *not* finished. I could right now make six more like her."

Olgivanna, who had witnessed the whole scene, with tears in her eyes got up and led Iovanna to the door.

At lunch the next day, Gurdjieff said: "Tapeworm sing 'God Save the King.' Like English people. But while this they sing, inside quite another thing they tell, just opposite. They say to the devil with the King. Others sing 'Internationale' and 'Marseillaise' and that makes middle part."

Solita said, "You mean that neutralizes situation, like safety valve?"

"Of course. Just why such thing is of value. Then can starving people sing, 'God Save the King' when such nonentity go by. Truth, nobody can have such fruit as this. Take, take, not pity."

Miss Gordon said, "That's what worries me all the time, Mr. Gurdjieff. To think we have such thing when others have nothing, are starving."

"*Mees* Gordon, *Mees* Gordon, may your mentation not be such."

"But you tell in your book when some people have much it means that others must have nothing."

"Yes, I tell how is."

"But why should it be so?"

"I not tell why. Eh, Kanari?"

"You always say fact is fact."

"Is exact. Now explain."

Said Solita, "It is explained in a chapter of your book—'Man's Understanding of Justice is an Accursed Mirage.'"

"You see, M*ees* Gordon; not enough read my words, also must think about what read, otherwise empty will remain."

At the café on the first day of June Solita said, "You said the other day that starch is holy thing, God thing. I wish to ask you if it is because, like amber, it has three forces in it—carbon, hydrogen, and oxygen."

"Now I not answer question because you go too far. You have one hundred kilos too much curiosity, your enemy. Before you had one thousand kilos, but still too much you have. I advise you recognize enemy and full stop make. Also another constatation I make. Something wrong your sex. Sex very important thing is, like light, like air you breathe, food you eat. If you are in five parts, two of your five parts depend from sex. You must more normal live."

Said Solita, "Cannot even think about such things. I do not wish, I have no time. In twenty-four hours I have only four hours for myself and I must use them for sleeping."

"Then lopsided you will be and I can nothing do, for this depends only from you."

At lunch the next day there was a Persian musician who was copying Gurdjieff's music.

Gurdjieff made a long speech in Russian to Dimitri. When Gurdjieff went out to the telephone, Solita asked Dimitri, "For heaven's sake, quickly tell me what he said, what he was talking about?"

Dimitri looked at her sheepishly and said, *"Vrai, je n'ai rien compris de tout cela."* [Truthfully, I understood nothing of all that.]

At Gurdjieff's request, Solita had been treating his patients with two electrical machines he had invented. They were very complicated with different adjustments for each.

"Every person is not polarized alike," Gurdjieff explained.

Solita found the color in the tubes beautiful—like neon—which even Gurdjieff admired. "Something in color *is*—like life. And sometimes in colors one color something of itself it even has—especially in electricity."

Speaking about the Persian musician, Gurdjieff said "He is half woman. Such representative of art have too many 'feelings.' We have name for such in Russian, one word, meaning prostitute-in-trousers."

Later, "You must now have three states—active, passive, and *life state.*"

At lunch at the end of the first week in July he said, "Now I constate Sardine has changed. Not so much antipathicism as formerly when everyone wished to push her away. Sardine, something of woman you now have. You are not soft *merde* now—kind that is result in morning from too much eating some one kind thing because you like, not because hunger have. But not yet are you hard kind. You are in middle. Words exist in other languages for these different kinds *merde*. In some languages words exist also for different kinds of blood. Never word blood use alone, but one of these words to say what kind is."

Still looking at her, he continued, "Today you eat like sparrow. You know sparrow cannot eat much, but peck, peck. Spoil for others."

"Like canary?" asked Solita, hoping for more details.

"Kanari I not know."

"A little you know,' said Solita, "because once you said is *svolosh* bird."

"I know of course a little but I not know canary *behind* like sparrow. Sparrow I know like myself."

Miss Gordon said, "Yes, you used to paint them to resemble canaries. I always wondered if that were true or a fable like the ladder in the desert. Stilts in sand and ladder."

"No, those stories true, only ten percent is fantasy. That reminds me how I suffer when Soloviev died. For three months I was not myself. Such friend was—more than brother. I love him more than a mistress. You all notice something fishy today with me?"

"Well, not fishy, just unusual," answered Solita.

"Unusual with me is fishy. Just today I carry [wear] corset, so all is changed, even my mind."

"Yes, today you talk."

"What egotist you are. Sincerely tell, how now your tapeworm?"

"Is sleepy," replied Solita, "but I will not let it sleep."

"I do not like your tapeworm, mees. You understand why? You understand what I told?"

"First thing, but not second thing."

"Well, try to understand next thing."

One afternoon they picnicked at Vernon on the hills overlooking the valley and river. Gurdjieff gazed a long time, sighed and said, "Ah, great nature!" After a long pause he said, "What millions lie dead there from past times! And if all of you are such as they, you too will finish as such."

There were cold chickens, fishes, loaves, the greens Gurdjieff called 'vegetables,' melons, Armagnac. Gabo had not gone with them, so Nicolai had to do everything and received all the scolding. He spilled his drink and blamed Solita. Sardine fed her dog Tuppy.

"You know," Gurdjieff said, "some people not even have dog. Nothing they can put selves into."

Louise thought that this meant approval at last for Tuppy!

"*Mees* Gordon, you not eat vegetable?"

"Not today. I'll eat them tomorrow."

"Ah, tomorrow. Well I know this disease. Often I tell tomorrow not exist. Is only today. What must be done, must be done today. It is now or never. Next day twice as hard, day after four times as hard. Only you can count on today."

On Friday, August 13th, Frank Pinder, a pupil who had first met Gurdjieff in Tiflis when he was a colonel in British intelligence, came to lunch.

Gurdjieff's brother Dimitri was very ill and Gurdjieff said, "He really die three weeks ago—now is only artificial."

During the toasting to Compassionate Idiot, Pinder asked what it was.

"Everyone is idiot, even God," Gurdjieff told him. "But when these idiots see another who another kind of idiot from themselves, they become angry and curse him. This is very characteristic of these idiots. Now compassionate means that among this company can sometimes exist idiots who know that all are idiots together so they pity all and not become angry. These are compassionate. I am unique idiot so I am no more this idiot compassionate."

By mid-August Dimitri, ill with cancer of the stomach and intestines, had two nurses. "By next week," said Gurdjieff, "it will be finished. It is time, in nature, in any case."

Dimitri died the last week of August.

Solita sat in the Café de la Paix with Gurdjieff that morning. He told her he had managed to keep the cancer inactive for twelve years, but when Dimitri quarreled with him three or four months before, he had gone to a German doctor for relief and that doctor gave him a medicine that was poison for him, made the "flower" grow on the cancer.

"When they sent for me at last," Gurdjieff said, "it was too late. All could do was give such thing as keep him alive artificially. But he in truth died three weeks ago and if today I joke it is because already I pass through experiences of his death. I will put him at Fontainebleau—my three near ones, mother, wife and brother, all one place; and very original place. Nearly all family now dead."

Said Solita, "Your new family that loves you can never be the same."

"No. Blood thing so strong for me. But real family, sisters, nieces, not love but hate me. Because I am source, it must be so. Never I give them enough and for this they hate me in their hearts. For what you can buy black dress, Kanari?"

"If necessary, I can find for 150 francs," said Solita.

"Yet each woman ask me 600 francs and there are eight woman. I gave just half what they asked and all angry on me and curse me in heart."

After Dimitri's funeral, Gurdjieff left and did not return to Paris until September 5th. He moved into his brother's apartment, at 6 rue des Colonels-Renard near the Arc de Triomphe.

He told Solita: "Man is such that he can only be egoist. He is so made. But sometimes for an hour or two, what he can do is to look around him, see what is, how is and make program accordingly. Only this will show him how he should be. I hate man. He is *merde*. Because he has brain he philosophizes with it. Give him a rose and he thinks it is *merde*—not recognize. Give him *merde* and he says it is rose. He has lost good clean instinct that even animals have. They know the difference between rose and *merde*. Now because such day I will drink Armagnac. In mornings with such troubles as now, I make nervous, make elephant from fly. But with this Armagnac fly is not elephant. Fly is—fly."

On October 19th, just two years from Solita's first evening with him and a year to the day when he had told her to review all her science studies and report to him, she brought to him at the Café de la Paix her report on her year's work, her conclusions and discoveries. He gave her permission to read it and looked at her chart of head and body systems to which she had applied the Law of Three for certain exercises. When she finished reading, he said nothing. Finally, she said, "Perhaps I was impudent to compose such a paper for you?"

"Not impudent," he said. "Even I thank you. You have unconsciously given me answer something I was searching for my book, about future of humanity. If you have found such thing, others of future humanity also can do. This what you have enlighten for me."

"I can't believe it, Mr. Gurdjieff."

"You can believe," he replied. "You have initiated yourself."

In early November, Gurdjieff said: "There is voluntary and involuntary sin and there is also voluntary and involuntary goodness, or good deed."

He asked Solita for a word, one verb, in English, that means "take blessing from above and pass to someone below."

She didn't know.

He said it exists in Greek in the gospels. He said that Jesus knew his nonentityness and should he return, he would be very angry that people thought he had said he was God.

Gurdjieff said, "Pray today that God sleeps—then only can the devil and his friends help me. I have more friends among devils than angels. When God sleeps is the only time the devil is free to do what he wishes, for good or for evil."

Later, Gurdjieff said, "If all *real* words and meanings in each language were taken and from them one language created, it would not be necessary to go to school."

On January 12, 1938, the day before his birthday, Gurdjieff was talking to a doctor at lunch.

"Pity you not understand what I tell Dr. Hambachidze—a Russian saying which could offend in English. This expression means thick-ass, and when is thick in that place, everywhere take on such thickness, even brain and of course understanding. Such thickness always means round idiot, same thickness on all sides."

Looking at Margaret he said: "Yakina, objectively you are round idiot, but subjectively something sometimes you understand in life—something else you have—you can make stop on round before continuing. So let you be official square for toast. This objective round is not altogether your fault, is result of your education, your past life. Fault is in your past, how you lived gives such result today."

At the toast to the Square Idiot, he said: "Yakina, pity such fat you have. You had once divine thing—divine possibilities. But now is too late. You have terrible ass."

He looked at his Christmas tree. "In general such tree is *merde.* Anyone can make, only when *you* make, is subjective, you lose something of yourself. But when I make, is objective for all humanity. Can be like medicine for you. If you sit and look for two, three hours, you can remember all your childhood. From such *merde* thing, I make butter. Same thing what I do with my music and my kitchen. I make another vibration from these ordinary things. Truth, after look long time at this tree in beginning of new year, you can have food for whole year. Man can look and not be just animal."

In mid-January at lunch there was one yogurt on the table, near his place, and Solita passed it to him.

"Aha, she wish remind me, but not for my sake. Is because she also like. Look how she manifest her ego, wish for herself and not will think pass to neighbor. Kanari, this dish is for all, not just for you."

To Georgette he said: "Not eat such food with fork—must finger use for seven day pig; for birds must always be finger. Ancient people all this custom have."

To Monique at her toast, "Let God or devil help you. Choose."

Asked Monique, "What is the devil?"

"Whatever you wish. Everyone thinks of the devil in a different way. Choose how you think of him now, not what you will think a month from now."

To Yakina at the toast to the Square Idiot: "Let devil help take you from your present center of gravity. I wish devil help you put this another place. You know what place, yes? Let be such conjury. Ass also is question of taste, like devil. Half of humanity like only such as yours, other half just opposite. Understand, Yakina?"

"No, I don't think so."

"Kanari, not explain her. Only scientific man can such thing explain. You have not science for such explanation. You understand what I told? Not altogether, I think, only almost. Is life thing, not such idea with which you write your article."

He looked carefully over each person's melon rind and pointed to Georgette's, at which she desperately begins to peck with a fork saying—*"Je n'ai pas fini, je n'ai pas fini!"* [I haven't finished, I haven't finished].

Gurdjieff said, "Such thing makes me nervous. Nowhere on earth now can such melon have, no one today can eat such, each one cost not less than 350."

Solita began to saw at her rind. Margaret virtuously dug into the deepest places and so had a clean conscience.

"Most active element," Gurdjieff said, "is under, close to skin are the mineral salts. And this you would defile."

A few days later at lunch Gurdjieff said: "How you, Yakina? Hungry after [steam] bath? Then with such dish as we have, all is roses, roses."

"Yes, too good, I suspect."

Solita, seeing he had not understood, said, "She means she is suspicious that soon must be thorns."

"Always is so when too many roses. Roses, roses. Now must begin to make only roses rose. Then rose-rose-rose, thorn-thorn-thorn, thorns-thorn and thorns-thorns. I will begin to make and you, Kanari, and Mees Gordon and Sardine think how can make for her also, each one of us one part. I have thought, that is one-fourth part; Kanari also? That is one-half. In Yakina's past, all her can-ness (ability-to-do) was in her—(makes downward gesture). When I first saw, I thought was only such representative of art as have will-lessness in one place. You understand what I tell, Marguerite?"

"Yes."

"No. If understand you would not carry [wear] such thing."

He looked at the rows of bracelets she wore on each arm.

"Eheu! Life such idiot thing. What good life has dog. He at all times wish only eat, only one tapeworm has. But biped-man has three tapeworms to satisfy. But some people have two tapeworms atrophied. What was that saying—blessed he …."

The Rope supplied the words and they all repeated together:

"Blessed is he who has a soul. Blessed is he who has no soul. But grief and sorrow to him who has its inception."

At the end of January Solita went to the Café de la Paix and found Margaret sitting with Gurdjieff. Her face was so distressed that Solita waited until she left. The previous day she had said to him, "I see I irritate you, Mr. Gurdjieff, so I will go."

When Solita sat down Gurdjieff said—"I nervous and your friend come talk empty to empty. So I tell her I explain to Kanari who know my language. She too light for this work, too American. In life she perhaps have something good. But not for our work. I thought when she first came that after she had contact with me, something would collect in her empty place, but now I see is not so. Such empty life leave empty place. In fact I could tell is piece of meat with emanations. Good formulation, eh?"

Said Solita, "I think the reason is result of philosophizing for years with Orage's New York group."[2]

"Yes, like that she is victim of self-observation."

145

"Perhaps not too late, Mr. Gurdjieff. She has such wish to work, be different. She truly knows there is nothing else in life but your work. Don't send her away."

"Well, I will see what I can combinate for her. She must all stop make, wait, begin again another way. She has only automatic mind, she not understand that of mind is two kinds and she quite not have real mind mentation. You explain her, but not use my words."

When Solita spoke to Margaret she was stricken and cried, then rebelled, then said she "disliked that man." Finally, she decided to face him the next day and ask again for some task.

At lunch, near the end of February, there were only Solita, Miss Gordon, and Margaret. Gurdjieff soon began again on Margaret's plumpness. He asked Solita to supply a word which she refused to do.

"When have money will find new secretary. Your obligation is to help when I look for word. Yakina, you were perhaps a beautiful child? You can thank this you are now spoiled. You are now receptacle for *merde.*"

Margaret, stalwartly, "Yes, I know."

"Must be so with such child. Everyone spoil, parents, young man. Child not study, not learn. If beautiful face have man or woman, always I know is *merde.* If lawyer or engineer I need, never I choose beautiful face—*merde* is. I choose monster. He is not spoiled. He study when young, is clever. This is fault of education and parents. Now late, time has passed. You no longer are hard— just liquid now begin. Fault of your past that you are now empty."

"What shall such person do?" asked Margaret.

"Get on table—do some new titillation."

"I don't mean in life."

"Ah, now very expensive costs such help. If for moving Kanari, castor oil costs 25 francs, for you will cost 50 francs. Now you must pay for your past."

2. Gurdjieff has been working with Margaret since May 1936. Her shell has still not cracked. That Solita says in her defense that it is "the result of philosophizing"—another way of saying what to Margaret is "conversation"—is true on its level. That Solita speaks of the "years with Orage's New York group" cannot be true as Orage's group only began in March or April 1924 and Margaret left America in June 1924.

Asked Miss Gordon, "What can she do?"

"Man is man. He cannot be otherwise. He is such that he can never change his body. He can only be as he is because he is the result of heredity. But his mind he can educate and with this control his animal body and not be its slave. He must at all times struggle and as his mind grows stronger, so will his weakness grow stronger. This is good thing, it makes for more struggle. It is not good if body at once lies down. He must command, he must direct. Easy not eat if not see. Only is difficult if he sees before him—and then not take. This will make something for him in another place. Something he can use.

Solita said that Janet had quarreled with her bitterly over her devotion to Gurdjieff. "Please tell me what is Janet's animal?" she asked.

"Ah, again, m*ees*, curiosity you have."

Five minutes went by without anyone speaking.

"Now one secret I will tell. Not only is tapeworm in stomach of man, other worms are also. Perhaps you have seen in *merde?*"

"No. Only in books as usual."

"Ach! Well, worms, such snakes as I tell about, is different kinds in stomach of man and of them all, one is always chief in this universe of stomach. He commands all and from him this chief in struggle of stomach-universe, from him depends of what consists the psyche of this man and what is his animal."

Gurdjieff talked for twenty minutes, a monologue of which Solita could not understand a single thing and told him so when he stopped.

"Of course not. Only I tell you this to give you taste of such thing."

On March 12, 1938, Hitler had annexed Austria to cheering crowds. In September 1938 Hitler postponed his attack on Czechoslovakia and met with prime ministers Chamberlain and Daladier from England and France, respectively, and Mussolini—the prime minister of Czechoslovakia was not invited. In what was called the Munich Pact, Hitler walked off with the Sudetenland. Then in March 1939, Hitler invaded the remainder of

Czechoslovakia and in April formed The Pact of Steel with Mussolini. Fears of war were everywhere.

Gurdjieff was to visit America in August 1937 but that was
canceled with the death of his brother Dimitri. That September
Alice suddenly fell ill with an intestinal obstruction—acute
inflammation of the peritoneum and gangrene—and underwent
an emergency operation that lasted five hours. A close friend of
Alice's suggested to Kathryn a group called Unity in Missouri, to
have their prayer circle pray for Alice. Kathryn sent them a telegram with the relevant information and said she "felt less alone."
She also of course informed Gurdjieff who also made something,
she said, "with all his will for a distant disciple in peril."[3]

Alice had a long convalescence during which she avoided all
conversation about the Work. "I suffered in silence," said Kathryn, "waiting for her to come back to our common aim, refusing
to admit the gathering evidence that she had lost her desire to go
on." Though she still would see Gurdjieff when he visited New
York, Alice's interest in the Rope never returned and she slowly
drifted back into her former life.

Kathryn had been employed by a travel agency, Ask Mr. Foster,
and persuaded her boss to send her to Europe for three weeks to
search for new business possibilities. In July 1938 Kathryn sailed
alone for Paris. Gurdjieff did not mention Alice until the third
day. He took Kathryn aside after lunch and told her of his disap-
pointment that Alice had not come as well.

"She did not know what work I made for her," he said, his tone
full of sorrow. "Every night, for her, I made special séance. Now,

---

3. Why Kathryn would take this suggestion is not clear from what she
wrote in *Undiscovered Country*. Apparently, from how she presented the situation, she never saw the connection between the Missouri prayer circle praying
for Alice—mixing its vibrations with those coming from Gurdjieff—and
Alice's subsequent resistance to the Work. Alice had subscribed over the years
to a journal that the Missouri people published so their name was not unknown
to Kathryn. Theirs was a way of devotion but it is not a way of development.
To have allowed the mixing of the two when Alice was without any discrimination or defense is unfortunate.

no longer can I make this. I have not the right." He shook his head and added, "And about her, now we no longer speak."

The lunches and meetings went on as usual until April 1939 when Gurdjieff decided to go to America, with Solita accompanying him as his secretary. Traveling with Gurdjieff was always a test for he was always teaching, creating situations that put people "in galoshes." Before the trip Solita had given him a roll of dollars to use for tipping on the ship. On the train to Le Havre Gurdjieff said he had no money, he'd spent all the dollars. Used to his ways, Solita simply smiled. They sailed on the SS *Paris*. On board ship he appeared in a beret too small for his massive bald head. It made him look a bit odd. Embarrassed, Solita tried to convince him to give it to her but he refused. During the day they often sat in deck chairs people-watching as they had at the Café de la Paix, Gurdjieff keeping up a stream of comment.

By the sixth day at sea the ship was shrouded in fog and there were icebergs. From time to time the foghorn blared. Solita told Gurdjieff that she organically hated the sound of the foghorn.

"Yet without could be unhappy situation," answered Gurdjieff. "You must like instinctively because is good thing. But you have wrong instincts and impulse for disliking because you not have education. Everything mixed in you of feeling and thinking. Of course everyone hates such noise—you are not the only one."

It was eleven o'clock in the evening when the SS *Paris* tied up at the docks in Manhattan. Kathryn, Alice and Louise, along with another group of students, were at the pier to greet them. The two groups stood by different gangways. As Kathryn said—"the Rope doesn't mix."

Soon, the gangway came down with a clatter, passengers hurrying off in long irregular streams. Solita, dressed with her usual Parisian chic, got pushed ahead of Gurdjieff. Vainly, she kept looking back but the crowd kept surging ahead. Soon Gurdjieff was well behind her. Every now and then she spotted the too-small beret atop his bald cranium bobbing up and down. The women greeted Solita enthusiastically but kept their eyes on the small beret. When Gurdjieff got near, he greeted each one, shouting—"Sardine!" "Th*een* One!" "Kroko*deel!*"

While the customs man checked his luggage, seven pieces in all, Gurdjieff passed out bonbons. The only item to be declared was a suitcase filled with false eyelashes. The customs man wanted $100 duty. Gurdjieff haggled, fussed and pleaded, all the time using his secret weapon, the language of the smile. Finally, the customs man gave in and Gurdjieff counted out $33.00. The hotels he'd stayed at previously in New York had refused to book him again. The "carpet and furniture disasters" from the clandestine cooking he had done in his room had made him *persona non grata*. So reservations had been made—living room, bedroom with bath—at the Wellington Hotel at 7th Avenue and 55th, only a few blocks from Childs Restaurant, Carnegie Hall and Central Park.

He held a meeting that night at his "office," Childs Restaurant, and on subsequent days, but after complaints from the manager, the meetings were switched to his hotel room. These were held twice daily, from noon until two o'clock and from six to eight o'clock. Solita, Kathryn, Alice and Louise came every day to sit and wait. His other pupils, waiting for an invitation, did not. Said Kathryn: "The old crowd doesn't seem to know anything about going and sitting. They wait to be invited. Meanwhile, we go and sit."

Gurdjieff was hardly unpacked before he set up a six-inch Sterno stove on a living room table. Solita was adamant about the danger and after a big discussion he moved the stove into the bathroom. The next day Alice bought him a large electric grill. Within days his suite became a restaurant, of sorts. Gallon cooking pots stood on the new grill, bread on the desk, pickles in the bookcase, watermelons in the bedroom. In his "pantry," the fire escape, he kept blocks of cheese, crocks, jars, pots, tins of caviar and bundles. Salads were in glass jars under his bedroom window next to the watermelons. In the bedroom in one bureau drawer he stashed a large roll of *lavash,* unleavened Turkish bread. In the bottom drawer, the five and ten cent store cutlery and paper plates.

Though there was no set day or time when guests would come, there were always four or five places set. A serious cook, Gurdjieff welcomed his guests with only a wave of a ladle. The Rope found his soups, as always, delicious, especially the chicken and apricot soup and the grape-leaf spiced soups with meatballs.

The food cooked, Gurdjieff took his place at the head of the table, the red tasseled fez slightly askew on his head. Before the soup course, he rolled cheese and greens into *lavash* which he ate first.

One evening, unexpectedly, there was "Armagnac trouble." Château de Larresingle had run out. A quick search of nearby liquor stores revealed it was no longer imported. Whiskey became the drink of choice for toasts. That emptied, he poured his own special home-brew. This was a concoction of triple-distilled alcohol (from his perfume industry) as a base mixed with lichee nuts and small pieces of toasted lemon-skin and then shaken.

"A frightful drink," said Kathryn, the most courageous imbiber of all the Rope, "so strong it eats varnish off table."

Garbage was a problem—what to do with the bones and rinds and assorted inedibles piling up from their meals. The women commandeered wastebaskets, emptied their contents into boxes and bags, which were then neatly wrapped and tied. As Gurdjieff's guests left, each was handed a "gift." Puzzled, Gurdjieff asked about the gifts. When he was told, he wondered where the gifts would be disposed of. In the middle of Times Square, he was told. "Of course," he agreed. "Most important place, put in."

Two days later, Kathryn was the only one at dinner. Afterward, Gurdjieff invited her into his bedroom only he did not drink. He asked her to sit on his bed and tell him a story—"With *tzimuss*," he said.

Then he said if she would lie on the bed beside him, it would bring "fulfilling."

Kathryn, in galoshes, said she didn't understand.

"Not mama-papa, you not understand," he told her. "Man when tired sometimes can fulfill, [by] having passive beside him. Then can he be passive. This very complicate thing I tell. Woman all is same. Man can be woman. Just this fulfilling when rest together—without mama-papa business. You not understand. I far go."

"I'm a Swiss cow perhaps," Kathryn said.

"No, Normandy cow. You not hear about Normandy cow? All world, in all language, know is normal cow. Not have big here (where udder would be) or here (where other organs would be) but all same—though average have—still give big. In Tibet, one Normandy cow give one liter daily. This one litre what one Normandy cow give equal five liters what ordinary cow give daily. You have such for me. You are here—*friend.* I not feel I must be so-so (gestures politeness)—or nervous. Even I can eye keep shut. No one come in door to kill. You sit, you are near."

Kathryn felt the importance of what he was saying but could not understand. She put his cigarettes on the night table, and prepared to leave. He invited her to come dinner the next evening at eleven o'clock when they all came from the steam bath.

Kathryn knocked at his door at two minutes to eleven. All the men who had gone with him for the bath sat with him around table—Donald Whitcomb, Fred Leighton, Stanley Speigelburg, Martin Benson. No women had arrived yet.

Said Gurdjieff: "Eleven exact, I tell. Then will women come."

Exactly at eleven o'clock Rita Romilly and Lillian Whitcomb arrived.

Gurdjieff announced a special sitting for women, so the men gave up their seats and went into the living room. Even while Gurdjieff talked, the men continued to talk, arguing politics. Once Gurdjieff interrupted what he was saying to the women, and listened to the men. Then he turned to the women and said—"Hear how they beat each other!"

Kathryn didn't like the disrespect for Gurdjieff, for the women. It was, she said "a new atmosphere for me—different from what I have known in [other] Gurdjieff gatherings."

Fred Leighton, an old student who Gurdjieff had stayed with for a time when in New York, came to lunch one day. He told how in the American West there was an expression, "Say it with a smile".

"Of course," answered Gurdjieff, "because then he think you joke. You notice … never anyone take offense anything I say? Even you know what words I use. But never you see man angry with me when I tell. You know why? Because I am cynic.""

Leighton said Gurdjieff didn't mean 'cynic;' he was not a cynic but a 'skeptic.'

"Excuse—not skeptic," said Gurdjieff. "Skeptic means: you believe, I not believe; you hope, I not hope. I know this word from Greek. You know I know Greek roots. Cynic is word. Perhaps you not have in English."

Leighton, told him the word didn't mean what Gurdjieff meant. He didn't want Gurdjieff to be a cynic.

Gurdjieff said, "Cynic is the word. Cynic means a man who is not afraid to tell truth, exact how is, yet never he offend people when he tell because he is so right, he tell so exact. Never they can be offended, because the truth he tells."

The political situation was worsening in Europe. Germany, ignoring its agreement to the Munich Pact, had occupied the remainder of Czechoslovakia, Franco had defeated Republican Spain, and Italy had invaded Albania. Gurdjieff's students tried to convince him to stay on and settle in New Jersey. But he refused and on May 19th he and Solita sailed for France on the SS *Normandie*.

That June, Georgette's book *La Machine à Courage* nearly finished, she, Margaret, and Monique prepared to leave their rooms on the rue Casimir Pèrier for a vacation at the lighthouse at Tancarville. The last of her luggage packed, Georgette was hurriedly dressing when she looked in the mirror and saw a strange sight. "Monique," she called, "look at this curious little swelling. I wonder what it is?"

Both Monique and Margaret went to her room and found Georgette with a puzzled expression staring into the full length mirror.

The two women didn't look at her but looked in the mirror as well. They, too, saw the swelling.

"Evidently it is nothing," said Georgette in a dismissive voice. Then she added "… but it is rather curious."

"No," agreed Margaret, "it is just a little swelling, it couldn't mean anything."

But nevertheless what they had seen in the mirror had created a question. Georgette was willing to ignore it, but Margaret, who had a strong practical side, insisted that instead of leaving for the light-house they stay the night and the next day stop by the American Hospital. Margaret's Citroën loaded with luggage, the women dressed for a long holiday in Normandy, they drove to the hospital just to get an opinion. What Doctor Thierry de Martel said hit like a thunderbolt out of the blue. The swelling, the doctor told Georgette, was a tumor. If it wasn't surgically removed, it might become malignant. What had been merely curious suddenly loomed as life threatening. Though shocked, Georgette had battled illness before and won. An operation was out of the question.

In a trice, the women's whole world turned upside down. "Without the slightest sign of illness," Margaret said, "without a trace of warning pain ... within twenty-four hours, on a cloudless summer day, by the merest accident of a glance in a mirror—an observation, a question, an examination, a verdict ... our world stood still facing a word—cancer."

The women went to see Gurdjieff. He treated her a number of times but the cancer was too progressive. They then crossed the channel a number of times to see a doctor in London. But, again, without result. Throughout the summer, Georgette refused the operation. It was only at the end of August that she at last consented. By then, however, the whole world had come to a resounding—*stop*....

The long-speculated war with Germany was no longer possibility but reality. On September 1, Hitler's armored divisions invaded Poland. France and Britain declared war on Germany. It was no surprise. For months the military call-to-arms posters had been pasted on city and village walls—*Appel Immédiat!* Other posters told people what to do in case of a gas attack or instructed what to do with car headlights and private and public lamps during blackouts. The palaces of Fontainebleau and Versailles had been closed as had the Louvre and other state museums, their artworks shipped off for hiding in the provinces. Steel helmeted troops entrained at Gare de l'Est for northern frontier fortresses and the impregnable Maginot Line, while relatives, wives, girl friends and mistresses waved and cried.

The only operation the American Hospital at Neuilly was performing was a planned evacuation to Etretat on the Normandy coast. In the midst of what Gurdjieff would term a "mass psychosis," the women drove thirteen kilometers to Orgeval to stay for a week at Noel Murphy's house. Janet was already there. Solita, breathless and heart pounding, had just arrived. They traded bits of information, even astrological forecasts—the moon, Jupiter, Venus and Mars had all come together that month—and listened in shocked silence to the short wave radio reports from London and New York of the German advances. The women covered their windows with blue paper so that no crack of light might be visible to enemy planes and stocked up on provisions such as candles—though now only sold singly and not by the box—matches, sugar, soap, cotton, toothpaste, iodine and aspirin. Staples like sugar, flour and rice, although unavailable in larger quantities, could still be purchased by the kilo. The women avidly read last copies of the *Paris Soir* and the *Herald Tribune*. "Everyone coming out from Paris brought news, as you bring candy to your hostess," remarked Margaret, "and the one that predicted Paris would be bombed that night became the most exciting guest."

Margaret, Georgette and Monique waited in Orgeval a week and then drove on to Tancarville and rested a few days. To calm her nerves and to keep from thinking of Georgette's illness, Margaret read mystery novel after mystery novel—she had brought twenty from Paris. On the appointed day they drove to Etretat, a large village, for Georgette's operation, but there they learned Dr. de Martel was still in Paris. Returning to Paris was much harder than leaving. The roads were lined with cars, buses motorcycles, bicycles, carts, anything that could move and carry goods. Baby cribs, pets, bedding, luggage, canisters of extra gas, food—whatever could be packed or strapped on was taken. Weaving in and out of oncoming traffic, pleading, cajoling, the passing Parisians giving them crazy looks, the women slowly worked their way back to Paris.

Doctor de Martel was found and on September 12th the operation performed. "I got it all out," he assured them. Whether or not it was successful, he said, awaited time's verdict. While Georgette rested in their rooms at the rue Casimir-Pèrier, outside her window people frantically hoarded as shops closed, shuttering their windows and gating their entrances. Paris soon looked a ghost town. At the end of September, Margaret drove to Orgeval to say goodbye to Janet and Solita, who were leaving for America on October 5th. (Janet had previously planned this three month holiday in the States in addition to a visit to Indianapolis to see her mother Mary who was sick.) Margaret, Solita, Janet and Noel had breakfast together in Noel's kitchen at five in the morning and a half hour later in a heavy fog said their good-byes at a crossroads, Margaret standing alongside Noel, both waving, as Janet and Solita drove off for Bordeaux.

Once Georgette was able, Margaret and Monique loaded up the Citroën again in preparation for the long drive back to Tancarville. Arriving at the château all was silent. Either everyone had left or was in hiding. Finally, a servant was spied. Georgette's brother-in-law had just died, he informed them. The châtelaine was grieving in her room. They found her praying, talking of the cross, crying that she *"loved* the cross." As Georgette comforted her, Margaret stood silent, remembering that never once had the châtelaine spoken of the cross during all the years they had lived with her.

Margaret thought of Gurdjieff in Paris, how cut off they were from him. But he had said, "I have given you enough for years." The women talked to one another of his teaching, what was particularly special to them, and they resolved not to become entwined in associations of war. "It is a madness that will pass," said Margaret, "only to be succeeded by another. In the current madness even Hitler isn't to blame—he's merely a tool of Nature: on the theory that Nature needs certain emanations and gets them—millions of human beings agonizing over war—all those vibrations filling the invisible universes .... The wish to go on, the struggle not to fall back—all this makes a friction that produces combustion ... and out of these energies springs a fire."

Overwhelmed with Georgette's illness and the war, Margaret continued to immerse herself in her mystery novels. Two or three times each day Monique unwrapped Georgette's bandages.

Expectantly, the women looked for signs of healing. But the wound refused to heal. Georgette, refusing to accept that what she had was cancer, insisted that word never be used. But cancerous or not, the wound was not closing. What to do? Return to Paris? Too dangerous. Stay put? Impossible. America seemed the only hope. Once again, the women bought extra tanks of black market fuel, gassed up the Citroën and loaded its luggage rack. Margaret at the wheel, they left Tancarville for Hendaye, a village near Biarritz, only a few miles from the Spanish border. The plan was to cross to Spain, drive to Lisbon and book passage to America. Stopping at an inn on the way, Georgette wrote in her diary:

> An evening of fatigue ... and I coughed so much that my wound opened. Standing before the mirror of the inn, as the blood slowly flowed, I saw my image as Jesus of inferior quality—a carnival Jesus. In Tancarville, ill after the operation, I had fallen into a state of personal anguish—at every moment, stupidly, I felt fear. That fear continued—during a month I felt horror in my veins, in my bones; and then, as I grew stronger physically, my moral suffering increased until it overwhelmed me. I lived a despair too great for a human being.

Things began to brighten when—although almost imperceptible—Monique noticed Georgette's wound had begun to heal. Redressing the wound became an expectant ritual. The wound healed every day until only one tiny point remained open. Margaret was overjoyed. The future, her future with the lovely, dear Georgette, began to open up again.

Nearly two months of quiet but certain jubilation followed. But then in the waning days of November, inexplicably, Georgette began to lose ground, the wound began to open again. But then just as suddenly, the wound began to close. Over the short wave radio a warning came that all Americans must leave France or risk being interned in concentration camps. The thought of leaving Georgette stopped Margaret's heart and she thought immediately of the two revolvers she kept hidden in the car. Another difficulty loomed. Not life-threatening but still serious: money was running out. Working was impossible. How would they live? Miraculously, on November 20th Georgette received a letter from a New York publisher. Margaret and Monique crowded round as Georgette opened the letter and withdrew a check for 28,300 francs, an enormous sum. Maeterlinck's *The Blue Bird* had just been filmed and the publisher had printed a deluxe edition of Georgette's *The Story of the Blue Bird.* Fortune's wheel had finally begun to turn. After so much darkness, light.

Inexplicably, at the end of November Georgette's wound worsened and continued to do so through the Christmas holidays. Georgette refused to give in to it—"I have only had an accident. I am not sick at all," she declared. In the beginning she had steadfastly refused to accept she had cancer; now she was not even sick. Finally—as if the gods were playing with them—her wound began to heal.

Progress continued into 1940. All but one tiny area was healed. By this time, the Germans had completely sealed off the Spanish border. There was no hope of getting through. So in February 1941, the three women left Hendaye for Le Cannet, a small village three kilometers above Cannes on the Riviera. In the hills overlooking the shimmering blue waters of the Mediterranean, a friend had rented a tiny cottage for them. Climbing up the winding road from Cannes, the women found Le Cannet awash in colorful flowers and delightful fragrances. Georgette's recovery not only continued but she began to bloom. Once again the oppression lifted. Georgette was going to make it.

In May, Mussolini threatened to bring Italy into the war. If so, southern France could easily be bombed. Again the women packed up, fleeing Le Cannet for Bordeaux with America the final destination. All along their planned route—Brignoles, Arles, Montpellier, Toulouse, Auch, Condom, Langon to Bordeaux— the roads were empty. At the American Consulate in Bordeaux they filled out applications and handed in their passports. The SS *Washington* was scheduled to sail on June 8th. Margaret and Georgette could get visas but not Monique, as Belgium, overrun by Germans, no longer had status as a nation. Absurd, of course, but French officials, in the midst of a great defeat, said Margaret, "had become more self-important and more enamored of red-tape than ever." Georgette said—"Ah, the terrible scourge of the world is the nature of most human beings. It terrifies me. What is this evil which, suddenly, without a real reason, makes the heart that loves close up, the mind become deaf, and a kind of blind force set people against each other?"

Unwilling to leave Monique behind, the women set off for Bayonne. It was near enough to Hendaye and Spain that they could sail for America as soon as Belgium had again become a nation. In Bayonne, they went to the Préfecture to get *visas de sortie*. Their passports were sent back to Bordeaux with the necessary request papers. Days passed. Finally, word came—their passports were lost.

Meanwhile, on June 10th, Paris had fallen. On the 13th, the French government in retreat to Bordeaux, Paris was handed over to the Nazis as an "open city." Georgette's doctor, Thierry de Martel, committed suicide declaring, "I am over sixty, I expect nothing more from life, and I don't want to see the Germans march down the Champs Elysées." Which was, of course, exactly what happened. Hitler, his troops goose-stepping down the Champs Elysées before him, stood triumphant in the rear of an open black Mercedes convertible as it proceeded slowly down the grand boulevard, his arm raised in the Nazi salute. Top-ranking Nazi officers drove to the Invalides to view Napoleon's tomb before dining at the Ritz, while their soldiers hoisted red, black and white swastika flags atop the Eiffel Tower and every government building. All was well for a while, but soon the Nazis began the ransacking of Paris, carting off anything of value, machinery, Gobelin tapestries, surgical instruments, milk, mutton, sweet champagne, even French bed linen.

Outside the city, there was only barrenness and emptiness. The roads leading to the cathedral town of Senlis, to Laon, Beauvais, Les Andelys and Vernon were all empty except for the occasional bicycle, the roadsides littered with the debris of fleeing refugees. Throughout the flat, once well-tended landscape lay the rotting corpses of French soldiers, half earthed-over. In contrast, the German dead were buried neatly wherever they died, wooden crosses with name plates marking their graves in wheat fields, grape vine-yards or some villager's chrysanthemum bed.

The occupiers wanted to be seen by the occupied as *des braves types, tout de même*—"nice fellows after all"—but the mask was difficult to maintain. In Fontainebleau, for example, a little boy had made a *croque à jambe*—stuck out his foot—and tripped a passing German soldier. Immediately, the local *Kommandant* had ordered that all the town's citizenry on the approach of all soldiers must now step into the gutter. Wherever the resistance, in what-ever form, the Nazis tightened the screws.

Bordeaux was soon choking with refugees, all clamoring for shelter and food, thousands of cars blocking city streets, their flee-ing owners not finding accommodations, sleeping in their cars. The Battle of France now lost, eighty-four year old Marshal Pétain, victor of the war of 1914–18 with Germany, succeeded Paul Reynaud as Prime Minister and the last government of the Third French Republic petitioned for an armistice.

Refugees now, Margaret, Georgette and Monique in Bayonne found themselves in the center of the Occupied Zone, their dreams of America dashed, Georgette's condition growing worse. Once the armistice was declared, observed Margaret:

> The French became very moral, I could no longer appear in slacks on the street without attracting a crowd of enraged Frenchmen; the ones who had most enjoyed American ways and freedom now declared that it was America that had caused France's downfall. They yelled epithets at me as I walked the block from the garage to our hotel, until I felt that a French revolution was forming behind me. For once I had to keep silent and reach the hotel quickly without appearing to hurry.

It was not long before Germans marched into Bayonne:

> They were all tall and thin, except for one, and the first thing they did was to invade the chocolate shops under the arcades. Their uniforms were far superior, in cloth, color and cut, to the French; they had metal hooks around the

waist to hold their belts, and the hooks were placed low enough to give every man a long line from shoulder to waist. As they walked in groups through the streets I couldn't help watching the beauty of their rhythm. They all had it—a long legato stride. And they drove their cars differently from any Frenchman; you could always distinguish a German foot on the accelerator by the quick force and dash of sound.

By the end of July, the women thought the best they might do was to get exit visas to return to Le Cannet, which was still in the Unoccupied Zone. Receiving substitutes for their lost passports they got exit visas to leave Bayonne. Once again, they bought ten extra five-liter fuel canisters in the black market, filled up the Citroën's 107 litre gas tank, packed up the trunk and half the back seat to the ceiling, loaded the luggage onto the luggage rack, and set off for Orthez, a small nondescript village. It lay at the boundary line between the Occupied and Unoccupied Zones, the women reasoning that it might be too small to have a checkpoint.

Margaret took the back roads they all, by now, knew so well. There were few cars on the road, now and then a tractor. It seemed like they had reasoned rightly. Coming round a bend, however, up ahead they saw the outline of a German soldier, rifle at the ready. Young and bored, he eyed the women cautiously, slowly surveyed the luggage and canisters, without a word took their papers and made a show of going through them, but his interest was not in their papers.

"Cinema stars?" he asked Margaret.

Margaret smiled and was about to say "No, we're writers," but realizing his next question would be what did they write? she stopped herself.

"Yes," Margaret said as only Margaret could say it, "*cinema stars.*"

Once again the gods seem to be with them. Margaret once said, "I have a single superstition," said Margaret, "that the gods are for me and that anything I want will happen if I play at it hard enough. I can't say work at it because anything I work at never seems to come out right. I never could have talked French if I had worked at it. I just wanted to talk, felt impelled to talk and in three weeks I was talking."

In Le Cannet Margaret rented a little box of a house, Chalet Rose. It had only three small rooms, two bedrooms and beneath them a studio-kitchen. All it lacked was a bathroom. Money was tight. Ernest Hemingway, perhaps hearing of their plight from Janet Flanner, wired four hundred dollars. At seventy to the dollar, Margaret was able to change it into francs. Georgette sang and worked on her book *La Machine à Courage*.

Margaret and Monique had hoped that Georgette's condition would improve once back in the color and fragrance of Le Cannet. It did not. The swelling in fact grew larger. By April Georgette's arm had outgrown human proportions. Amputation was considered but refused. Instead Georgette began a correspondence with Jane Heap in London, telling Jane that because of the division between the Occupied and Unoccupied Zones of France, her fear was that she would be cut off from Gurdjieff in Paris.

Jane wrote back:

> You can never be cut off, unless you yourself fail to understand yourself in relation to him. It is never an action, an event, a mistake that cuts one off ... it is some non-activity in the verb to be. You remember his chapter 'Good and Evil' [in *All and Everything, First Series*] there is much talk about serviceability to God, and lacking this serviceability the being does not cease to exist but he ceases to be ... serviceability meaning of value in the design or plan .... As long as we have this as our highest wish, and make efforts to create a positive neutralizing force in ourselves, we are contributing to absolute good and cannot cease to exist in the mind of God. No more can our contacts with Gurdjieff be cut off. One side of him you see manifestations of ordinary man, but the other side you must know is always impartial, timeless .... Give my love to Florence Nightingale Anderson. Bless her heart, I was always afraid I'd be ill and that she would nurse me.

Since that day two years before when Georgette had noticed the unusual little swelling, the fear of her death had hung like an unpleasant odor over Margaret and Monique. Though all their travels, the ups and downs, it had hovered there silently in the background, always ready to spring forward, contained only by the women's denial. Now, in these last days, a change came about. "Our fear of death became quieter," said Margaret. "We entered that transition which leads from despair to destiny, from personal grief to impersonal tragedy, and which is like the shift that occurs in art—from stylelessness to form. I knew that our death-in-life was beginning its transmutation into the octave of life-in-death."

Georgette now began to talk in symbols and to repeat numbers over and over, *Un, deux, trois, quatre* .... [One, two, three, four ...] Margaret and Monique knew that she was referring to *Heptaparaparshinokh,* one of the two primary laws of life, and to the "I." At one point she said to Margaret very clearly—"You must not go always too fast, you will lose much; you must begin at do, not mi; build from do to mi, then pass the half-tone to fa—consciously." Margaret told her that she understood.

For a time, Georgette became obsessed with the idea that Gurdjieff would appear—*"Il vient, je le sais, il est déja la—il est entré par en bas."* [He is coming, I know it, he is already here—he has come in below.] That evening an inter-zone card came from Paris with the message that Gurdjieff had said she had *"beaucoup de courage"* [much courage] and had said she was a "friend." Hearing this Georgette's face transfigured and she said, *"Il a dit cela?"* [He said that?] She then spoke her last words, *"Alors ... nous allons mourir sans mourir?"* [Then ... we will die without dying?]

Later, cradled in Margaret's arms, Georgette Leblanc, seventy-two years old, drew her last breath.

Jane, upon learning of Georgette's passing, wrote to Margaret, "I read and re-read her last days as you tell them, and I think I know what she was trying to do and say. 'As you go, so we come again.' Georgette will never perish. Die we all must, but we can hope that none of us who has 'eaten' of Gurdjieff's food will ever perish."

Janet and Solita arriving in New York the second week of October 1939, took rooms at the Hotel Earl across from Greenwich Village's Washington Square Park. In so doing, in a geographic sense, at least, the two women had come full circle for it was here in Greenwich Village that they had first met twenty-one years before. Janet wrote to Gertrude Stein she expected to return to France in January, but, ambivalent, she dawdled. By the time she booked passage, Hitler's armies were marching through Belgium. The following Fourth of July her plans changed dramatically when Janet spent the weekend on Long Island's Fire Island. Here she met thirty-eight year old Natalia Danesi Murray, an Italian who had once had aspirations to become an opera singer and actress. A handsome woman, stunning and dark-haired, Natalia had been divorced for several years and had a young son. Janet loved her easy laughter, great enthusiasms and her passion for liberty. The two began seeing each other on a regular basis. Janet was soon calling her new Roman friend, "Darlinghissima."

Solita, having lost Janet to Noel in Paris, now lost her to Natalia in New York. While she hadn't liked Noel's amazon manner, Natalia she simply didn't trust. Cold, duplicitous, possessive was how Solita found her. But, given her and Janet's pact of "absolute freedom," she simply had to stand aside. As for Noel, Janet had expected her to come to the States. Letters had gone back and forth since Janet disembarked. But by August 1940 Noel had resolved to stay on. Local residents, she said, could provide her with milk and bread, and vegetables she would get from her garden. Though Noel's arrival would have complicated matters for Janet, still she was angry.

In October 1941 Janet finally finished her profile of the legendary Germanic author Thomas Mann—"Goethe in Hollywood"— for *The New Yorker*. For over a year, she had worked on the piece in her usual painstaking and methodical manner, interviewing any one in the least connected to the subject, collecting mountains of small facts and anecdotes and entertainingly erecting them in support of some incisive concept. She had lunched with the author of *Buddenbrooks*, *The Magic Mountain* and *Death in Venice* and, rather than being impressed, had been clearly put off by his remote masculinity and the stiffness of his aristocratic and Teutonic heritage.

Her piece showed little appreciation for his genius and skewered Mann for using incidents in his family's life as grist for his books, a strange accusation inasmuch as she had done the same with her novel *The Cubical City.* Enraged, Mann called the piece "an insignificant piece of hackwork." Others defended her, notably the writer Alec Woolcott who told her she must "feel more comfortable now that you have laid your Thomas Mann *egg*.... If the result strikes you as a trifle dull, it is all the fault of Thomas himself. He is as interesting and artistic as Grant's tomb."

Solita and Louise Davidson, meanwhile, had both joined the American Women's Voluntary Services, a training center and clearinghouse for women volunteers wanting to serve in community or war-related jobs. As Solita wrote to Margaret in Le Cannet, "in this year everything has changed nearly down to the roots of life." Among the women volunteers, she told Margaret, she had met Elizabeth Jenks Clark, "Lib," a tall and stately young woman with whom she was now living. By 1942 Janet had moved in with Natalia, subletting part of Natalia's East Forty-eighth Street apartment, but still she could not fully break with Solita. When Solita and Lib moved West in the hopes of starting a new life together, Janet wouldn't or couldn't let go. She wrote to Solita often, talking about a new profile she was doing on the Hollywood movie actress Bette Davis which seemed so trivial, given America's entrance into the war, and still speaking about the guilt felt for leaving poor Noel in France.

For her part, Noel continued to live in Orgeval, getting the milk and bread she needed and growing food in her garden just as she planned. It soon became apparent, however, that she was being watched. A day came when she was told not to leave Orgeval and ordered to report weekly to the police. In September 1942 the Nazis arrested all American women living in Paris and its environs. The dragnet caught Noel, whom the Nazis classified as an enemy alien. Taken to Paris, Noel, along with Sylvia Beach and 350 other women, was put under heavy guard in an improvised dorm. The next morning the women were taken by bus and herded aboard a filthy train bound for an internment camp in

Vittel, a spa town. Noel was assigned a room with five other women in the Grand Hôtel, its stately old world elegance now marred by the barbed wire and guards with guard dogs surrounding it. It took six months, but the intercession of friends in Paris finally won Noel's release the following February, 1943. Still alive in spirit but her body showing the signs of her internment, Noel returned to Orgeval and her garden to wait out the war. Janet confided to Solita, who had returned from the West with Lib to live in New Jersey, that she no longer loved Noel as she had and that she would "try not to grieve about my infidelity."

The Magus Departs

CHALET ROSE. JUNE 1942. AFTER GEORGETTE'S DEATH, MARGARET WAS DISCONSOLATE. HER WHOLE WORLD HAD died with Georgette. SHE COULDN'T KEEP from grieving and dwelling on the past. In letters to her, Solita kept suggesting she return to the United States, but Margaret had little money. Solita wrote to Ernest Hemingway telling him of Margaret's plight and he sent the money to pay for her passage. So in June 1942, Margaret, fifty-six years of age, reluctantly left Monique and Chalet Rose and made her way to Lisbon where she sailed to New York on the SS *Drottingholm*. A photo of her taken just before leaving shows her looking tired and whimsical. The years had taken her beauty but the eyes were still alive.

Sailing to New York as well was Dorothy Caruso, nearly fifty years old, the widow of the famous Italian opera singer, and her two daughters. Like Margaret she was returning to the United States after many years abroad. Though her husband had died some twenty-one years before after only three years of marriage which produced one daughter, Gloria, she still carried him with her. Of his death, she said, "My state was beyond loneliness and longing; it was the silence of emptiness and unreality."

Two years after Enrico's death, having experienced periods of depression and desperation, Dorothy heeded the advice of a close friend and married an Englishman. Though the marriage lasted only three months, it produced her second daughter, Jacqueline. As the Caruso estate required that Gloria live in Italy four months out of the year, in the ensuing years Dorothy, and her daughters traveled back and forth between New York and Italy. With the 1929 Wall Street crash Dorothy, fearing that her daughters might be kidnapped, settled in Switzerland. In 1933, her daughters then eight and thirteen, Dorothy married a Frenchman and lived near the forest of Fontainebleau. Seven years later, the marriage ended. At the beginning of the war, Dorothy went to Southern France where she worked in the fields, sometimes as much as fifteen hours a day, planting potatoes to help hundreds of destitute families living in the Alpes Maritimes. In May 1942, hearing that all of France was about to be occupied, Dorothy and her daughters fled to Spain and boarded a ship for America. Though this octave of her life was ending, the new one looked just as empty.

"I was returning," said Dorothy, "after an absence of many transient years to New York—a gigantic city filled with strangers and forgotten friends, that once had been my home and was my home no longer. I faced a future without plan or purpose. After my rapturous past and my astonishing present, all that I had to look forward to was a life of ease and emptiness."

One of the passengers aboard the *Drottingholm* immediately attracted Dorothy's attention. Dorothy inquired about who she was but was reluctant to speak to her. Finally, Dorothy approached her— "I hear you published the *Little Review*," she said. It was like a clarion call. The women talked for hours. It was as if they had known each other always. When Dorothy returned to her cabin she told her daughters Gloria and Jackie that "I have heard things tonight that may change the course of our lives." When asked what it was she heard she found she could remember nothing of the conversation. Still, there was the abiding recognition "as if through revelation, that on this night, on a ship sailing towards New York, I had come at last within sight of a land I had sought since childhood. The magnitude of the revelation, the quality of the disclosure and the immensity of its effect upon me, erased from my mind all dread of the future."

This meeting at sea, between two continents, both at war, had the taste of fate for Margaret Anderson also. "It was as if everything had been decided and arranged for us from the first moment of our meeting," she said. "A little later one of her daughters said she hadn't known whether she would like me and so she asked me, 'What do you feel about poetry?' And when I answered, 'It's like a religion, don't you think?' ... she knew that everything was all right."

By the time they reached New York, the women's friendship had bloomed—"The last great friendship of my life," Margaret would call it. If such a relationship was new for Dorothy, it was equally new in another way for Margaret. For now she had a teaching to impart, one that she experienced first-hand, had suffered with as Gurdjieff had pointed her past her personality and into her essence and beyond that, perhaps, to a glimpse of real being. It was a world that Dorothy Caruso had never known or suspected.

Solita stood dockside with a dozen long-stemmed roses, smiling in the summer sun, waving and calling to Margaret as she disembarked. Seeing the large good-natured woman who came down the gangplank with Margaret, Solita immediately understood. The image, the recognition, were paralyzing. She felt dazed. What had happened at sea between Margaret and this woman was "irrevocable." Seeing the joy on Margaret's face, Solita said, "I recognized nothing but fate—which, for the first time in my life, I accepted immediately, without struggling."

There were embraces, warm and full, and with the luggage passed through customs, they all took a taxi to the New York apartment Dorothy and her husband had kept. There was no question but that Margaret would live with her. "I don't remember how or when," Dorothy said, "we asked her to live with us—it was as if she had always been with us. It happened as simply as the conversation."

The women lived well and easily together, sharing their life stories. Dorothy told Margaret that as an adolescent and young woman, her early life was filled with fear and rejection. Raised by her Nanna, she never saw her mother or father except at breakfast and dinner. At thirteen, her mother having been sent away to a sanitarium, and her Nanna having died the year before, she was sent away to the Convent of the Sacred Heart. During holidays she was the only girl not to receive correspondence, money, or clothing from her father. To bury the hurt, she quickly convinced herself that her father must be too sick to write or send things. After two years Dorothy returned home from the Convent to care for her mother who had also returned home, but soon became ill again and was sent back to the sanitarium. Dorothy, having experienced her father's coldness and anger towards her, asked to be returned to the Convent. Two years later, almost eighteen, her father sent for her to keep house for him. Of her father, editor of *Scientific American* and a well-known patent lawyer, she said, "I couldn't explain his dislike of me except that I bored him. He had a violent temper and I soon learned that he was unreasonable, blustering and egotistical.... When he returned home from the office at night, the sound of his key in the front door made my heart pound.... He exploded into angry sarcasm whenever I was ill... he berated me... he blamed me for the servants 'short coming' and glared at me across the dining-room table. As he took no interest or pride in my appearance, he allowed me only the most meager wardrobe—and that with such ill grace that at last I never asked for anything I could do without. I had to sit with him every evening in the library, too frightened to speak, yet afraid that my silence would provoke another outbreak of fury."

Margaret felt that Dorothy might have the talent to write and so she soon induced her to begin putting her experiences to paper. A routine was soon established in which they each worked on their writing during the day and, in the evening, after dinner, Margaret would take from a special folder the notes she had written at the Prieuré and at luncheons and dinners of the Rope and read them aloud to Dorothy.

To tell her story, Dorothy tried to enlist the help of a ghost-writer. The writer came one day to the apartment and Dorothy told her life story. The woman wept. She told her she was incapable of reproducing in a book the emotion that Dorothy had brought her to feel.

Dining one evening with Margaret in a restaurant, she confessed her lack of education and her desperation. "In all my life," she told Margaret, "I have accomplished only two things. I made Enrico happy and I've brought up my children well. Even that I didn't do myself—he set the example for me."

Margaret answered that there was more to education than

what one learns from books or another person. "You don't know what you have inside yourself—you've never tried to bring it out."

Dorothy protested that she did not know how.

Margaret stared at her a moment and with a sweep of her beautiful and handsome hand, pointed up at the restaurant's balcony above the dining room.

"Suppose there was a screen stretched across that balcony," said Margaret. "Suppose you were looking at a motion picture of your life with Enrico. Begin anywhere and tell what you see."

The next morning Dorothy began to write that she now did not remember her life with Enrico but she saw it. "And as I wrote even the picture that I was seeing vanished. All my other senses became involved; I smelled the hot Italian air: I heard Enrico speak again, and sing.... As if propelled by powers beyond my own, I finished the first draft of the book in six weeks."

Three months later, after editing and revision, the book—*Enrico Caruso: His Life and Death*—was ready for publication. When Dorothy read the manuscript over for the last time, she said, "I knew that the tragic end of the story I had told was not its ending." She would soon begin another book—this on the story of her life.

One evening Solita, and several other women, one of whom was Elizabeth Jenks Clark, Solita's new companion, came to dinner. When conversation turned to Gurdjieff and the Work, Dorothy questioned them—"What do you mean by his 'work'? What work do you do?"

She was told of the work at the Prieuré and the translation of *All and Everything*, of the sacred dances and music and the "inner work."

"What is inner work?" Dorothy wanted to know.

"Work on yourself."

In cryptic fashion, this was explained, but she was told she could really not do anything until she saw Gurdjieff. The conversation then turned to his book. Dorothy wanted to borrow a copy. She was told it only existed in manuscript and this was not to be lent out.

"Why not?" demanded Dorothy.

"Because you wouldn't be able to understand."

"How will I ever understand then?"

"When you go to him, you will see. Everything he says, every word he utters, is a teaching. Gradually you come to understand."

But what if you didn't understand—could you ask that he explain it?

"He rarely explains. He wants you to make great efforts to understand, from the hints he gives you. He purposely makes it hard. In his book he says that the key is always hidden far from the lock."

During one discussion the women resolved to keep the focus on the cosmology of the teaching Gurdjieff had brought. They spoke of the Ray of Creation and man's forgotten potentiality of acting not from one center but from all three and, in so doing, beginning to ascend the scale of vibration represented by the Ray of Creation, moving from one "world" of vibratory frequency to another.

Solita quoted Gurdjieff, saying, "One must strive for Being." If anyone wanted to understand more, it must be realized that it could only come through the emotional center, not the intellectual. At the same time, one must remember, she told them, that he had also said: "Study, study everything. Know yourself, then humanity, then the planet. Study forty-four hours a day."

"Is there anything to the teaching?" one of the women asked.

Margaret said nothing, seeing that her answers would be too long and involved. Everyone was silent. Margaret looked at Solita.

"Is there anything beyond all this, Solita?" Dorothy finally asked.

"Yes."

"What comes afterward?" asked Dorothy.

"Everything," answered Solita.

The war still raging, there was no hope of seeing Gurdjieff. Supposedly, he was still in Paris. How he was faring with the rationing and the Nazis no one knew. Miss Gordon had stayed behind with him when she could have easily left. It spoke volumes to the harsh judgments that sometimes had been made of her. Someone had said that Gurdjieff was still managing to hold meetings in his apartment with Madame de Salzmann and the pupils she had brought him. It was said that Miss Gordon had attended the meetings until 1943, when she was interned by the Nazis in a prisoner of war camp where she died (a rumor that proved true).

The years were wonderful and refreshing for Margaret after so many years of struggle. Dorothy and Margaret continued to talk about Gurdjieff and the teaching, played chess, went to museums, dined and took small trips.

In time, Margaret, ever the provocateur, interested in making Dorothy more aware of herself, pointed out that Dorothy hid her emotions behind good manners. "Let go," advised Margaret, "so that you can move from one state to another."

Just as twenty-one years before Jane Heap had asked her group to tell the story of their lives as a way of separating the essential from the nonessential and giving shape, direction and meaning to one's life, Margaret now suggested to Dorothy that she write a book about her life. "You must make every word count," Margaret told her, "but first of all you must find your form—the form that will be you and no one else."

But where to begin? Dorothy had no idea.

The question was presented to Solita who often dropped by with Lib Clark for a visit (a woman Margaret insisted upon calling "Lynn" for some reason, perhaps because Margaret's middle name was "Caro*lyn*"). She told Dorothy she should find those qualities in herself that made her different from others. "Those qualities," said Solita, "will be your limits and you must write within them."

Dorothy protested. What were her qualities? She didn't know.

Solita pressed her.

"I love children," said Dorothy.

"Lots of people love their children," said Solita, eyes flashing and smiling, "I mean special qualities."

Dorothy said nothing, just stared into space, the images of herself from times gone by passing before her eyes. Events, people, relationships she could see ... but qualities?

After a time Solita told her, "I think your outstanding qualities are judgment, justice and observation."

Dorothy looked from one of her three friends to another. "Margaret's eyes," she said, "full of strength and confidence in me. And Solita's eyes, coming to life in the life of a book. And Lib's— eager, encouraging."

In the spring of 1944, Janet Flanner's new love, Natalia, had received a commission from the Office of War Information and was sent to Rome. Janet, feeling more and more useless, moped. She wanted desperately to return to Europe and, pulling strings, by early November 1944 finally flew to London as an official army war correspondent for *The New Yorker*.

By the last week in November Janet was in Paris. She visited Gurdjieff and found him older and grayer but still very much a presence. The apartment looked run down, the carpets threadbare in places, but the pantry was full. He had convinced the local merchants that he owned oil wells in Texas and all would be paid at the war's end. She mentioned the names of the Rope to him. But nothing registered. It was only when she said "Kanari," "Kro*kodeel*," "Yakina," "Sardine," "Th*een* One" that his dark eyes flashed and a broad and knowing smile came to his face.

Leaving Paris she visited Noel at Orgeval. The two women had changed in appearance over the preceding five years. Janet's hair was short and white, her face more lined, its countenance sadder, the voice deeper, smokier. Noel was much thinner, her hands gnarled and worn looking, her great height now stooped. But the laugh and sharp humor were still there. Hemingway had stopped by earlier and let it be known that Janet was with an Italian woman. Janet wrote to Solita that Noel "accepts without question like a hind that is beaten the fact that I have an Italian friend." Janet feeling guilt, Noel a passive anger, the visit only lasted three days before Janet returned to Paris. But things patched up and Janet spent part of most weeks in Orgeval.

Janet finally told Noel about Natalia and the women made the best of it. In June Janet visited Natalia in Rome and Natalia came to Paris later in the summer. Noel was furious and demanded that Natalia never come to Paris again. In December 1945, *The New Yorker* sent Janet to Nuremberg to cover the trial of Reichsmarschall Hermann Göring and twenty-one other Nazis. She reported on the trial again the following February.

Earlier, in the spring of 1943, Kathryn Hulme, wanting to participate in some way in the war effort, had become a welder at the

Kaiser Shipyards in Oakland, California. Though she involved herself thoroughly in her job, the thought of how to see Gurdjieff again was paramount. In August 1944 she quit her job as a welder and applied for a post with the United Nations Relief and Rehabilitation Authority (UNRAA) which relocated displaced persons and prisoners of war. After a two-month course in field planning and operations, she was sent to Jullouville on the west side of the Cotentin peninsula in Normandy.

Three thousand Allied relief workers had been assembled there to help the nine million displaced persons uprooted by the war. Kathryn was put in charge of a team of a dozen other relief workers and in July 1945 headed out to begin work. Delays in getting the necessary papers gave Kathryn the time she needed to get to Paris to see Gurdjieff. The city was a shocking sight, its long broad boulevards bereft of traffic for lack of gasoline. Hurrying to 6 rue des Colonels-Renard, she rang the bell and waited, her heart pounding. From behind the door she heard a slow, heavy shuffling, a safety chain clinked, the door opened part way and there stood Gurdjieff looking at her with a slight scowl, she being in army uniform.

"It's Crocodile, Mr. Gurdjieff...."

"Kroko-*deel!*" he cried and she rushed into his arms, him repeating over and over in a hoarse voice, "Not expect ... not expect!"

He led her into the pantry and poured her a cup of thick black coffee. He looked older to her, more tired, his skin darker than she remembered. He passed her a cigarette, a Turkish brand, and they smoked and drank coffee together. She told him of her experiences since she had last seen him six years before and that Solita and Alice were also in uniform in America, working in a hospital unit they hoped would bring them to Europe. She told him, too, of the slides she had seen of Nazi concentration camps and the crematory ovens. "As he listened," she said, "hunched over and motionless, his face darkened and a vein in his forehead swelled and beat. I saw the wrath of God in that clouded countenance, a righteous fury that seemed about to explode, though there was no change of expression, only of coloring. He wanted her to stay for dinner but she had be back and so he said, "When all is finished there in Gair-mania, Kroko*deel*, you must come home."

In August Kathryn and her team got the necessary cards and headed into the US occupation zone in Wildflecken, in the northeast corner of Bavaria. The former training school for Hitler's S.S., Wildflecken was "home" to twenty thousand Polish DPs (displaced persons) jammed into sixty blockhouses spread out over fifteen square miles.

On Kathryn's team was Marie-Louise Hâbets, a Belgian nurse who had been part of the underground resistance and then served with a British field first-aid auxiliary following the Battle of the Bulge. Her eyes were deep blue, spaced far apart, and, though she appeared to be near Kathryn's age, her face was marble smooth and without wrinkles, not even small smile creases at the corners of her eyes. Marie-Louise kept to herself, was very self-contained and deplored all lack of self-control. With the impressions of the camp so heavy and dark, Kathryn said in rising anger—"*Le Christ est absent.*" Marie-Louise took her by the arm and led her out of earshot of the others and told Kathryn—"You must never again say such a thing, *jamais, jamais, jamais.* The Christ is never absent, especially from dark places. He is here in every one of His poor ones, very near to us, too … nearer than I have felt Him to be in a long, long time."

As time passed, the women grew closer. Marie-Louise, it turned out, was a former nun. She told Kathryn about her life as a nun and how she had spent seven years in the Congo helping lepers. The previous August, because of her hatred for the Nazis, she had left the convent and worked in the Belgian underground.

Kathryn, in turn, told Marie-Louise about Gurdjieff, the teaching of the Fourth Way, and the Rope. In the middle of June 1946, Kathryn invited Marie-Louise to go with her to Paris to visit Gurdjieff. She phoned Gurdjieff and told him she was bringing a friend—"Malou," as Kathryn now called her, had made her promise not to say she was a nun—and picked up a bottle of Polish vodka to give as a present. Gurdjieff led them back to the pantry. Malou, seeing the gourmet display of foods on his shelves, reacted at what seemed to her ostentation, but quickly recovered herself. Gurdjieff poured them Turkish coffee from his thermos and the conversation began. At one point, Kathryn brought forth the bottle of Polish vodka, setting it on the table with a flourish. Gurdjieff's eyes glinted as a mocking expression appeared on his face in preparation for his "play."

"*Look* what Kroko*deel* she, M*ees*!" he said winking at Malou. "She makes *big* ceremony for bringing one speciality she thinks does not exist in Mr. Gurdjieff's pantry!"

With that, he went to the pantry and, pushing aside some boxes, exhibited six liters of vodka along with a dozen other bottles of Armagnac, Calvados and Marc. Kathryn had also brought him cartons of cigarettes from the PX and these he threw on a shelf that was stacked like cordwood with American cigarettes.

"She *also* thinks, M*ees*," he said grinning at Malou, "that I do not already have very *very* good relations with the American Army!"

Malou was disturbed at his ridicule but Kathryn understood that this was his way of teaching. "What she had witnessed," said Kathryn, "was not a 'humiliation' but only a prod at the same old weak spot [false pride] the master had been poking at for years, but seldom quite as amusingly as this time. This is one of the ways he teaches, *mon amie....*"

Gurdjieff then brought out two boxes of sweetmeats, one of *loucoum,* a "Turkish delight," and one of chocolate creams which he divided up, patting the candies, flakes of cigarette ash falling like snow flakes on the boxes, giving Malou a sly smile. In time she relaxed. He looked weary and began to nap, his breathing labored, Malou now seeing him as a beloved old grandfather. She whispered to Kathryn how fatigued he looked and just then he opened one eye and smiled, his face suddenly coming alive, and he nodded at her, saying in hoarse French, *"Petite Soeur de Charité,"* [Sisters of Charity of Ghent] the name of her former religious order, and then dozed off, the two women taking their leave.

On July 27, 1946, Gertrude Stein died in Paris at the age of seventy-two. Margaret and Janet Flanner were strolling in the garden at Orgeval and Margaret congratulated her on the article she had written in *The New Yorker* about the fate of Gertrude's art collection—which consisted of twenty-eight paintings by Picasso as well as a portfolio of his drawings, and seven canvases of Juan Gris—in which Janet regretted not one had been left outright to Gertrude's companion of thirty-eight years, Alice B. Toklas.

"We all felt it shameful," said Janet, "that Alice had the right only to sell one or two in case she badly needed money."

"Shocking," Margaret exclaimed, "but it doesn't surprise me."

Later, Margaret wrote Janet a letter telling her what she thought of Gertrude. "Gertrude and I," Margaret began, "never changed our minds about one another. We got off to a bad start. The first thing she ever said to me: 'You have no right to publish young writers in the *Little Review* and not pay them.'"

"I was extremely irritated. I said, 'It's not a question of right, but of duty. No one else will publish them.'"

"This irritated her, and we went from bad to worse. I knew we could never be friends. There was something so hearty in her, and so much authority involved in the heartiness. She and Jane 'got on' marvelously, but then Jane could be hearty when necessary. I can't, and I can think of no one whose heartiness, combined with such serious self-love and intensity, could repel me as much as Gertrude's. To me she was a kind of commercial being, so practical, so implacable, so quarrelsome with the 'great friends' she loved and then detested, that I would have fled her daily presence in trepidation. My reactions to her were like my reactions to certain music—'Please don't play it in my hearing. I can't bear it.'"

After Gertrude's death, Margaret went to see Alice and they struck up a friendship and a correspondence. In one letter Alice wrote: "I am amazed at the importance of your gifts, and your *Fiery Fountains* has given me most intense pleasure. You have made the perfect phrase to portray yourself—'I do not live unless my heart stands still.'"

In June 1948 Margaret and Dorothy sailed for France. On June 30th, they found themselves knocking at Gurdjieff's door. A student let them in. Margaret found it dingier than she recalled, the colors faded, the furniture shabbier, and the dining room carpet worn through and showing large patches. But Gurdjieff, though seventy-six years old and looking tired, was his old self. Margaret found that he was "still as lavish as ever with his existence and his ceremony." He sat at the side of the table, instead of at the end, having lunch with about twenty students, all sitting and eating in silence. Gurdjieff ate with his fingers bits of lamb and hard bits of goat cheese and fresh tarragon leaves. To Margaret, he seemed more silent than in the days of the Rope. Unlike those luncheons, Margaret now saw that "there was teaching in all that he did or said, only its form had changed: he was teaching now chiefly through his presence."

After the meal, Gurdjieff began to speak. His voice was low and muffled and the syllables it formed in his Asiatic accent, Dorothy found meaningless. She could not understand a word he said. His every facial expression or small bodily movement, though, she found heartbreaking. "The kind of force he is using," she thought, "is wearing him out. Why must he go on doing it? Why do they let him? We should go home, we should not ask this tired man for anything."

As there were so many new pupils—English, American and French—Gurdjieff often spoke to Jeanne de Salzmann who then spoke to the pupil. Said Margaret, "After years of work with him her stature was now visible to everyone."

At the end when Dorothy and Margaret got up to leave, Gurdjieff said: "You come tonight for reading at nine o'clock. Then dinner after." So began their daily visits for lunch and usually for dinner. Before each meal *All and Everything* was read. Dorothy found the book boring. In answering questions, Gurdjieff spoke in a broken English she found barely understandable. He didn't talk about the teaching but chiefly about countries and nationalities, and always in a derogatory way which Dorothy found as boring and repetitious as the readings. Sometimes he spoke severely to students, especially those responsible for preparing the food. To Dorothy it seemed unjust. She recoiled at the public humiliation. Once a student defended himself and she said, "Gurdjieff's voice grew louder, angrier, and his eyes flashed. Then at the peak of rage he suddenly smiled, relaxed, and said, 'Bravo!' and offered the culprit his favorite sweet." This display left Dorothy more confused than ever.

Finally, the day came when she had had enough. She told Margaret she was leaving for the States. "What is there to learn," she asked, "just listening to that book, watching the others who never speak to me, whose names I don't even know, and watching Gurdjieff eat or play that little organ? I'm going home."

Margaret, knowing exactly what she was going through, as she had once gone through the same ordeal herself, told her in a neutral voice she must do as she thought best, neither urging her to stay nor to leave.

Dorothy didn't leave but for five days she stayed away. She began to suspect that perhaps Gurdjieff was teaching after all, just not in a way she had expected. She remembered then what he had said to her at their third meeting—"Inside you are rabbit." Yes, he was telling her what Margaret had: that instead of making an effort to act honestly, she had covered the emotions of a lifetime with good manners. Though she did not know it, her shell, the false personality with all its preconceptions and requirements, had begun to crack.

And so she returned to Gurdjieff. When she again entered the world at 6 rue des Colonels-Renard, he smiled, pretending to be surprised to see her. At the table, crowded with students for lunch, he teased her about her size. She didn't mind. "It was a warm and vibrant welcome," she later told Margaret, "and during lunch I felt a glow as if there had been established between us a new and special bond—a kind of unspoken sympathetic understanding."

After lunch Gurdjieff invited her to have coffee with him in his pantry room. There, among a cornucopia of fruits and sweets and wines and slender sausages of camel's meat and bunches of scarlet peppers and sprays of rosemary and mint, he took a beaten-up old thermos and poured her a cup of coffee from it.

"You want to ask me something?" he said.

"Everyone here seems to have a soul except me. Haven't I any soul?" asked Dorothy.

In the oriental manner, Gurdjieff picked up a piece of sugar and put it in his mouth and sipped coffee through it. Did she know the meaning of the word consciousness, he asked.

It meant to know something, she replied.

"No. Not to know something—to know yourself. Your 'I'. You not know your 'I' for one second in your whole life. Now I tell and you try. But very difficult. You try to remember say 'I am' once every hour. You not succeed, but no matter—try. You understand?"

She nodded. Something opened within her and she found herself telling him about her childhood in her father's house, of her time in the convent, and the goodness of her husband, her despair at his death, and about her children and how deeply she loved them. She told him she was not educated, that she didn't know what to ask or where to start from.

"You must help your father," Gurdjieff told her.

"But my father is dead."

"I know. You tell already. But because of your father you are here. Have gratitude for this. You are your father and you owe to him. He is dead. Too late to repair for himself. You must repair for him. Help him."

How could she help a dead man? Dorothy didn't understand. "Where is he?" she asked.

"All around you. You must work on yourself. Remember what I tell—your 'I.' And what you do for yourself you do also for me."

And so Dorothy began to remember herself and observe herself. She began to question her reactions and manifestations, began the work of not taking herself as an indivisible I and began to see that in fact she was indeed many "I"s and that her personality, false personality, had built a hard shell of niceness and goodness around her—that she was not true to herself, not authentic. After much work and suffering she suddenly saw her situation: "In the past I never revolted—not outwardly; I even felt I had no right to revolt. The other cheek—that rigid religious law ... it had cut a deep groove ... suddenly I have finished forever with turning the other cheek: because I, who am never angry, am standing beside myself in anger."

And she began to understand her responsibility to herself.

"I am the protector of my inner life. I have at last discovered that life and I will no longer allow it to be violated—either by claws or fangs or smiles. I will never placate again. I am as I say I am. My own truth matters to myself, more than my fear, and I will impose my truth.... I have finished with fear—I have experienced consuming anger. I shall never again keep silent, or turn away my head. I shall speak out and call the liar and the fraud.

"The incident that starts world wars is in itself insignificant. Somewhere in the forest lies a charred match...."

Gurdjieff, after dinner, often put his little accordion-piano on his knee and played. His left hand worked the bellows, while the right made music in minor chords and long haunting single notes. One evening he played for Dorothy and Margaret and several others. Dorothy was happy when he first began to play but when he finished she put her head on the table and wept.

She had spent a lifetime listening to music but didn't understand how with this music she could so quickly go from happy to deeply sad and then back to happy.

"I play objective music to make cry," said Gurdjieff. "There are many kinds such music—some to make laugh, or to love or to hate. This the beginning of music—sacred music, two, three thousand years old. Your church music comes from such but they don't realize. They have forgotten. This is temple music—very ancient."

In midsummer, while Gurdjieff had gone to the baths at Vichy, Margaret and Dorothy traveled to Giverny to see Monet's garden. Three days passed. Then word came—Gurdjieff had had an auto accident. His condition was critical. He was unconscious in a hospital in Paris. But when they arrived in Paris he was already back in his apartment. Though his ribs were fractured and his face and hands were covered with bruises and lacerations, he still wanted the readings and meals to continue.

The next day his condition worsened. The doctors thought he would not live. But on the third day he was again seated at his dinner table, the large head still a shining dome but his face a dark shadow. His lips were one purple bruise under his mustaches. A piece of gauze was affixed to his throat to hide a wound.

"I cannot eat," he said. "My mouth all cut inside."

Though his fingers were still lacerated, he painfully divided up the trout.

"You like?" he asked. "Then take."

At the end of a dinner at which nobody spoke, he stood up, putting a hand to his ribs, and said, "It hurts. Great suffering I have."

He began to walk out but stopped and said, "I thank you. I wish for you all that you wish for me."

Somehow over the next days he cured himself and soon looked younger than he had before the accident.

That December Gurdjieff sailed to New York on the SS *America* with Madame de Salzmann. Gurdjieff stayed in a large suite on the eleventh floor, this time, at the Wellington Hotel, as he had done on his last visit in April 1939. The daily regimen of lunch and dinner and the ritual toasting began. Meals had to be prepared for between fifty and a hundred-and-fifty people, depending on how many Gurdjieff invited and on the unannounced arrivals.

The Rope was there represented by Margaret and Solita, with Alice and Kathryn coming later. (Margaret brought Dorothy but apparently Solita did not bring Lib.) Other students of Gurdjieff's Fourth Way included Lord John Pentland and his wife Lucy with their daughter Mary, Christopher and Anne Fremantle, Tom Forman and his wife Tania Savitsky, the granddaughter of Madame Ouspensky, Olgivanna with her husband Frank Lloyd Wright and daughter Iovanna, Wilhem Nyland and his wife Ilonka Karasz and daughter Carolla, the Woltons, Martin and Rita Romilly Benson, Edwin and Dorothy Wolfe, William and Louise Welch with their daughter Patty, William Segal, Donald and Lillian Whitcomb, Paul Anderson, Fred Leighton, Lincoln Kirstein, Louise March, Peggy Matthews [Flinsch], Jessim Howarth and daughter Dushka [Sophie], Muriel Draper, Cynthia Pearce, Carol Robinson, Marian Sutta, Nick Putnam, Payson Loomis, Edith Taylor and her son Polo and daughter Eve [Petey], John Bennett, and Phillip Lasell.

"All debt liquidated in France," he announced. "I come to you pure, like new-born baby." Ouspensky's English group, he said, had paid all his debts in Paris which ran into millions of francs.

His health was even better now than before his auto accident [presumably 1924] and he wanted to buy a large château where he would establish his Institute. At one point while he was speaking, Alice Rohrer burst into the room.

"What! You not afraid to come?" Gurdjieff said.

"No, Mr. Gurdjieff," Alice answered.

"*Why* you not afraid?"

"Well—because I have known you many years."

During the toasts, Alice announced that she was no longer a squirming Idiot but a square one.

"Ha! Was automatic changed," declared Gurdjieff.

When the toasting arrived at Enlightened Idiot, the Director of the Toasts asked, "Anyone here?"

"No," answered Gurdjieff. "Yet have been times when everyone at table was."

Someone asked if they could bring their mother.

"Yes. Mother is my weakness. I loved my mother very much. I invite come lunch."

One day Gurdjieff went to see Madame Ouspensky in Mendham, New Jersey, at Franklin Farms, an estate that had been acquired for students to work on themselves. Ouspensky had died in 1947 and she gave him a draft of her husband's manuscript, *In Search of the Miraculous*. Thereafter, after every luncheon, Gurdjieff had a chapter read. He said, "Very exact is. Good memory. Truth, was so." At another time, "Is too liquid. Lost something."

At one meal he showed all the five-and-ten-cent gifts which he had bought for presents to take home. Of one gift he bought dozens and was especially proud.

"Small thing is," he said, "but for them in Paris is new and wonderful."

He demonstrated how he would present this "rare gift" from America with a bow. "The French will be awestruck," he said. He then handed the gift to Fred Leighton. It was a ten-cent folding bunion knife.

The night before Christmas, Kathryn flew in from Germany, stopping over en route to see her mother in San Francisco who was very ill. On arrival she found a letter from her sister awaiting her at her hotel saying that her mother was losing her memory and might not remember her. The next day she went to the Wellington and was able to see Gurdjieff alone and tell him of her mother's condition. Afterward, he took a bottle of colorless liquid from a cabinet. He told her to massage the liquid over her mother's solar plexus, then take a photograph of her, wrap it tightly in black paper so no light could enter, and bring it back to him.

After the Christmas meal, she said, "Mr. Gurdjieff, may I tell the children a story in honor of your birthday?"

Kathryn told a story about a four-year-old orphan who had boarded her plane in Amsterdam to fly to meet her new mother in New York. The child was so frightened that she kept talking to her doll in a fluty voice, rocking it in her arms, telling her not to be afraid. Kathryn repeated the story several times—"poor girl, no parents, four years old"—each time becoming more choked with emotion and tears. At one point, Gurdjieff handed her a handkerchief. That soaked through, she was given another. Then the large tablecloth was handed to her. When she took it, everyone roared with laughter, especially the children.

When finally she stopped, Gurdjieff addressed the children: "To this story, children, and most stories, must behave outwardly polite, thank even, say 'thanks, so-and-so'—but inwardly, not be touched, forget quickly. Now you saw Kroko*deel* tears. Ask *mère*, *père*, [mother, father] people you trust, what crocodile tears are. Very important to know."

Kathryn continued to cry. Gurdjieff had strong coffee with milk and sugar brought to her. Again, she began to talk of the "Poor girl...."

Gurdjieff interrupted her—"If again say same thing, we all pay Krokodeel money which she has to pay back later doubled." Even that didn't stop her. Gurdjieff finally scolded her for giving such stuff and nonsense to "my children."

One of the men had concealed a tape recorder under the couch to record Gurdjieff's words. It had picked up, of course, Kathryn's story of the poor little girl.

One day, speaking about the toasts, Gurdjieff said: "Unique Idiot is highest thing and in stone or static thing is lowest. Between the two is our scale or measure. Scale is from *merde* to God. First time one starts up the scale automatically proceeds as far as number 16. This is easy. For going down, is difficult ... because [must] go down with consciousness. Second time go up, can go beyond 16."

At lunch the next day Gurdjieff's suite at the Wellington was jammed wall-to-wall with students, their overcoats piled four feet high the length of the foyer. Early arrivals sat cross-legged on the floor around the sofa, leaving everyone else to stand. Gurdjieff sat on the sofa, one leg as always characteristically tucked under him. He parted his large white mustaches with the thumb and index finger of one hand. Finally, he took a letter from his pocket and handed it to J. G. Bennett saying in a low voice: "Read, read—is for everybody." It was a circular letter to all his students announcing the decision to publish the *First Series* of *All and Everything*.

When the toasts began, Bennett announced that he was "Gurdjieff's oldest pupil," not mentioning that he had left Gurdjieff in 1923 with a promise to return and did so only twenty-five years later. Gurdjieff put him in the Round Idiot category—"those that never stop, but day-night-year-round continue being Idiots."

Two weeks after Christmas, Kathryn returned. She told Gurdjieff that when she got to San Francisco she massaged her mother as Gurdjieff had told her. Somehow what she did brought back her mother's memory. She was able to talk with her, but only temporarily. Kathryn gave the photograph to Gurdjieff. He asked about the black paper. She had forgotten. He did not rant but simply shook his head, as this omission now made his task harder. He then gave her an exercise having to do with her mother. During the reading, Kathryn worked the beads of the black chaplet Gurdjieff had given her and other members of the Rope fourteen years before. At the reading's end, he looked at the chaplet and then at her, Kathryn said, "with quite the most lovely smile I had ever seen." Without a word, he put out his hand and she gave him the chaplet, she thought to hold. He passed a few of the beads through his fingers. He held up the chaplet for all to see.

"It mother thing …," he said in a hoarse husky voice, the word *mother* pronounced in tones of love.

Without a word more, his only facial movement being a nod of satisfaction, he dropped the chaplet into his pocket.

Later, Gurdjieff had Kathryn's "Christmas tape" played. Everyone convulsed in laughter. Kathryn, embarrassed, braved it out. However, each time she visited he ordered the tape played. Again and again, day after day, she heard—"Poor little girl, no parents, only four years old…." She pleaded for mercy—"*no more tape!*"—but he did not relent. On her last visit, no longer self-conscious and in reaction, Kathryn actually heard herself, heard Kroko*deel*. She said, "I wept genuine tears…. I was hearing only my now lugubrious voice carrying on like a wound-up talking machine beneath the sounds of the master's mirth."

Approaching Gurdjieff to say goodbye, she thanked him for his help with her mother, for the new exercise he had given her, and especially "the merciless last lessons he had given me which showed me to myself as I had never seen myself before."

These would be her last words to her teacher, the man she called "Master."

In mid-February 1949, Gurdjieff and Madame de Salzmann sailed back to France on the *Queen Mary*.[1]

1. It seems odd that Solita did not return to Paris as others did, given their close relationship of previous years. This raises a number of questions. Why do Solita's notes of Gurdjieff's visit to America in December 1948 abruptly stop after a month or so? Why is Lib Clark, her companion, not mentioned as having been present during Gurdjieff's visit? Margaret had brought Dorothy and Gurdjieff was open to having visitors so there was no reason not to bring her, if in fact that was the case. Solita knew as early as June 1945, when Janet Flanner first visited him, that Gurdjieff was alive. Given the conditions of postwar Europe, it is understandable that she did not return. What creates a question (perhaps easily resolved) is why it was not until October 1949 that she finally went to Paris but this apparently only because Janet invited her and paid her passage. Solita's reports to Margaret and Dorothy about Gurdjieff's passing and his funeral are heartfelt and sincere. But this still does not answer the question of why she waited so long to see him. Could it be that something happened between Gurdjieff and Solita in New York? Or, as with Janet previously, Lib fought against her renewing her relationship with him?

When Gurdjieff returned to Paris, he resumed the daily luncheons at once. Margaret and Dorothy also returned but for some reason Solita stayed in New Jersey with Lib Clark. Lord Pentland and his wife Lucy came from America as did Cynthia Pearce, Peggy Matthews and Dushka Howarth. Among those coming from England were Jane Heap, Elspeth Champcommunal, C. S. Nott and his wife Rosemary, Dr. Kenneth Walker, Russell Page, John Bennett and his wife Elizabeth, as well as Jessie Dwight Orage. Interestingly, Dr. Maurice Nicoll refused to come, as did Dr. Francis Roles, who had taken over Ouspensky's groups. From France came Véra Daumal, Pierre Schaeffer, Henri Tracol with his wife and their daughter Lise, Bernard Lemâitre, Alfred Etievan, Pauline de Dampierre, and Hubert Benoit.

In the summer Gurdjieff decided to go to Chamonix to take the waters. Four cars were quickly assembled, crowded with students and boxes of Russian croquettes, bags of croissants, melons, apricots, chocolate bonbons, of course, and large thermoses of strong black coffee.

Gurdjieff's car led the way, he driving at pell-mell speed, stopping only once for a half hour's nap by the side of the road. Despite a week in Chamonix he was still tired. He had grown thinner and his skin still showed a gray pallor. He was coughing and in pain. Dorothy sat beside him on a bench while porters arranged the luggage in the cars for the return trip. She told him that she wished she had met him twenty years before.

"Today it's too late," she mused. "I realize now that I am nothing, and it's the loneliest feeling in the world."

"Ah," Gurdjieff retorted, "you are no longer blind. Your eyes now open—you begin to see."

Back in Paris at his apartment one day at lunch he said, "I have worked hard. My book will soon be published for everyone to read. After I will go away, far, where I can rest."

"But will you come back?" someone asked.

There was no reply.

Another said, "We will follow you wherever you go—will you go to California?"

Such questions Gurdjieff never answered. But this time he looked at the questioner and smiled and said, "Perhaps California, perhaps farther."

A few days after the middle of October, Dorothy and Margaret were to sail with him to America but he had become ill and postponed his trip. Gurdjieff told them to go ahead and be in New York to welcome him. Before leaving, Dorothy went to see him at a café. She found him sitting alone. They exchanged a few words, then sat in silence. Finally she said to him—"Mr. Gurdjieff ... the 'I' which I am trying to develop—is this the soul that survives after death?"

He waited so long to answer she thought he perhaps hadn't heard her. Finally, instead of answering, he asked—"How long have you been with me?"

"Almost two years."

"Too short the time. You not able yet to understand. Use the present to repair the past and prepare the future. Go on well; remember all I say."

She was concerned about his health and told him so.

He moved slightly in his chair. She heard him groan.

He told her—"I must take habit of pain."

Then he extended his hand toward her and they said goodbye, she walking away and him sitting there in what she remembered as "the shrill sunlight."

She and Margaret boarded the ship and were at sea between two continents again.

Jane Heap, who had continued meetings and readings of the *First Series* throughout the war, now brought her people over from London. Crossing the channel she told them, "If Gurdjieff asks you something, don't tell him because whatever you say I said, I *didn't*." In Gurdjieff's presence, she told them, they were to be free and on their own. "He's a multitude. But if you watch, sometimes you see the sage pass by." Sensing their tenseness, she gave the reassurance, "Whatever happens, whatever he says to you, I endorse you." There was no need for warning. After their first meal, Gurdjieff told them, "Do not be afraid anymore. You are at home here. I am your new father." There were toasts and teachings, indirect usually and sly, at the luncheons and dinners and unexpectedly they were also filled with humor—as one said, "delicate jests, the broad jokes, the gales of laughter that sometimes swept through the room, easing [the] unbearable tensions." The magus was still at work.

Solita arrived in Paris the beginning of October 1949. Janet had paid her passage as she was doing a profile of Léon Blum, the French socialist leader, and needed Solita's editorial help. The animosity Janet had felt toward Solita's devotion to Gurdjieff had abated, as had the jealousy Solita felt toward Noel and Natalia. Solita took a room at the Hôtel Vendôme where Janet was now living and together they all visited the old haunts like the Café Flore and the Deux Magots. The visit was a happy one. Solita visited Gurdjieff as often as she could, while running errands for Janet, typing as Janet dictated her Genêt's "Letter from Paris" and editing the Blum profile.

It was just like the old days. The war was over, everyone was thankful, joyous, filled with affirmation for the future. Students from America, England and France were swirling around Gurdjieff. While much older, there was still the magical radiation of energy. Though the body was worn from the weight of years of his unflagging attempt to establish the ancient teaching in the West, the mind and the will were still alive and fresh. Movements classes were being given at the Salle Pleyel. There were the luncheons and dinners and nightly readings of the *First Series*. The manuscript of this great work had been sent in type and galleys were now being read in preparation for publication. He had people looking for an appropriate château like the Prieuré where he could reorganize the Institute for the Harmonious Development of Man. As in New York in early 1924, everything looked bright and full or promise.

But then—just as in 1924—it all changed to its opposite. Gurdjieff's condition, always precarious, suddenly worsened. On October 16th he collapsed. Though he revived, he was noticeably weaker. Then his condition worsened again. Finally, on the 26th he was taken to the American Hospital. Said a student:

The ambulance men brought the stretcher to his bedroom, but he wouldn't have this, and walked out into the hall and got on to the stretcher there, sitting back, saying "Oy!" as he always did. He did not dress, but wore pajamas, and his red fez on his head. He sat upright on the stretcher, and was carried away like a royal prince! All the family were clustered at the street door (the crusty old *concierge* was in tears!) and as they carried him across the pavement he made a little gesture, a sort of wave, with his hand and said, *"Au revoir, tout le monde!"* The last sight of him was as he was carried into the ambulance, his cigarette between his lips.

At 10:30 A.M. on October 29th, George Ivanovitch Gurdjieff died. "I have seen many men die," his doctor said. "He died like a king."

On a sudden three-day leave, Kathryn Hulme had arrived in Paris on Saturday, the day before he died. She had joined Solita in the lobby of the American Hospital at Neuilly, remaining until it closed and then returning the next morning, Sunday, the morning he died. He was brought into the hospital chapel. A bearded Russian priest arrived and from the foot of the bier began to chant prayers in a lovely golden voice. Kathryn peered into the face of her teacher, the man she had called Master, and she thought—"Never to hear my name called again by you ... Kroko*deel*, Kroko-*deel!*..."

Dorothy and Margaret landed in New York on October 31. A few days later a letter arrived from Solita addressed to both of them. Margaret's hands trembled as she read the letter to Dorothy: "We are nearly in despair. Yesterday and today and the days to come are the worst in my life.... He's wearing his best suit, bought for the American trip. He is lying on a divan, covered to the throat with a pale coverture which is piled with red roses, pink orchids, white flowers; on either side of his head are two enormous bouquets of violets. The chapel is lighted with candles. His face is like a statue's.... Madame de Salzmann has been absolutely superb. At the service yesterday she sat near his head with white face, closed eyes from which the tears slowly flowed.... The grief is terrible, silent, and has a really objective quality of dignity. Of my own grief I will not speak; it is a small part of the common catastrophe.

I shall always be grateful to those powers that allowed me to be here to see him before he went away from the planet earth. But I shall never be able to describe the noble beauty of his dead face."

On Monday Gurdjieff was taken to the Russian Orthodox Church. At the foot of the bier had been placed a little icon of St. George. Kathryn knelt down before it before passing with the slow-paced line of mourners toward the head of the bier. As she looked at the beloved countenance of this man among all men who had changed her life for all time, she suddenly heard the inner voice of that which she thought had died, her Crocodile, telling her—"Kiss him goodbye ... *don't be afraid!*"

The following Wednesday, November 2nd, the man some called "teacher" or "Master," others "charlatan," and who for himself was a magus, was buried not far from the Château du Prieuré in the cemetery at Avon. Wrote Solita:

> The crowds stood along the street to watch him brought out [of the Russian Church in Paris] and put in the great funeral carriage, his flowers placed on top. The family rode with him. The hundreds of others rode behind in the cortege [put in accent mark] in many private cars and four enormous autobuses. The streets were jammed, closed to traffic for blocks around the Russian church, and other crowds gathered to watch the spectacle. I went with some of the rich silent English, old followers of Ouspensky's. Through the old familiar roads, streets, towns, turnings, forest to Avon ... In a cruel icy sunny wind we walked by the hundreds through the cemetery gates, following him to the family plot. I saw the grave torn open in the rocky watery ground, deep, deep, horribly deep....The porters let him down into it. A great sigh came from the people—the only sound they had made, when they were together, since he died. The priest came to the rescue with his chanting. Later everyone passed by the terrible hole, cast a pinch of earth down on to the box, knelt, made the sign of the cross, and passed on. It was over. He had disappeared from us for ever.

G. I. Gurdjieff in 1949.

G. I. Gurdjieff lying in state.

The funeral cortège, November 3, 1949.

A Russian Orthodox priest intones a final prayer at the grave site in Avon.

Working With Life

N EW YORK. 1950. THE *FIRST SERIES* OF GURDJIEFF'S *ALL AND EVERYTHING* WAS PUBLISHED, AS WAS P. D. OUSPENSKY'S book, *In Search of the Miraculous,* a detailed report of the teaching Gurdjieff gave during his Russian period. Over the years, Gurdjieff had personally trained small cadres of people to carry on the teaching. The various work groups previously established in America, England, and other countries organized themselves around Madame de Salzmann, who had worked closely with Gurdjieff since their meeting in Tiflis in 1919. Members of the Rope might have taken their places within the ongoing teaching, but as Kathryn Hulme said, "How could one attach oneself to one of the work groups, once having fed at the Source?" Of course, that wasn't the point, but if not understood it was not to be argued.

Following Gurdjieff's death, all the women of the Rope returned to their separate lives. Solita left Janet in Paris to return to New Jersey to live with Lib. Alice, apparently unable to come to Paris to see Gurdjieff, had married. Louise worked with a theater in Connecticut. Kathryn returned to the States bringing Malou with her. Motoring across the country, they finally chose Phoenix, Arizona, as a place to settle. Kathryn began her book, *The Wild Place,* about the displaced persons camps, and Malou-worked as a nurse in a local hospital. Though raised as a Protestant, Kathryn attended Catholic Church with Malou, eventually converting.

Margaret and Dorothy continued to live in Manhattan. Dorothy said of the precious days she had spent with Gurdjieff:

> He was gentle with my soul. It was a soul that had not grown up, as I grew up. It had been timid, but trusting.... Gurdjieff gave it courage. From his mysterious and conscious world he guided it with the kind of understanding he called 'objective love'—the 'love of everything that breathes'; and 'it' responded with unlimited trust—the highest type of love there is, I think, in this immediate and unconscious world.
>
> Nothing is so great or so true as the trusting love of a child. It doesn't matter whether he has understood your words or not—it is the way they are spoken that matters. And the way they are spoken creates in the child the love and trust he returns to you. This is the emotion that Gurdjieff, and the 'conditions he created,' created in me.
>
> I can repeat our conversations, interpret his silences, describe his appearance, define his doctrine, yet I can only give the slightest indication of the change that took place in me after knowing him.
>
> I was aware, before he died, of this process of active and increasing change. His death, instead of ending the process, accelerated it. And then, one day, I understood what had been happening. I had transformed something in myself: the change was Me.

Having found her inner life through Gurdjieff, Dorothy soon found herself disconnected from life in Manhattan.

> Isn't it agony to have to entertain people who are old friends but with whom you no longer have anything in common? It is as if you screamed at the top of your voice and knew all the time that they couldn't hear you. What you say aloud to them is not ever what you want to say. It is with people who hear you when you are silent that you can talk. I feel so guilty, now, when I am with the others, that I never stop chattering. I am so afraid they are going to find out how they drain me that I

deluge them with a flood of silly words, and flatter them in order to make them go on talking, so I can rest within myself while listening with my unweary outer ear. How hurt people would be if they ever found me out, and so I go to almost any length of stupidity to save them from the blow of revelation.

Her friends always wanted to know—"But what good did all this do you? What did Gurdjieff do to change you? What did you actually learn from him?" From her own experience with Margaret, she understood how great was the gulf between her friends' understanding and hers, and so she always spoke as simply as she could. She told them:

> I began to see myself as I really was—a mass of old habits, of silly gestures and foolish words; merely a repetition of everything I had seen or heard. I learned about justice, compassion, mercy. I learned about 'objective love.' I learned that the more you hold in of yourself, the more powerfully you give out.
>
> Gurdjieff was an idea in the form of a man. The inner part of him, the idea, he allowed no one to see. He never, by word, gesture or expression gave any of his essential being away. That was his secret, his spiritual mystery. But it was a mystery only because he did not choose to let us know. Otherwise he would not have been a conscious man.

Margaret felt as Dorothy did about Manhattan life, and so the women soon moved to Riderwood, Maryland. There they lived peacefully, sharing their thoughts and feelings, gardening, and doing all the wonderful ordinary things of life.

The security and contentment, after so many years of struggle, were a dream come true for Margaret. Dorothy had become the third great love of her life, a woman who gave Margaret the deep and motherly understanding she had never received as a child, and who was also well-off enough financially so that what Gurdjieff had once called "the material question" was now no longer a question.

For twenty-some years Margaret had worked on the manuscript for *The Fiery Fountains*, the second volume of her memoirs.

It was an evocation of love as portrayed through the relationship between her and Georgette. Carefully edited by Solita, it was published in 1951 and received excellent reviews. Wrote the poet and writer William Carlos Williams:

> We forget, men and women alike, that we're not going to live very long, even if we shall not be shot in a military sortie or give up the ghost at the birth of our first child. It isn't going to last many years, not above an average fifty, so what we want we'd better go after at once, without loss of time and without compromise.
>
> Margaret Anderson wanted about her a certain quality of beauty, not now and then but all the time. Everything else had a leaner value for her than that. She has gone straight toward that objective: to surround herself with those people and those mortal things, which she loved.
>
> But to be so uncompromising, so inflexible, so catholic in one's desires involves supreme courage and determination. Margaret Anderson has gone where her taste required that she should go to realize those wants at great cost. The account of her journeys and the descriptions of the persons she met and loved on her way makes a book of supreme interest.
>
> It is besides a history of the heart during the past quarter century shot with bitter strands but dominating the pattern still shows the crimson, silver and gold of a flaming spirit that attacked and won many a fine victory for art and the good life.

Janet Flanner, always a stern critic of Margaret's, liked the book enormously. She praised Margaret for having made the reader "believe in love." She wrote to Margaret:

> That you have preserved yourself in words makes an invaluable record, for you have to be read to be believed. Furthermore, to make readers actually believe in the existence of love is the hardest task for a writer. In your book through your sensibilities and their weight you establish the reality of love as a *fact*. You gain a remarkable concentrated personal quality in your report of all you touch upon or list and on this accumulation a landscape line, as it were, is achieved, with variations in it which keep the reader gazing at what you tell as it moves uphill to its high point of loss and tragedy.

This was quite a recognition for Janet, for, as she once admitted, neither she nor her sister Marie loved themselves, and so were not capable of receiving or giving love. "Without any affection for oneself," Janet said, "there is no communication with oneself and so I am lonely in my heart each hour of the day and if awake at night. Nothing but regrets, errors, mistakes—none of which can be loved. I fancy poor Marie feels the same."

Though never a member of the Rope, Janet remained in its orbit. She continued to reside in Paris. She felt she was getting old. "One is old when one no longer believes in the possibility of change," she said. "Change won't come true, nor dreams by day, for I never dream at night and so I am wide awake for the rest of my life, eyelids open in shock and tears. I felt not only without faith in my future but now my past has arrived and that it now becomes inescapable."

A keen and fearless observer of life and herself (in the ordinary sense), Janet had long been disgusted with her continual intellectualizing of her emotions. Now, as she grew older, at crucial moments her emotions would break through and she would "sit and weep." The specter of her father's suicide had remained with her all these years. Priding herself on being objective, a realist, she was not one for sentimentality, but with the passing years, she had become more nostalgic. "I suffer so from sheer sadness," she said, "that I can hardly stand being alive."

Though her accomplishments as a journalist had brought her many awards and accolades—Ben Bradlee, Jr., the famous editor of the *Washington Post,* called her "a paragon of foreign correspondents—the one with the first class brain, plus the best senses in the business"—more and more she questioned her worth. "I have manufactured journalism for nearly a quarter of this century," she said. "Nowadays everyone manufactures. Few create. If an individual knows the difference, and I do, the failure to create leaves only one conclusion: one has manufactured." One could see a culture's style of thinking in its style of writing, she believed, and American writing for her was nothing more than "a melange of Freudianism and advertising, our complete absence of an idea or thought, just action."

She wanted to be thought of as "honest, outspoken, kind and good." And most people thought of her in this way. But to keep relationships going with Noel in Orgeval, Natalie in Rome and New York, and Solita in New Jersey, she had to constantly supply the necessary small lies, duplicities, and subterfuges that such a life required. As she wrote to Solita, "nothing can be the same, my darling, as time changes it, with each human change, giving deformities and looser relations."

Solita, still living in New Jersey, kept up a correspondence with Janet in Paris, Margaret in Riderwood, and Kathryn and Malou, who moved to Los Angeles after a year or so in Phoenix. She and Lib would later move to Orgeval.

In London, Jane Heap and Elspeth Champcommunal continued to share a house in Hamilton Terrace. Elspeth had long since retired as the chief designer for Worth. Jane made craft items and jewelry which she sold along with other handmade art objects in her shop, The Rocking Horse. Despite her diabetes, Jane had continued on with her groups and they had grown. Jane had accepted at once the leadership of Madame de Salzmann and worked closely with her.

Not much had been seen of Alice Rohrer, "Th*een* One," who married an Italian named Gusto and with time had become more distanced from Gurdjieff and the teaching. Louise Davidson, "Sardine," lived in Ridgefield, Connecticut, and was involved with a theater group in nearby Westport. Despite the distance and differences in their lives, the Rope kept in touch by postcards and holiday and birthday cards.

In 1952 the book Dorothy had been working on since the mid 1940s, *Dorothy Caruso: A Personal History,* was published. It was in this year, too, that she was diagnosed with cancer. She fought bravely but on December 16, 1955, died. For Margaret, it was the second of her great loves who had died in her arms. She wrote to Janet: "Georgette's death was more objective. Her loss was inconceivable to me, but her death was somehow impersonal ... she was physically so fragile that we thought she might die at any moment." Still, Margaret had never given up hope about Dorothy recovering. Until the end Dorothy had remained strong, with many plans for the future. The night before she died she had telephoned Margaret from the hospital and told her—"I love you so tight I'll go out in the street and let all the cars run over my two hands." Concerned about how Margaret would take her death, Dorothy asked her daughter Jackie, "Do you think Margaret will be all right alone? I mean really *alone?*"

"Of course I am all right," Margaret wrote to Janet, "but I hear myself walking through the house crying out loud like an animal, and I can't stop—don't want ever to stop, it's the only relief."

In June 1956, deep grief hanging about her like a never-lifting fog, Margaret packed up and sailed for France. She returned to Le Cannet to live with Monique at the Chalet Rose. It was wonderful to see Monique after more than fifteen years. She was a comforting influence and the familiar surroundings helped, but still, grieving remained. She wrote to Solita, "For months after Georgette died I had an image: one of her large photos (the one we called the 'smile') was beside my bed, and when I wakened I always had to turn my head in that direction because she seemed to be just to the left, and a little down, as if she were a deep well from which she sent up to me the most consoling words. I can't tell you how long this persisted—it was like a healing. Duffy's [Dorothy] death affected me differently: she still seemed so strong, it was so pitiful that she should stop being near me. Georgette's leaving me was like a classic tragedy—something great and impersonal that had to be, and that left her still beside us. Duffy's was personal, unnecessary, and so, so unprepared for—both by her and by me. That's why my suffering was more subjective, and I had no way of making it stop."

One night Margaret happened to reread a little book of poems that Dorothy had written.

> Just little child verses, but making you know exactly what kind of child she was. She had so many hopes and fears, she was so brave, she was always talking about how people could be good and courageous; she had so many longings, she was so lonely, really; she was always understanding people like shepherds

alone at night, and old peasants and poor priests—(Yeats' "little priest, asleep upon a chair"); always remembering her 'friends'—kind policemen and nannies and poor children; loving so many animals—cows and horses in fields, and little brown owls, and 'gullible sea-gulls'; her fish, 'Isabel and Ferdinand'.... Always so wistful and then so disappointed—'But that's silly.' Always so optimistic, always putting up a brave front, always thinking about the miracle of the mustard seed; almost boastful about being able to suffer nobly and not make other people suffer; almost defiant with gratitude, and always thinking of God. This is why I loved her, why I came to understand her 'essence.' She was always, in nearly all ways, that child; and this always made me cry. And still does.

One day walking back and forth in the small garden at Chalet Rose, Margaret looked out at the sparkling blue of the Mediterranean below. She felt nothing. Alarmed, she told herself—"You must think of something else, force yourself to—something that will make your mind concentrate on other years and days." She went back over her life story, looking for something that would be worth writing. Then she recalled how years earlier an American publisher had asked a German friend of hers to write a lesbian novel. The idea excited Margaret. Instead of the usual lesbian story in which the lesbian is saved by a strong man who rescues her from her isolation, loneliness, and guilt, Margaret wanted to write a story that would affirm feminine love. As soon as she began to write she realized, "I was saved."

Titling her novella *Forbidden Fires,* Margaret wrote of her obsessive romantic love for Josephine Plows-Day, "Tippy," the English actress who had scorned her. The character of "Kaye" in the book was modeled on Jane Heap, and that of "Claire Lescaut," Georgette. "All the story," Margaret declared, "is either literally, or essentially, true—except for one episode," the ending. But Margaret said, "It could have been—as I see when I reread her [Tippy's] letters today; but I was too stupid—I never stopped arguing and I never could convince her. Alas, alas!—but I almost did, and that's something."

In 1958 Margaret took the manuscript of *Forbidden Fires* with her when she went to visit Solita and Lib in Orgeval. Solita, a harsh and uncompromising editor, customarily liked little of what anyone wrote. To Margaret's surprise, Solita kept exclaiming to Margaret as she read—"Perfect." "Very, very funny." "Lovely." "Very Proustian." "This is what I call good writing." "This time you can make some money."

Margaret sent the manuscript to Knopf, Simon & Schuster, and Viking. They all turned it down. Margaret's treatment of the subject matter was too radical for contemporary readers. The book did initiate a correspondence between her and Kathryn Hulme on the nature of lesbian love.

That July Kathryn wrote to Margaret that she thought the novella "superbly written—spare, clean, witty in so many places ... compressed to a quintessence almost too rich for my blood ... I think you handled it magnificently." But Margaret's depiction of romantic love among women left Kathryn cold. "The forced suppression of one of the centers when so obviously all three were ready to lift this love to its highest peak, as on a pyramid" was a kind of murder. "There had to be some kind of killing done at each meeting [between the women] ... or so it felt to me ... and I experienced rage at the thought each time. You never once wrote the word 'chemistry,' you never even say it existed ... but it was there for me through all the pages and its murder at each meeting seemed hideously needless.... You see how totally inadequate I am to even begin to understand such a thing as romantic love subsisting on music, letters and instantaneous intellectual understandings...." The romantic love the novella depicted is "an emotion of which I would be totally incapable of experiencing. It is certainly not lesbianism to me. Lesbianism is a much more 'natural' emotion than this rare state you present so beautifully.... I have always believed there is a place for a real lesbian work ... but not as moonbeam."

A month later Margaret wrote back: "I never imagined that my feelings and emotions were rare, I thought everyone involved in romantic love felt as I do." She knew that Solita agreed with Kathryn but Margaret believed that anyone of her type would always experience "moonbeam." Romantic love in the world's literature offered a thousand proofs of emotions just like hers. "Through all the ages, all men and women of romantic tendency, and especially lesbians of the romantic type, feel as I do; they never talk of any other kind of emotion; perhaps I'm a little extreme, but I know I'm not rare—unless you want to contrast me only with the bourgeois."

Margaret especially did not agree that lesbianism is a much more "natural" emotion than she depicted. "In all the lesbian love I've known no single experience has lasted very long as 'being in love,' simply because of that 'natural, simple' attitude—to me obvious, unenthralling, uncompelling, unfascinating, unobsessive, unalluring, un-Chopin, un-moonbeam—down-to-earth 'naturalness' that means almost nothing to me."

In contrast with earlier years, Margaret, though always intense, had developed a sense of humor. She closed the letter with, "Well, you know how much I do thank you, and you'd better not keep it up because you'll tempt me to correspond with you at length, which would be ruinous to you."

Margaret and Kathryn's discussion about lesbianism occurred within the context of a much larger subject—*ecstasy*. Margaret and Solita had debated it for years. Finally, Solita put her thoughts in a long letter:

> Dear Martie,
>   You want me to go on with our correspondence about *ecstasy?* I'm going to accept, since it has made me continue to formulate:
>   The word itself, according to the learned and tranquil Skeats, is merely 'enthusiasm'! The Middle English definition was 'a swooning, a trance.' (That's you). The real root meaning is *ek* (out of) *astasis* (state or condition), meaning out of one's normal or ordinary state. Therefore you have never have ecstasy. Ecstasy, your lovely curse which makes people looking at you think you take dope (which you call 'making something out of nothing'), is what Gurdjieff calls "pouring from the empty into the void."
>   I want to know, evidently, what can't be known. I do know, from Gurdjieff, that all laws are based on electricity; and that 'Ecstasy' happens undoubtedly in the filling of our somatic batteries.

First and fundamentally: the capacity for ecstasy depends on the amount of electric energy in the body's cells—the quantity and quality. Second, it depends on the distribution and arrangement in the body's batteries in a certain kind of person. (Heredity enters here.) This kind of person is a natural magnet for those images outside himself—but which he himself produces as if by mirrors. Therefore 'onanism': enjoyment of oneself, with one's power wasted and without benefit (word means doing good or creation). If this results in art—you remember what Gurdjieff calls art! Since the sex batteries are the strongest, containing as they do the quintessence of the life force, ecstasy people are strongly sexed (I have known people who prefer their ecstatic imaginings to straight sex).

The possessor of the capacity for ecstasy—nervously organized, electrical energy running—feels a need to project the overwhelming currents of energy whenever a magnet approaches that attracts his conditioning. When great magnets such as romantic love, music, nature as art, a mania for God are lacking, the capacity expends itself on trifles—daily-living-magnets—and becomes exuberance, when it isn't a trance.

This capacity for Ecstasy, plus the capacity for Work (in the Gurdjieff sense), plus high intelligence, plus 'will power' are what make a master like Gurdjieff.

This electrical content is the emotional gift of fire, the fire under that 'vessel' which the alchemists wrote about so guardedly. This fire, forbidden by Gurdjieff to be expended except in his Work*, is what is used for development. *(This does not mean that Gurdjieff repudiated a normal sex life.)

It is (by 'exercises') stored in the principal battery and by certain treatment is refined into the 'agent', another alchemical term. This agent is the divine power that a master uses even through walls or at a distance, for healing, influencing, teaching, seeing your organs, reading your thoughts and emotions, hypnotizing, making 'miracles.' All self-development (in a man who can 'do') on his capacity for harnessed ecstasy.

Perhaps this is what Gurdjieff meant about you when he said that you had had a chance at real 'work' because of your love for the ecstatic state; and added, 'Pity, once you had something.'

I hope you like this formulation. My brain is being cleaned of cobwebs. Write something else that will make me think, please. Oh, I miss our 'conversations'! Namely, you make me angry enough to formulate. You had better answer this at once

[I'm] dying to know what you have for a reaction. I think it's pretty good, myself, and certainly you couldn't find anything like it in any book in the world, if I do say so myself. I could only think it out because of certain things he told me.

Margaret replied:

What can I say except that it all sounds wonderful, and that I hope it's true. How can I know whether it is or not? How can you know? 'Sent through walls for healing'?? I know this is what Georgette felt and really believed. I wish I could enter into contact with such mysteries. Will the doubting Thomas in me always hold me back? Could anything be more curious than my total trust in Gurdjieff and my total ignorance of his knowledge? But it's not curious at all it's the state of half-mankind, I suppose—the half in the outer circle, where I think I don't belong.

I have heard Jane say that Elspeth and I are the kind of people who can put more effort into hanging-back than in going-on.

In 1953 Kathryn Hulme's *The Wild Place* won Best Non-Fiction Award from *Atlantic Monthly* magazine. The day that Kathryn was to fly to Boston to receive the award, Malou seemed unusually thoughtful. Finally, she asked Kathryn what she would tell her editor if she asked for the subject of her next book. Kathryn didn't know, but said she would think of something.

"Why don't you suggest *my* story, a bit—how do you say—fictionalized, of course?" she asked with a shy look.

This was the story Kathryn had dreamed of writing ever since the Wildflecken years when they had talked of her life.

"Why now? Why? After nearly ten years of guarding your secret?"

"Because ..." she said steadily, "I think it might *do some good.*"

Kathryn finished the manuscript in two years and in 1956 Malou's story—*The Nun's Story*—was published. The book was an immediate success. Among its many readers was the actor Gary Cooper who strongly suggested to his friend Fred Zinnemann, the director of *High Noon, From Here to Eternity* and *Oklahoma,* that he make it into a movie. The rights were quickly sold to Warner Brothers with Audrey Hepburn cast as Marie-Louise Hâbets, "Sister Luke" in the book. Said Audrey, "It wasn't just that I wanted to play a nun. The book appealed to me, the movie had a good director, and the part was suited to my nature."

Several years earlier, Kathryn and Malou had moved from Phoenix to Eagle Rock on the outskirts of Pasadena where they bought a small redwood house set on a hilltop. Audrey Hepburn lived in the Los Angeles area as well. Every afternoon for several weeks she visited the women to learn the basics of being a postulant—how to perform her orisons, Hail Marys, and other offices, as well as how to approach an altar or kiss a silver crucifix. Malou, suffering from high blood pressure, worked only part-time as a private nurse and she took Audrey to a hospital to study operating room procedures and to learn how to use surgical instruments. They spent one afternoon in a research laboratory familiarizing Audrey with Bunsen burners, test tubes and microscopes.

To research the role, Audrey decided she wanted to spend some time in an actual convent. Her first choice was the Sisters of Charity in Ghent, Belgium, where Malou had trained. But there were problems. The book had infuriated many in the hierarchy of the Catholic Church. Its harsh depiction of convent life—the flagellation, kissing her superior's feet, being ordered to fail exams to teach humility—and that also a nun who had broken her vows had made a great deal of money by telling her experiences was not something to be supported. The French Catholics, however, less concerned about retaliation from the Vatican, invited Audrey to stay at the Order of the Sisters of the Assumption at Froyennes, near Paris. Warner Brothers, of course, was also asked for a substantial cash contribution.

Production began in 1957, exteriors shot at the convent at Froyennes, in Ghent and the surrounding Belgian countryside, while the film's interiors were shot at Cinecitta in Rome. Near the end of January 1958, Fred Zinnemann, Audrey, the cast and crew also went to Stanleyville in the Belgian Congo (now Kisangani, Zaire) to shoot. For four days they shot in Yalisombo, a real leper colony located on an island in the middle of the Congo River, some forty miles downstream from Stanleyville. Location shots were finally completed in early March.

A real friendship had developed between Audrey and Kathryn and Malou in the weeks she had spent with them learning to be a postulant. And so when she returned to Rome where the last scenes were being shot, Audrey wrote to them—"Delving into the heart and mind of Sister Luke, I have also had to dig deep down into myself. Thereby having done a bit of ploughing of the soul—so to speak—the seeds of all I have experienced have fallen on neatly prepared ground, and I hope will result in harvesting a better Audrey."

Kathryn immediately wrote back: "Your utterly delightful and most moving letter from Rome most certainly 'took the wind out of our veils'.... Without a blush, you see, I steal one of your most enchanting expressions to describe our open-mouthed wonder at your facility with words. Who ever would have thought you'd have such ability with words, along with all the other great gifts those proverbial cradle-fairies endowed you with? In a way, it is grossly unfair. If the good fairies had given you just your looks, that in itself would have been enough, would actually, almost have verged on the unfair. But then your artistic talent. And now we discover your warm and witty facility with words...."

Alice Rohrer and her husband Gusto had visited Kathryn and Malou in 1957, staying in a nearby motel. Alice, liking the area and the closeness to friends, had a house built down the hill from theirs, and in January 1958 she and Gusto moved in. Though it was a special time for Kathryn and Malou—the film of *The Nun's Story* was soon to be released and advance notices were exceptionally good—it was a gloomy time for Alice, who had to cope with her husband's increasingly black moods. Within three months, she decided she wanted a divorce. To obtain legal counsel, in early March she went to San Francisco, staying with Lily, a younger sister who kept Alice's financial affairs in order. Kathryn was to give a lecture at Mills College in Oakland that same month, so the women quickly made plans to get together. Kathryn and Malou would drive up to San Francisco, give the talk and then they would have dinner with Alice on Wednesday, the 12th.

That evening Alice met Kathryn and Malou at their hotel and they had a drink in their room where they could talk in private. Alice had just come from the lawyer, she said, and all that she had to go through to get the divorce was astonishing. Then she said, "Now, we are finished with that subject. Now we play."

Kathryn told her it was her evening and they would do whatever she wished. Alice's favorite dinner spot in San Francisco was the English Room at the St. Francis Hotel just up the block, so the women simply joined arms and walked to dinner.

"I feel all my blood moving back into me again," said Alice.

"All you need, darling, is to be out on the town with the girls for a change," Kathryn told her.

Kathryn was going with Malou to Hawaii to research *Old Salt,* a book she was writing, and as the women walked up Post Street they made plans to include Alice in what they all soon were calling "the New Life."

Alice bought them a drink in the bar and the talk circled around finding Alice a house in Hawaii, where Kathryn and Malou had decided to live. At one point the conversation shifted to Gusto.

"Oh Katie, to think that I should have brought such trouble to your doorstep at this special time...."

"Darling," answered Kathryn, "where else should you come but here?"

At dinner in the English Room they talked of all the travels they would do together. Alice ate well, ordering grilled French chops and raspberry sherbet for dessert.

"She ate all the little petit fours," Katie said, "that came on all the sherbet plates—first Malou's, then mine, picking them up with that little bird hand, and saying, 'You're sure you don't want them?'"

After dinner they went to the theater to see the French mime Marcel Marceau.

Entering the theater, Alice exclaimed, "Katie, I'm like an old country woman, it is years since I've been in a theater."

"This is only the beginning, darling," said Kathryn.

Alice was enthralled with Marcel Marceau and Kathryn told her as they walked out of the theater that she was sure she would love him because "he is a pixie person like yourself."

Though Alice protested that she wanted to take a taxi, Kathryn and Malou drove her to Lily's in Kathryn's car. It began to sprinkle as they drove up to her sister Lily's little house. Alice asked them not to get out of the car, she would pull her coat over her head and run up the stairs. Before she did she put her arms around Kathryn's neck and gave her a tender kiss on the mouth.

"It was so warm, so loving," Kathryn said, "and she squeezed me and said, 'I've never had such a wonderful night in years, Katie.'"

They made plans to meet again on Friday and take Malou to the Fairmont Hotel for lunch.

And then Alice was out the car door, coat over head, in a dash for Lily's door. The door opened, closed, Alice threw off her coat, saying to Lily, "I really ought not go out and eat so much"—and dropped to the floor, dead.

Kathryn and Malou had returned to their hotel and gone to bed when Lily phoned. They immediately dressed and returned. Alice was on the bed. Kathryn leaned over and kissed her cheek.

She said to Malou, "She's still warm...."

Malou took her by the arm and led her out of the room.

Kathryn felt absolutely nothing on Thursday.

Late Thursday evening the autopsy report showed that Alice Rohrer had died of coronary thrombosis, ruptured myocardium.

Friday morning Kathryn woke up sobbing, her mind's eye filled with images of Alice, her "Nickie," throughout the years in her milliner's shop, the travels to North Africa, with Solita and Jannie in Paris, with Gurdjieff at those incredible luncheons and dinners with Solita and Margaret and Georgette and Louise—it all flowed like clear water in a slow mountain stream.

The waves of grief that gripped Kathryn were so strong that she felt she might lose her sanity. Malou comforted her, saying that "God must love you to have given you that very last hour of Alice's life, given you the joy of giving her everything she wanted

212

in those last hours—and in all the familiar places where your relationship had first begun."

The funeral was held at Grey's Mortuary on Saturday at two o'clock in the afternoon. Kathryn had sent a huge wreath of white gardenias with a swatch of pink camellias at the top and some green and pink lily leaves tied like a bow. It was placed on an easel at the head of Alice's casket and bore the names of what Kathryn called her "Paris sisters"—Solita, Margaret, Louise, Janet, Lib, and Noel.

Kathryn and Malou together sent a great blanket of white carnations and white stock falling around like fringes. Lily bought her the chiffon dress she always said she would want "to go away in."

Alice had told Lily "if ever anything happened—not to let people look at me." But Alice's three other sisters had driven up from Los Angeles and so Lily left the casket open.

"Alice looked very beautiful," said Kathryn, and there was, as she pointed out to Lily, "a secret little smile about her mouth, as if she were playing possum."

At the service, Tchaikovsky's *None But the Lonely Heart* was played, the piece Alice had told Kathryn must be her funeral music if she died before Kathryn did.

Gusto attended the service, and Kathryn and especially Malou went out of their way to be nice to him.

After the service Alice was to be cremated and her ashes sent East to repose beside her mother's grave.

Kathryn and Malou headed back to Los Angeles, driving as far as King City in solid sheets of rain. By the time they arrived home, they found a letter from Janet Flanner awaiting them. Janet had been in Paris when Alice died, but the telegram Kathryn had sent her at *The New Yorker* had been forwarded. Janet wrote:

> Condolence and deep sadness at the death of our wild strange homeless Alice, always without a permanent address in this world, all her life through. Except for you; I suppose you, Katie, were her permanent street, house and heart number where she resided. My dearest Katie, how long it has been, with the Citroën car through which we met you both in the [Café] Flore, then the years of laughter

and travel and jokes and darling Alice's incorrigible incredible letters. She was one of the strangest wandering spirits I ever met, in any orb, I appreciated and loved her, her refinement, her confusions, her aspiration, her errors too as much as any other great quality of her temporary connection with the world as we knew it. She knew it on different levels. One material. The other where? In her own ether.

Over the years Alice and Kathryn had had an extensive correspondence. Alice had kept all of Kathryn's letters and, as Kathryn had never kept a diary, she was interested in reading them. "There would be in those letters," she said, "certain reminding phrases which would have diary-quality of telling me how and what I was in those years." When Kathryn visited Alice's sister Lily, she said she had destroyed them all. "This was best for all concerned," she assured Kathryn.

Lily was known as the "good sweet sister," the one who had faithfully kept Alice's accounts throughout the decades. The year before her death Alice had rewritten her will bequeathing to Lily some $3 or $4 million while giving her four other sisters $5,000 each. Alice knew that Kathryn's books and the film had left her "taken care of" and so left her out of the will. "I was a little hurt naturally," Kathryn said. When they had discussed the rewriting of her will, Kathryn had asked Nickie not to remove the clause about Kathryn having selection rights over her library (Kathryn had given her most of the books) and possibly a bibelot or two. Alice had indicated she hadn't done so. But she had.

Alice's will appalled Kathryn. It showed, Kathryn felt, "the covetousness which wrecked our Nickie." Seeing what the money quickly did to Lily was even worse. "She will eventually become," said Kathryn, "the quintessence of the avarice of which Alice was only the essence."

Kathryn visited Lily on January 16, 1959, ten months after Alice's death. Kathryn said her heart sank as she saw the house decorated with Alice's great Mexican silver platters and furniture and Lily decked out in her sister's jewelry. Lily talked of all the things she was going to do with the money, take a long tour to see all the places that Sister saw and to have "a good time as Sister wished." "I let her talk," Kathryn told Solita in a letter. "I even drew her out. Never was Krokodile more strong, showing nothing, nothing, as her plans unrolled." And when Lily served her tea, spooning the sugar with a charming silver spoon garlanded in roses and Kathryn told her she had seen that spoon before and showed her the scrolly "H" on its handle, telling her it was one of her friend's silver bridal pieces, Lily exclaimed "It is, Katie! Then I shall love it just that much more!"

Later Kathryn told Malou what had transpired (but omitted speaking of the silver spoon because of Malou's increasing problems with her high blood pressure). Malou thought a moment about the burning of the letters and the fool's inheritance.

"You know, Katchka"—Malou's pet name for Kathryn—"there is a Flemish phrase to describe Lily." It was how one says "checkmate" to an impossible sight—"She is a cow in a lace collar."

Kathryn saw Lily's future. "The horror and unhappiness of being captive to her possessions, the inevitable (and justifiable) fury of the cut-off sisters rising about her.... Nothing in her past life prepared her for the position of the power she now is in.... and so she becomes 'a cow in a lace collar!' A multimillion dollar cow."

On the way home with Malou, Kathryn reviewed her life with Alice. She saw how she had given everything to Madame X, the princess in potential, who she felt only needed her to show her how to be a princess in fact. "The totality of thought and emotion which went into that endeavor may be called wasted by some," mused Kathryn, "but not by me. It is not often on earth that one is given such opportunity to go whole hog. This is my real inheritance from Alice.... she was, wish or not wish, the agent that gave rise to this rare and wondrous experience...."

As disappointing as Kathryn's experience with Lily had been, both Kathryn and Malou were overjoyed when in spring 1959 they attended the premiere of *The Nun's Story.* A few weeks after opening to excellent reviews, it received Oscar nominations for best direction, screenplay, photography, score and picture, and best actress for Audrey.

215

Meanwhile Audrey was in Durango, Mexico, about 600 miles south of the U.S. border, making her first western, *The Unforgiven*, with director John Huston. Twenty-nine years old that May, she had just discovered she was pregnant. This, together with the memory of having been thrown from a horse as a child, made her frightened at the prospect of riding. Told that a stunt double would be used for most of the scenes, that she had only to ride a horse for about fifty yards, she finally agreed. She would be astride Diablo, a white stallion formerly owned by President Batista of Cuba, which was to canter over a particular spot by a riverbank. However, the combination of Audrey's uneasiness, the camera lights, and sudden movements by the crew caused the horse to suddenly buck. Audrey was thrown and landed on her back. Several vertebrae were broken but, though badly hurt and in pain, she did not lose the baby. Malou had her brought back to Los Angeles in an ambulance plane and Audrey stayed at her and Kathryn's home for three weeks while Malou cared for her.

In July, the night of the awards, Audrey, seven months pregnant, was in Switzerland and wrote to Malou:

> Dearest most Precious Lou,
>
> Just loved your letter and thank you from the bottom of my heart. Tonight is the big night and you will all know the results.... No news will ever be more glorious for me than when I heard I was going to be the chosen one to play Lou-Luke—or when you said you'd come.

Though the New York film critics had earlier voted Audrey the best actress award, the Oscar for best actress went to Simone Signoret for her role as an aging woman in love with a young man in *Room at the Top*.

In 1960 Kathryn and Malou, finding Los Angeles more and more crowded, decided to move to Kauai, Hawaii.

Kathryn Hulme and Marie Louise Hâbets

Audrey Hepburn as
Marie Louise Hâbets
in *The Nun's Story*

217

Kathryn Hulme, Fred Zinneman, and Audrey Hepburn discussing *The Nun's Story*. Los Angeles, 1957.

Audrey Hepburn, in costume as Marie Louis Hâbets, on location in Africa.

Solita Solano and Isak Dinesen in Rungstedlund, Denmark, June 1962.

The Rope's Last Days

C HALET ROSE. JUNE 18, 1961, MONIQUE SERRURE DIED. SHE HAD BEEN SUFFERING SINCE 1958. MARGARET HAD KNOWN Monique for 37 years, had lived with her from 1924 until leaving for America in June 1942, and then again after she returned to the Chalet Rose in June 1956. Monique's death was a tremendous loss. Three days afterward Margaret wrote to Solita, "Georgette died, but there was still Monique ... Duffy died and there was still Monique. Now there is no background, and for the first time in my life I don't know what to do.... At first there was the relief that her suffering was over, and that I could rest a little.... Then suddenly all relief, fatigue, all the horrors (of which I've never given you any idea) were effaced; there's nothing left except my missing her."

In the last years, as often happens when people grow older, Margaret had become less tolerant of a number of her friends. In the wake of arguments, either she or they simply stopped communicating. The friends she did have all lived elsewhere—Solita and Lib in Orgeval, Jane in London, Kathryn in Kauai, and her sister Lois in the States. She would not live with any of her friends—she valued her independence above all else and also wanted never to burden them. Returning to America with its lack of civility was out of the question. She understood she would have to make the best of living alone.

At Christmas time, having passed her seventy-fifth birthday, Margaret was quite ill for about a month. Her heart was acting up and, a lifelong smoker, she found she couldn't walk up stairs without losing her breath. Having been known for her amazing vitality and ability to quickly recover from any illness without the aid of a doctor, she found her condition startling. Finally, not getting any better, she went to see a doctor. He gave her the first real check-up of her life. Her aorta was not functioning well, he told her, and gave her medicines. They seemed to work. But then a tooth abscessed and her cheek blew up like a balloon. This passed. She continued smoking and listening to Chopin, reading magazines and newspapers, buying cat food for her black cat Bébé, and correcting the page proofs of her forthcoming book *The Unknowable Gurdjieff*. Published in September 1962, the book was a success and brought Margaret accolades from the Rope, and many fan letters.

Empty at first, Margaret's life at Chalet Rose had slowly settled into a routine which she found both pleasurable and stimulating. As she told Solita: "When one has lived alone a long time one enters a fixed pattern of habits that is difficult to break. The habits have been imposed by the great and unique pleasure of being free to follow all one's impulses, to do at all moments what one most wants to do. I have no 'tasks' that bore me except the obligation to answer fan letters. The rest is silence—the concentrated pleasure of work, the constant use of the mind, the reward of watching one's progress. To live day by day, each day exactly like the other, has become such an ideal life for me that I hesitate to change it. In such a state of life, the thought of other activities becomes almost frightening. They loom, they seem too difficult, become exaggerated, gigantic. Thus, to buy a suit: a great chore, involving deep reflection as to the perfect material, color, design.... All this is too ridiculous, I know, but it's my present state ... and can be called, if you like, the approach of age."

Margaret's book had prompted Kathryn to think of writing a book about Gurdjieff as well. The following spring she and Malou visited Solita and Lib in Orgeval and she decided to get Solita's opinion. The women, of course, were all glad to see one another after so many years. They sat in the garden having tea. Kathryn and Malou talked about their new home on the magical island of

Kauai and the filming of *The Nun's Story* and their admiration for Audrey. Solita, in turn, told her friends about having written to the Danish storyteller Isak Dinesen, whose real name was Baroness Karen Blixen. Solita had told Dinesen of her high regard for her *Out of Africa* and her story "The Deluge at Norderney," the latter about a woman's center of gravity returning to her after menopause, making her witchlike. They had begun a correspondence and last year Dinesen suggested that they should meet in Paris. The women found they had a like empathy. Dinesen asked Solita to call her "Tania" and invited Solita to visit her at her ancestral family home, Rungstedlund, not far from Copenhagen.

Tania had married her cousin Baron Blixen-Finecke, a famous big game hunter, in 1914, and gone to Kenya to run a coffee plantation. A ladies' man, the baron had numerous liaisons. Four years after they arrived in Kenya, Tania met the English aristocrat, big game hunter and safari guide Denys Finch-Hatton and fell in love, *la grande passion*. Unlike her husband, Denys appreciated literature and knew the classics by heart. In time they became lovers, she writing stories avidly, he acting as her "muse." In 1921 Tania and her husband divorced. She and Denys never married, as for him it had no appeal. In 1931, when the price of coffee unexpectedly dropped, the plantation had to be sold and she returned to Denmark. Denys died in an airplane crash shortly thereafter. Forced to live with her family once more, she reinvented herself as the storyteller taking her family name of Dinesen and adding a masculine pseudonym, "Isak." In 1934 she published *Seven Gothic Tales*. It was an immediate success as was *Out of Africa*, published in 1937, which was one of Solita's favorite books.

The women had much to tell one another and the conversation was going well. At one point, Solita asked Kathryn if she had any ideas for a new book. Kathryn mentioned Margaret's *The Unknowable Gurdjieff* and said she was considering writing a book on Gurdjieff, as well. The blue of Solita's eyes immediately flashed and she came forward in her chair—"I am completely against it," she said.

The discussion went back and forth between the two women. Despite Solita's adamance, Kathryn held her ground. Lib and Malou looked on, sipping coffee, saying nothing. Finally, unable to sway her, Solita told Kathryn flat out—"You don't have the talent for it."

Solita relented a bit before the visit ended. If Kathryn must do this, she said, then it must be written as autobiography. She reasoned that with the *First Series* of Gurdjieff's *All and Everything* already printed, his *Second Series* to be published the next year, and the final *Third Series* in preparation—anything but an autobiographical account would, in effect, be interpreting Gurdjieff's presentation.

Later, sensing Kathryn's resistance, Solita waited until Kathryn went upstairs to pack and pulled Malou aside. "Make her do it," she declared, "if she must, as an autobiography.... Make her do it."

By the time Kathryn and Malou returned to Kauai, Kathryn had come to see Solita's reasoning.

And so Kathryn sat down to write *Undiscovered Country*.

That June, Lib drove Solita in her Jaguar to Denmark to visit Tania at Rungstedlund. Solita and she were almost the same age; Tania, born Karen Blixen, seventy-seven, Solita, seventy-four. Both had suffered stultifying early family lives which they escaped through marriage to men they didn't love who took them far off to foreign shores—Solita to the Philippines, Tania to Kenya.

Though they had much in common, Solita said she realized that if she and Tania were to have a significant communication it would not be through words.

"Our words, at least to begin with," said Solita, "would probably be conventional and on the surface, but we would meet through our tacit agreement on those matters which can dispense with speech. As it turned out, this is the way it was."

Lib, not having met Tania and not invited, stayed behind at a hotel and Solita caught a taxi. Tania lived at her ancestral home of Rungstedlund on the main road between Copenhagen and Elsinore castle. Arriving in early evening, Solita found Tania and Clara Svendsen, her secretary and nurse of eighteen years, waiting for her at the door. Tania's appearance had radically changed since their previous meeting a year before in Paris and she now needed

Clara's support to move. Still, she gave Solita a beautiful smile and embracing her said, "Solita, I am so happy that you could come to my house. Thank you for coming." Clara embraced her as well and her dog Pepper leapt on her, wagging its tail.

"Now," said Tania, "perhaps you would like to go to your room; dinner is early here, in fact in five minutes."

Five minutes later Solita was led into the dining room by Clara who then helped Tania to her place at table. She always sat at the end, with Clara and Solita at each side. Members of the Rope had often talked of various people they knew being "civilized," of having achieved a high degree of "sophistication." "Here," said Solita, "was the paragon—without the minutest flaw in her behavior and observation. I had known from the first that she was not feminine, but made of rock and fiery elements, like a volcano; and she knew that I knew it…. I often felt that I was in the presence of someone who dwarfed the human race."

At the table there were long silences in which Tania would easily enter into a contemplation lasting as much as three or four minutes. There was no chatter, no banalities or straining for conversation. "Each of us," said Solita, "was allowed her own freedom for inner life renewals, mingling of impressions, sorting all into the compartments that were waiting oh so gratefully with the assurance that someone would not dissipate each precious event before it could be assimilated." By a glance or a word Tania would communicate the realm in which she was thinking.

Said Solita, "Sometimes it was almost like being with Gurdjieff for that kind of understanding. The rest of our companionship was of the utmost harmony in which I made myself into an instrument for her to play upon, to get 'answers' from, and those of an immediacy I had been schooled in at Mr. Gurdjieff's table and have not been called upon since to use in life. This kind of 'game' she understands and thoroughly enjoys."

On another day, three men, one a well-known writer but all uninteresting, came to lunch. When they had left Tania asked what Solita thought of the writer.

"I thought he was very brash," said Solita.

The word "brash" neither Tania nor Clara knew. When it was explained Tania said, "Yes, isn't it curious that he has never learned how to behave."

After one of their first dinners Tania spoke a little of her days in Africa.

"I should have gone up with Denys in the plane that day [the day he died]. It was then I should have died," she mused.

"I consider that thought treasonable and egotistic," said Solita. "You have no right to wish you had not used your genius in this world. You have given beauty and inspiration to thousands, as well as untold delight, and also have been an honor to your country."

"How true!" cried Clara.

At that moment Tania's face began to change, her eyes filling with light, and she said, "What you say makes me very happy."

"This in all the visit," said Solita, "was the only time I stood against her in the faintest way, it was my only self-assertion."

The next afternoon Tania asked Solita to come out to the verandah. From a large untidy box of old photographs, she held two out to her.

"Here is Denys," she said, "as a young man at Eton.... Here is a Greek head he then so much resembled.... And here he is, many years later. You can see that he has already lost much of his hair from the temples, but I think it did not spoil his good looks."

Solita found him quite beautiful in a classical Greek way. "I have never seen such a mouth for beauty, on man or woman," she said.

Other photos were shown, mostly family portraits. Finally from the box Tania withdrew a large passport photograph.

"This was myself more than thirty years ago."

"But, Tania, it looks like a young Indian rajah with that turban. How fascinating."

Tania put it back in the box. Then taking it out again, she asked, "Would you like it?"

Though Solita found Danish food excellent, Tania could eat very little, nothing more than spoonfuls of soup, perhaps a forkful of vegetables, a bit of the dessert. Her cook, Tania joked, was always glad of guests so that she could test her skills before they were forgotten. Over the years Tania had had a number of serious operations. In one a great part of her stomach had been cut out; in another a nerve had been cut off from her spine and instead of curing her pain had made it worse. She was nearly always in pain.

"I'm so sorry that you are suffering," Solita said.

She turned away, murmuring, "Don't sympathize." Then added, "Yes, it is a nuisance."

Later she said, "In my former life, I enjoyed food and was an expert on cooking and good wines. Now everything I eat tastes disgusting. But I love to see others eat and I even ask people to tell me what they have had for dinner."

Tania never appeared in the mornings, so Solita was free to walk in the park, read, or, as she said, "just enjoy my emotions." After dinner the second night Tania asked, "Do you mind if I have a game of *besigue* with Clara?" Then after a pause she added, "You know I need it." It is her version of a card game "idiot's delight," it seems, and Clara had kept an account of their nightly winnings for years. So Solita read beside them until ten o'clock when the evening tray of cherry brandy, cookies, and biscuits for Pepper appeared. They would sit and sip and have a cookie and enjoy what Solita described as "the semi-silence in the balm of nerveless ease, unknown in the country of my birth." At the end of every night Tania would embrace Solita, always saying, "I am so happy you could come to me here."

The only surprise during Solita's visit was a curious episode that occurred every night. She had, on a chance impulse, brought Tania a box of "best-in-the-world" Belgian bonbons, and these were taken from a drawer of the sideboard after dinner. Tania received the gilt paper-wrapped box from Clara, herself untied the gold string, opened the box with care, selected two bonbons, passed the box to Clara who took but one. Slowly Tania ate her two, then repacked the box with its gold papers and tied it up again! Back it went into the drawer like a treasure.

One afternoon they drove to a great château for high tea and a tour of the enormous rooms filled with family portraits, Aubusson rugs and museum-quality furniture. Then they drove on to the ancient cluster of buildings where Tania's niece, husband and four boys lived, an old family place where Tania's mother had lived for a while. On the way Tania told the driver to go to the site of an old castle, now sunk, over a bridge and by a stream. They stopped there. Tania said, "And here is where I wrote 'The Poet,' the last of the *Gothic Tales*. And over there is the house in which he lived. I thought you might like to see it for yourself."

On the last day of Solita's visit, Tania looked exhausted, without vitality. She looked so bad that Solita feared that this would be the last time she would see her. The next day, before lunch, Tania said she had been in great pain all night. Clara gave her some medicine at the table, and she went to the porch while Solita packed.

When it was time for Lib to arrive in the car, Solita passed by the verandah. There was Tania, sitting slumped, head bowed, asleep. Solita and Lib packed the car and Solita went to say goodbye. Through the window, Tania had seen the Jaguar, and Lib, too. Clara came out and told them, "Tania feels better and wishes to go with you to Elsinore."

Lib drove and Tania sat beside her. She waited in the car while Solita and Lib made the tour round the castle as quickly as possible. Driving on to Copenhagen Clara went to see her mother and Tania invited the women to tea in a chic restaurant. While Lib parked the car, Solita helped Tania to a table, going slowly, step by step. On the way she told Solita, "Oh, your friend is charming!"

When they were all seated, Solita said:

> There came upon her a transformation like all the street lamps lighted at once. With us both before her and tea ordered, she set herself out to enchant. This was the first time I had seen this aspect of her—this inanimate invalid who had crept forth as if from a death bed, now became from the shoulders up a true siren with electric lamps for eyes, a restored face of high beauty and a speech that flowed on without stopping for an hour—the vedette of her youth and books. She recounted adventures, tales how she had come to write her novel *The Angelic Avengers* (the one written under an assumed man's name of Pierre Andrezel), dev-

ilishly endeavoring to make me say 'I had liked it,' which I refused to do.

She said, "Oh well, anyway it was well-constructed and was a Book-of-the-Month choice in America." I made no comment to that, so she said quickly, "Oh of course, I realized that it had nothing of the quality of my real work," and I said, "It certainly did not."

Lib and Solita were enthralled and scarcely spoke. "Tania," she said, "glowed and those magnificent eyes burned as I have never seen eyes burn, or imagined it possible for fire to burn without physical fuel."

At one point Solita said—"Oh, how beautiful you are!"

And she returned, "You should have met me fifty years ago."

That was the last the women would see of her, for three months later on September 7, 1962, Tania, Isak Dinesen, the Baroness Karen von Blixen-Finecke, died.

Returning from Denmark, Solita and Lib drove down to Chalet Rose in July to spend several days with Margaret. All they could talk about was Isak Dinesen, so much so that Margaret—who had written her as well and never received an answer—said they were still "under a spell of enchantment." Since Monique's death, Solita and Lib had been concerned about Margaret's living alone. This was likely a factor in Lib telling Margaret she had bought a peasant house in Orgeval, larger than the present one. It had two guest bedrooms and bath. Lib asked Margaret to come for Christmas, she would be their first guest (Solita and she were leaving for America and wouldn't be back until then). To top it off, Solita and Lib asked Margaret to do all the interior decoration. "I shall go mad with happiness," said Margaret at the prospect, "because the house is really ideal; has extensive gardens and everything else that one wants." Margaret, of course, tried to get Solita to talk about Gurdjieff but Solita refused. She was a "veteran" of Margaret's conversations. As Janet Flanner was to say: "The Orgeval lunches invariably developed, by the second cups of coffee which ended them, into small verbal wars. These were Margaret's particular delight, and if she was able to say, as she drew on her topcoat to go home, that she'd never had better conversation, it was her way of acknowledging that she had been involved in battles with almost everyone at the table and felt that she had triumphed in most of them."

With Solita no longer willing to engage directly in such conversation, Margaret did the next best thing. She wrote Solita a letter in which she had a conversation for both of them:

> For several years I have been longing for a renewed discussion about Gurdjieff and his ideas, their value and their mystery. There are still many unanswered questions in my mind, and my special friend, I believe, could answer some of them. But she is a sparring-partner who dislikes discussion. Nevertheless I keep trying to "draw her out."
>
> *Me:* Let's have a real conversation.
>
> *Solita:* You can't have it with me. Ask someone else. I have no interest in questions and answers.
>
> *Me:* I could of course talk with the various Gurdjieff groups, but they would answer, "You'll learn nothing by arguing, only by 'working.'" And I'm sure they would be right.
>
> *Solita:* Then why not stop arguing, and boring people with questions?
>
> *Me:* Well, as Berenson said, "Being that God has given me a passion for argument, let me enjoy it." But I'm no longer asking to enjoy it. I am merely asking what you think Gurdjieff really believed about death and an after-life.
>
> *Solita:* I don't know.
>
> *Me:* What did we go to him to learn? And did we learn it?
>
> *Solita:* Gurdjieff said that the search for a soul has always been man's principal preoccupation.
>
> *Me:* As so many others have said! Such a truism is well-known to me, and doesn't answer my question.
>
> *Solita:* The human mind cannot cope—wasn't made to understand the universe. Will it ever? Decide for yourself.
>
> *Me:* I can't decide for myself—which is why I asked what you had decided.
>
> *Solita:* (Silence.)
>
> *Me:* If the human mind can't cope, why then did we take our *minds* to Gurdjieff? Why did he ask you to help N's *mind*? Why did you say that R's *mind* wasn't capable of understanding Gurdjieff's teaching? And isn't it you who

said that there was no pupil of sufficient intelligence, no *mind* in the same *gamme* [scale] as Ouspensky's? And that therefore no one understood anything transformational?

Solita: Yes.

Me: Well, if there's anything that I dislike, it is contradictions.

Solita: Everything is paradox.

Me: Everything shouldn't be. You say that recurrence and survival aren't the same thing, and you say that Gurdjieff denied eternal recurrence. Did he then also deny survival? I've never been able to find out—from his talk or his writing. What do you think?

Solita: (Silence.)

Me: One would almost be willing to die to *know* something.

Solita: Many have felt the same.

Me: Another well-known truism. Since you exercise such economy in discussion, why not economize in truisms?

Solita: (Silence.)

Me: One last question. Can you tell me today why you went to Gurdjieff 35 years ago?

Solita: For an aim in life which I could respect.

Me: In any normal interchange of opinion, I would ask what that aim was.

Solita: (Silence.)

Me: I would then ask whether it's necessary to go to Gurdjieff for such an aim. Haven't thousands of people found "respectable" aims without his help? - great artists, great scientists, Dr. Schweitzer, Peace Corps, etc.?

Solita: No, no, no. Now enough. And your exasperation is childish. Accept not ever to know the unknowable. Please put your flaming mind in cold storage.

Me: Your negatives cause me a kind of despair. Must you always throw a feather-bed over my mind?

Solita: (Silence.)

Me: I know why Jane, Georgette, Dorothy and I went to Gurdjieff, and I've always assumed that you had gone for the same reason. Must I now associate you with only a "respectable" aim? Why do you condemn (in Gurdjieff's well-known phrase) all discussion as "a pouring from the empty into the void?"

Solita: Because discussion is nothing but curiosity. In other words, titillation.

Me: I can think of no one who had more curiosity than Gurdjieff. And of no one who devoted more of his life to communication.

Solita: I do not believe in, and want no part in, what you call communication.

Me: Très bien. Then we must continue to regard Gurdjieff as a man miraculously possessing some kind of higher knowledge of which we understand very little, even after years of study, but in whom we believe as people believe in a messiah?

Solita: Yes.

Me: A marvelous answer. With which you know I don't agree.

In February 1963, Malou, having in January just passed her fifty-eighth birthday, took a refresher course in nursing at St. Francis Hospital in Hawaii. It was her first contact with a nun's community since she had left her order nineteen years before. "The first day," she said, "gave me shivers." She had thought the living accommodations would be dormitory style but she was given a room. "It was like going back into a cell." she said. "When I saw the iron bed and bare bureau, the crucifix on the wall and no running water in the room I was reminded of my vow of poverty." She sat in the hospital's chapel and watched the sisters praying. "They were tired at the end of a day's work and still they knelt and prayed without moving for a half an hour and more. There is no mediocrity in the bunch of them. A mediocre nun could not stay in a convent. I thought to myself, 'To think I was once one of them. Why couldn't I take it?' Still, I do not have the answer."

In September of 1963 Kathryn sent Margaret a draft of *Undiscovered Country.* Margaret wrote back immediately. She had two criticisms. One, what was "Wendy"—Kathryn's name for Alice—doing in the book? Two, forget the autobiography. The book should be a "monolith," it should focus entirely on Gurdjieff. Kathryn wrote back and reminded Margaret that not only was Alice an original member of the Rope, she was also an important part of her life. Defending the book as autobiography, she said, "At the risk of sounding fatuous, I think any 'selling point' in this book will be what happened to me, the Nun author with a considerable readership gained through that accidental 'best seller.' The average general reader is not interested in Gurdjieff ... never heard of him, would drop a book cold if it seemed to be only about an unknown mystic."

The following year on June 18, 1964, Jane Heap, eighty-one years old, died in the house she had long shared with Elspeth Champcommunal in Hamilton Terrace, London. Since the late 1920s she had battled diabetes but continued to lead groups until her death. On June 22nd, just four days after Jane's death, Elspeth died. Now, of all those who had attended Jane's meetings in Montparnasse, only Margaret, Solita and Janet Flanner remained. The impact on Margaret must have been profound. All that was left now were still and silent memories. If the reality and mercilessness of what Gurdjieff called *Heropass* was not known before, it certainly was so now.

In 1964, the same year Jane died, Fritz Peters published *Boyhood with Gurdjieff.* Well-written and giving many illuminating anecdotes, it mentioned little of Margaret and attacked Jane. Margaret doesn't appear to have had a relationship with the boys. Not once in her three volumes of memoirs did she mention raising them. Raising children is always problematic and for Jane to have agreed to raise two young boys—for neither of whom was she legally or morally responsible—was an act whose generosity and self-sacrifice only a mother could know. Jane's letters to her friend Florence Reynolds show a real caring and pride in the boys. Fritz's publication of his book the same year as Jane died—it would have been in character for him to have sent her the manuscript or galleys—may have been only a coincidence but it gave her, were she interested, no opportunity to give her side.

In 1965 Kathryn finished the final draft of *Undiscovered Country.* She gave it to Solita for a last editing. To put oneself under Solita's editorial thumb was to invite self-inflicted torture, but the price Margaret, Janet and Kathryn paid was always worth it. Solita rarely liked anything. As Margaret said, "She hates most all material, all writing manners, treatments, techniques, general ideas, etc. She has few loves—Dinesen's *Out of Africa* is perhaps her favorite book in the world. She says she loves Léautaud, some Stendhal, some Gide, Proust, and Katherine Mansfield's description of her brother's death.... She loathes all novels." Solita's earlier criticisms of *The Nun's Story* had been so sharp that Kathryn felt herself "struck dumb." She realized, however, that they had made it a much better book, so she voluntarily subjected herself once again.

In 1966 *Undiscovered Country* was published. Kathryn sent a copy to Margaret at Le Cannet. Margaret immediately wrote her: "I was so moved that I had to cry. I have always had a certain pride in my own Gurdjieff book, but after reading yours I have no pride left. I felt only as if I had been so superficial that I don't like myself. All your effort, your work, your real love for him, all your real emotions are there."

Kathryn also sent a copy to Louise Davidson who was working at the White Barn Theatre in Westport, Connecticut. "Katie darling—'Krokie,'" wrote Louise, "I've just given your brave and masterful 'effort' a second reading with complete concentration. As you already know Sardine took over the first with joyful flips in air—not on sand. *Undiscovered Country* brings G. closer, and with Love, than anything I've read about him. A vivid picture of the Work and your life in relation to it. Not one superfluous word. Your writing flows from the heart with tremendous impact. What a struggle to put the right words on paper to describe a spiritual adventure and of such magnitude, for words are material, not spiritual. I too pray that your book will reach the hearts of many people. I know that is what you want most, but we have to face the unhappy fact that 'messengers from above' are too often scoffed at and thought ridiculous sometimes to the point of being absolutely 'nutty.'"

Blessed with beauty, intelligence, talent and great vitality the oncoming of age was difficult for both Margaret and Solita. Their lives had been so full and meaningful and filled with adventure and friends and now the inevitable contraction came with the slow and irretrievable loss of their great physical and mental gifts and find themselves entering a time both saw as increasingly barbaric and meaningless was to feel a gnawing pain difficult to soothe. From time to time Solita and Lib would drive from Orgeval to Cannes to see Margaret. One time after dinner they were having coffee at a local café and both Margaret and Lib had become exhausted by Solita's empty chatter. Finally, Lib could stand it no more and said:

"Darling, during the last years there has been only one occasion when I've seen you control your nervous manifestations and that was when we were chez Tania [Dinesen]. You were so determined to make a good impression that you never acted as you do now, all the time. You behaved attractively and normally, you stopped all your hysterical chatter about nothing, you acted like a sensible human being. So you see that, if you want to, you can behave intelligently."

"Perhaps," said Solita. "Depends on my audience."

Margaret and Lib had many talks about why Solita acted so. "Lib attributed it to Solita's being a rejected child. "She has compensated for that," said Lib, "by drawing attention to herself in every possible way she can—by making scenes with waiters, by acting 'superior' to her friends, by eternally boasting about her knowledge of Latin and Greek and Sanskrit, and by refusing to take part in any situation in which she isn't the instigator."

Margaret saw Solita as two persons. "One," Margaret said, "who was almost insane with nerves; and the other—intelligent, human, lovable, a devoted friend, generous beyond words; a person who writes beautiful poetry, pure prose, who is an editor of genius and who has taught me all I know about writing."

The years of living alone had taken their toll on Margaret. On February 8, 1967, Margaret—eighty-one years old, her three great loves all gone, Monique gone, her health precarious—wrote:

> I have no more courage. Life has been so wonderful that I prefer to end it rather than to live less wonderfully.
> Today my life serves no purpose, and no person needs my devotion. My death at such a moment becomes à propos [fitting]; and it will release my friends from over-devotion.

Everyone has always been too kind to me—even Gurdjieff, who knew at once that I had no real courage or strength. I cannot face accident, helplessness, lingering illness, and becoming a burden to those I love.

All is in order—will, letters, and 'presents' to everyone.

To die now is best, so don't be sad. Once more, again and again, my gratitude to all of you, and all my love.

Martie

Whether this note was written before or after Margaret moved from the Chalet Rose into the Hotel Reine des Prés is unclear. In any event, happily, she did not take her life. It was clear to her, however, that she could no longer live alone with only her cat Bébé for companionship. "I had become a person," she said, "who at least knew what fear is, and who fears it. I had to seek some kind of security. The only kind I could grasp at was a hotel room, where people would protect me if I became ill, or if I couldn't protect myself from losing my mind."

To move into the hotel, as animals were not allowed, she had to put Bébé to sleep. Her living quarters were even smaller than at the Chalet Rose. There was no garden to walk in and only one room. It was high-ceilinged, its walls painted a pale color, with a bed, a too-small square writing table, and a small gas stove. Margaret's possessions were few. Books, records, a phonograph and a few clothes. A tall, energetic woman blessed with an uncommon beauty and zest for life, Margaret had greatly dwindled over the years. After Monique died, she had eaten less and less, becoming so thin that all her clothes had to be taken in. Except for two inexpensive sweaters, she had not bought any new clothes for five years. She did not want to be seen by anyone. She brought just three photographs with her, of Georgette, Jane, and Dorothy. Though she still insisted on smoking, emphysema made walking even short distances difficult. The hotel bath was only one flight up, but she could not manage the forty steps. The one time she had gotten up the stairs, she had needed help to get in or out of the tub. For washing, she began using the bidet on her floor. Though she couldn't make cocktails any longer, because using a shaker would have taken too much effort, every evening she would still pour herself a little Cointreau or mix it with brandy, and drink it without ice—"That always gives a pickup," she told Solita. As always, in accordance with her Scottish ancestry, she lived frugally.

Solita, impatient with Margaret's economies, wrote to her: "But you must spend money, it's crazy to be so cautious." Replied Margaret, "I refuse to be a burden to my friends.... when I become helpless I shall have to go to a clinic and that costs money." In actual fact, though she had no social security, Dorothy had willed her money and Michael Currier-Briggs, Jane Heap's student, had managed to sell Jane and Margaret's papers to the University of Wisconsin for $70,000. Margaret received half and, always generous, immediately gave away $15,000 to her sisters, Lois and Jean, and to Fritz, Solita, Lib and many others.

The transition to living in a hotel was difficult for Margaret, as it would be for any older person, but especially so for Margaret who all her life had been able to control and put her stamp on her living environment. After ten months in the Hôtel Reine des Prés she wrote in her diary, "What am I doing in this hotel room?—this alien place where I am now 'living'? I am experiencing reality. For the first time in my life I know what it is; for the first time I feel that I am looking straight at it. I've heard it talked about, written about, but I have never experienced it until tonight. My refusal, always to accept it must have been that I suspected in advance its future horror; and now, as a consequence of this first-hand knowledge I feel for the first time what insanity must be—why people resort to madness instead of accepting reality face to face."

She had been reading Alberto Moravia's *Ennui* and, depressed, had gone to bed at eight o'clock. She had awakened at midnight. "The awful realities of this unnecessary book," she wrote, "have plunged me into such disgust and astoundment that I began to write these notes. I feel as if this book's portrayal of raw, uncouth, shocking, hopeless, doomed humanity has engulfed my wonderful, personal, innocent, infantile life to the point that I can't even remember it. Is it true that people live like these people in Moravia's book? If they are people, then what am I? I am some other breed. I have never known anything like these arid, nauseating lives—they are outside my imagination. I insist on this point [as] it keeps me from feeling insane."

At one o'clock in the morning she awoke again. To give herself strength to write, she mixed herself a Cointreau and brandy. She took a drink and wrote, "Oh, my memories! A life that could create what it wanted, needed, demanded. And then a real miracle—Gurdjieff, with his suggestion that we could live outside the pattern of human madness and impotence. What has become of that miracle? It has become a memory—but a memory so strong that it helps me to understand this incomprehensible night of my life."

At three she awoke again. It was cold in the room though she had kept the gas stove on. At the mercy of her imagination, her mind associated the warmth with the cold Nazi concentration camps and tortures—"How can I ever sleep again, when nightmares of these tortures I have never suffered leave me as lacerated as if they had happened to me."

She asked herself, "Where does your life go when it leaves you? I'm not being fancy: I've had something in me—in my brain—which is no longer there. To be without it leaves a curious feeling, rather like another sensation I've so often had when I read a novel. I take mental snapshots of the characters' backgrounds which exist in my imagination as definitely as if they were factual."

An image of a house Colette had depicted in *Cheri* (the book that Janet Flanner had translated) came to her. "This house exists so clearly in my brain that I could photograph it; but what happens to the photograph when I stop seeing it? If everything that exists is material (as Gurdjieff taught), of what substance is this imagined house composed? Could I touch it? Could I photograph it?... I see the table where the characters are dining when Chéri says to his mother, 'I gather that your memory is breaking down. Do you think anything short of solitary confinement will cure it?'"

Finally, the long night ended. Into the room came the sun's early rays. "Enough insanity. It's now morning and I return to what is left—still left—of my life. It consists of one indestructible element: the fact that I know I am more fortunate than most people, more protected, more befriended, and that I never stop feeling the deepest gratitude for such blessings."

In time Margaret adapted to her new life. She continued to listen to Chopin and all her favorite composers, write letters and relive the cherished memories of another time. She also worked on the manuscript for the third and final volume of her memoirs *The Strange Necessity*. Published in 1969, it was not advertised and initially did not sell well. It did bring her some new acquaintances. Near the middle of the year a man began to visit her once a week but he was not what Margaret called "a conversation-friend." She said she knew that by the way he entered her room.

> He walks into my room completely oblivious of the vibrations filling it, which are nearly always electrical. He doesn't close the door after him. I ask, "Will you please close the door?" He does. "No, you must close it until you hear it click; otherwise it will fly open." He makes it click. Then I ask, as I do every week, "Will you please take the pink cushion out of your chair? Otherwise it will be crushed." This accomplished, he talks for an hour without thinking of anything but the impression he is making. The impression on me is of unclosed door and crushed cushion. But he is content, he is unaware of the dead person I have had to become in order not to make him aware and unhappy. But now I must ask him not to come any more. I have known him for a year, which means that I have conversed about the door and the cushion fifty-two times. That is too often.

Of Solita she said: "I still have a charming and intelligent and very special old-time friend who is more than capable of 'conversation' if she were ever now in the mood for such indulgences. She isn't, but even her negatives stimulate me. I love disagreement as much as agreement."

She was mugged once outside the hotel and had a bout of grippe and later pneumonia but recovered, and by early 1971 felt her health had almost returned to normal. "As long as I stay in my room and type, go to the dining room, or across the street for magazines and newspapers, I can breathe naturally. But to walk a block

I have to sit down twice on a bench because I begin again to be breathless."

On October 14, 1971, she wrote:

> And now I've just had another of those "visions" for which I can find no reason, explanation or description. Perhaps they should be called fantasies—"Imagist."
>
> It was the strangest—and, I suppose, the most essential— experience of my life. I had been feeling remorse for many things (chiefly for things I hadn't done), and suddenly great tides of—emotion—real emotion—began to sweep over me.
>
> I was sitting in my green armchair, and a solid circle had been drawn around me, over my head and shoulders. My room became silent and heavy and dark and I began to live in the circle. I was detached from all life except that which took place within this circle; I saw that my real "I" was there, expressing itself strongly—an "I" that bore no rela- tion to the "I" of the person who had written the day before: "That damned R!!" and "Don't give her my love."
>
> In the encircled "I," I was ten years old and "Nantie" had been telling me about religion. I rebelled over some of the "facts" she presented, I couldn't believe that the world had been created in six days. I argued and argued. But I believed all the rest that she said, in the way a religious con- vert believes. My young life had all the comfort described by people who believe in a personal God.

Fritz and Margaret had kept up a correspondence but of late his letters were filled with anger. They had gotten on well for the most part over the years. Their times together were always extreme—either absolutely wonderful or horrific. Though there were long periods of silence, they had always managed to patch things up. Now Margaret felt she couldn't go on writing. "I miss him greatly—his friendship, intelligence, and companionship" Margaret said, "—but I can't see him again. He becomes dangerous when he resorts to madness—he could destroy my life, to say nothing of others." He had written some angry and accusatory letters to his mother Lois, ending with the vow that he would never write to her again and were she to write to him, her letters would be returned unopened.

Of late, Solita had been drinking more and more. Lib wrote Margaret that she had taken Solita to lunch in Paris to see a friend:

> Solita drank too much (as always raised her voice too much, usurped the conversation, etc). After lunch she *teetered* with my help into a taxi. At the Gare St. Lazare there are now moving-stairs instead of the old ones—very steep and high. I wanted to stand behind Solita, *just in case*, but she wouldn't allow it. Just before reaching the top, when the stairs meet the floor of the big *salle* [waiting-room] of the station, I saw Solita fall over backwards, thumping, head downward, all the way to the bottom of those steel moving stairs.
>
> I rushed down, against the up-moving stairs as Solita was being carried up by them (feet forward, still on her back). Two strong men and I were unable to lift her until she arrived at the top of the stairs. With superhuman strength (from terror), we managed to put her on her feet and held her upright until she could speak. A miracle that she was not killed, nor any bones broken; not even a bruise anywhere. I think that her fur coat saved her life. *Aussitôt récupérée* (as soon as she recovered), she demanded a drink in the station café. Afterwards, great difficulty in getting her up those high and dangerous train steps.... I live in constant fear.... *Adieu et à bientôt*, my dearest *real* friend.

By mid-1972, however, Margaret's health began to fail. It took many minutes for her to get up and out from an armchair, and in going to a restaurant with friends her walking was so painful due to her lack of breath that she almost had to be carried.

> *Darling* Sweetie—your remorse.... I *must* cure it. Present situation MY fault: I gave up planning when I knew I shouldn't. I could have gone to Paris hotel (Voltaire?)—though not yet having Vaduz made that sound impossible. I could have been happy even in that little hotel facing your Orgeval church, waiting for that tenant of Lynn's to die, but I just got discouraged, which was uncharacteristic and changed my destiny. So will you please realize all this, for always. Can't bear it that you suffer.

"Always makes more sense today. Yesterday I was so weak I had to go to bed, rather worried. Hotel staff *very* worried, called doctor. He tried to come but couldn't—too much work, said would come today. But today I feel strong again, can stand up, walk and feel in right mind. So you see. (He'll be here any minute.) all this good news should cheer you—such a bouncing creature!

I want no lingering invalidism like Georgette's and Duffy's [Dorothy]: I want my heart to decide when to stop. I will agree. Do you remember my telling you once that [Rudolph] Steiner said all people die as they have lived? I believe it now—Georgette, Duffy and Monique did. So I should just go into a dream.

What a letter! You see that, after working too hard, I can't write at all.

If I should reread this scrawl I probably wouldn't send it.

So it shall be dropped in the box next door.

Once more, love,

M. C. A.

The following February she wrote to Solita and Lib in Orgeval: "I experienced Death this morning." She had awakened and didn't know whether she had died or was still living. She told herself, "not to move and perhaps you could endure the moment." She did not know what would happen when she went to breathe again. She thought of coughing to prove to herself that she was still alive. "Is this the way Death always happens?—one second more to endure—here or there—which side is Death? Not a word I'm writing is one-tenth of what I was feeling."

The next month she wrote saying, "I don't want to write this letter, but feel that I should: better to give you a small shock now than a large one later, when you're unprepared for it. Last week I became so terribly ill that I could no longer breathe until I had sat still for an hour—agonizing suffering."

The doctor came quickly. He recommended she go to a clinic but she refused. She had finished what she was working on. He began a daily regimen of serious injections. Said Margaret:

Now I am living a sort of wheelchair life, never leaving my room, trying not to leave my armchair. Forgot to say that I was sure I was dying. Wasn't afraid of that, couldn't accept more agony. Be assured that I am not suffering morally. Yesterday I fell asleep, wakened not knowing what day, what hour, it was. My memory is now almost completely lacking and will, I suppose, grow worse. Never mind—will do my best.

Where is my life? Is it leaving me? Have I come to this high, pale, empty room in order to watch my life die? Or to watch my life become insane? I would take suicide pills tonight if I were "real" enough to know what they are, what I should ask for at the pharmacy. I don't know the name of these pills, I've never even taken sleeping pills; I wouldn't know how many suicide pills to take.

My life—my "unreal" but veritable life—has been a succession of miracles which I can barely remember tonight. But they were there—operating in a personal universe created by my relationship with Georgette, Jane, and Dorothy; we four at different intervals lived a reality of our own, unknown and unchallenged by the world around us. Now even Bébé has disappeared from that world—the day came when I had to have him put to sleep.... I couldn't bring him to a hotel.... I took him to a vet who loved him and gave him a *calmement* [tranquilizer] before the *piqûre* [injection], so that he would feel nothing. But this act was too much for me. My knees trembled so that I couldn't drive the car, I had to take him in a taxi to the vet's office. Bébé—my little black cat who trusted me thought I was strong, I thought I could stand it, I thought I could pack up my life and my things and come to live in a hotel room where I would be protected from fears. I needed no protection from loneliness; I have never been lonely—I have had Georgette and Jane and Dorothy to remember. We lived as other people don't live and they continued to live with me in the Chalet Rose. Therefore, I had never known boredom or loneliness or desperation or mindlessness.

The end was approaching and Margaret seemed to know that. Despite all, she wrote to Solita, her "Sweetie," until the very end. In the middle of August 1973, a letter was delivered to Solita in

Orgeval addressed with the familiar large and bold handwriting, but now not quite as large or bold.

Said Margaret, "I prefer to stay on in this room until my heart stops beating. I can work a little, see my useful friends from New York and London. Then I shall be willing to die. I don't want to prolong my life."

"Your *unbelievable* letter," wrote Solita, "just here. My heart stopped twice. Your prediction of death (oh, no!! Not yet—I refuse your pessimism, your 'logic'.) Your physical state as you recount it makes me sob and sob. *You,* my beautiful one ... *No ...* And how beautifully you state your thoughts, you who say you cannot write! You can write all right. And you do."

Margaret had called her at Orgeval and Solita wrote, "The reason I did not speak to you on the telephone was because I was afraid I would cry. Your letter broke down any possible concealment of my concern for your being so ill and one of the most painful aspects that haunts me is that it's my fault that you were allowed to go far from us to live. We could have sedated you, put manacles on your wrists and locked all the doors (from *the outside, of course*)."

A week later another letter. "You said you could come in September," wrote Margaret. "Come. Come, soon as possible. Minute by minute I am dying—no one realizes."

Solita was in very fragile health and could not go.

Another letter in mid-September. "I no longer dare to walk across the street for my papers and magazines—I stop breathing." Fortunately, she had found a clinic that cost not much more than the hotel and, as she said, "I shall even have a bathroom of my own!" She found the situation "grotesque" but "we shall not treat it as a tragedy. I shall continue as if it were the opposite."

In September Solita wrote: "Dear Martie, what is there to say? I live on agony, despair, whiskey and sleeping pills. You think you are dying: you are tied to a bed. I know I shall die this year and I'm tied to a house. *I cannot get to you*—at least not yet. Can I ever? The nurses say you are better. But you know best? Oh darling, my Martie, how can these 'facts' be true? I live in a fantastic nightmare."

And on October 17th she wrote these last lines to Solita: "i must never spend anoyjer [another] like this one. i am dying and the head nurse will pay no attention. i can't breathe. the agony is so terrible that i must write it."

And with that, on October 17, 1973, Margaret Anderson, eighty-seven years of age, drew her last breath. She died of emphysema. Margaret would have truly delighted in the fact that the *New York Times,* with which she had fought over the years, still didn't get it right. Its obituary reported that Margaret Carolyn Anderson, eighty-two years old, died on October 20, 1973.

As Solita wrote to Margaret's sister Jean: "Long *long* suffering. No religious service. No cremation. Buried as arranged years ago in [a] plot (Le Cannet) with Georgette and Monique—three names, one stone. Many flowers, several friends from London, articles in the *New York Times, Time* Magazine."

On June 3, 1974, *The New Yorker* published an essay, "A Life on a Cloud: Margaret Anderson" by Janet Flanner.

> She was the born enemy of convention and discipline—a feminine romantic rebel with an appetite for Chopin and for indiscriminate reading. But conversation was her real passion. She had early the visionary conviction that only artists were capable of stimulating talk, and that she would be better off dead than failing to be a listener to such talk, if she could just find it.... Her visible beauty enveloped a will of tempered steel, specifically at its most resistant when she was involved in argument, which was her favorite form of intellectual exercise, as I, who knew her for many years, can attest.... One of the things that made Margaret insupportable to other women of spirit was a belief she had developed in her own infallibility, which, of course, made her unbearable.... Her nature was so solid that it reduced Margaret to the two opposite elements always uppermost in her own personality—violent agreement and violent disagreement, both accompanied by characteristic spirals of her taunting laughter. She meant to taunt no one, however, as her nature was affectionate, but she had a split mentality, based on her addiction to argument.... In her *The Fiery Fountains* she unexpectedly became an invaluable writer on

the emotions. She writes on the classifications of love, on the varieties of love, on romantic love, on amity, on perfections of friendship, furnishing an extremely interesting and rare analysis of these states of feeling. In a section subtitled "The Art of Love," she remarks with aphoristic felicity, "In real love you want the other person's good. In romantic love you want the other person."

Janet concluded the essay with what Margaret had written in *The Fiery Fountains* as the final summation of her life:

> I wonder why I have wanted to write this story of my life. I know it at first hand, but so incompletely that it has little meaning. It has been so happy and so sad, as happy as flowers, as sad as moonlight—a happy life that loves the saddest music. It has been a striving and a failing; a development and a diminution; it has been proud, and egotistic, and modest; aggressive and unassuming; alert and unconscious; hopeful and, I fear, lost. It has overflowed with thankfulness and remorse—a life like any other, but which has seemed to me so different, so special, and so blessed as to be unique. The blessings I wanted were love and music, books and great ideas and beauty of environment. I have had them all, and to a degree beyond asking, even beyond my imagining.

Two years after Margaret's death, Solita Solano, age eighty-eight, died at Orgeval on November 22, 1975. Janet Flanner, age eighty-six, died in New York on November 7, 1978. Kathryn Hulme, age eighty-one, the last of the Rope, the special women's group Gurdjieff created, died on Kauai on August 25, 1981.

Before she died, Kathryn Hulme, Gurdjieff's "Kroko-*deel,*" had written, "Life has been bleak since my lines to Solita, Lib, Martie and Jannie went dead. Gurdjieff used to tell us, 'I pity you, when you no longer can sit at my table. Such suffering you will have....' (Starvation for his ideas was what he was talking about.) Go down the scale a few octaves, and the same thing can be said (or could have been said) by Solita and Martie ... and Jannie from another kind of table.... Starvation is a many-faced malady."

Epilogue

I
T IS NOW SOME SIXTY YEARS SINCE THE GROUP OF WOMEN
WHO WERE TO FORM THE NUCLEUS OF THE ROPE FIRST MET
every Monday evening at Jane Heap's apartment in Montparnasse. The lives they lived have long passed, and yet through their
books and their archived material they continue to speak to us of
themselves, their questions and difficulties, triumphs and failures,
and, most importantly, for those interested in the teaching of the
Fourth Way, their work with Mr. Gurdjieff.

Reflections of how hard Gurdjieff pushed and challenged them,
how intimately he worked with them, still live in the record of the
many luncheons and dinners together and the trips they took with
him to Vichy, Cannes, Lascaux and elsewhere. What we may make
of this is for each one of us to ponder and work with. Respecting
that, this author would now like to offer some of his own impressions and interpretations, not in any attempt to persuade but rather
to probe, to engage and to challenge, the material.

For those not familiar with Gurdjieff's method of teaching—
he often warned it should not be imitated—his treatment of the
Rope, how he called them "dirty" and often spoke of *merde*[1] (see
"Personas and Inner Animal" in the appendix) is sure to offend on
paper now as once it did in person. Why would these intelligent
and gifted women put up with such coarseness? Why would Miss

Gordon, Solita and Kathryn and Alice and Louise go on with a reading of an unintelligible manuscript far into the night, night after night? Why would Solita continue a relationship with a man who had her wait for him for two hours in a café to which he never intended to come? Why would Margaret subject herself to such personal humiliation at his hands and yet return again the next day for more of the same?

Psychologists would no doubt shrink and frame Gurdjieff's actions within the compass of ordinary psychological terms, but that is to miss, grossly, the gold of the moment. The women's love for and loyalty to the man they recognized as their teacher, the magnetic bond he established with each of them—this is the silent stream, the living radiant heart in which all interaction waxes and wanes. It is the very substance of the moment, its living immediacy. The *real* food Gurdjieff served at his daily luncheons and dinners was prepared in Being. The role he might play, his words, his actions—these were its mere surface reflections. The deep nourishment was in the substance. To identify with his machinations, to be put "in galoshes," as he said, immediately disconnected heart from head, cut one's lifeline to the living silence of the real world.

The teacher trying to trap his students into identification, the students working not to identify, to remain free of their reactions—that was part of the taxing, frustrating, maddening and ingenious conditions Gurdjieff created. The teaching he brought is not a way of devotion but of self-development, of conscience and understanding. What is being developed is *individuality* in the real meaning of that term—one who forges within the integrity to withstand the heat of opposites, the "yes" and the "no" that keep one a slave of psychic and vital forces. What Gurdjieff offered at his table was the active manifestation of Divine Love,

---

1. Gurdjieff used this word not just with the Rope but with everyone. Previously, he had used the word "fertilizer," but then after he studied the American language he changed the word to "shit," as it was, he said, "real ... an honestly expressive word that gave the proper flavor of that particular human condition." See Fritz Peters' *Gurdjieff Remembered*, p. 24.

offered in so outrageous or offensive an outward form that only a fundamental discrimination could separate. "I wish you do not like *merde,*" once Gurdjieff explained to the Rope, "so I first make you feel like *merde,* only from there can one begin."

But what of Gurdjieff himself? Why would he accept these women as students? There can be no question that his viewpoint regarding questions of gender and sexuality was rooted in Tradition. What then of the Rope? Perhaps there is a clue at the very beginning of its formation. Gurdjieff, at dinner with Solita, Kathryn and Louise, mentioned he was planning to start a new group and that they would be its nucleus. The women, of course, were overjoyed. Gurdjieff quickly cut short with, "You very dirty...." But then he added, "...but have something very good—many people not got—very special."

Solita began to cry.

"Must not cry."

"But I must," she answered

"Must—but must not."

Have something very good—many people not got—very special. To what, exactly, is he referring?

The answer may lie in the life of Madame Vitvitskaïa, the most memorable female portrayed in all his writings, and the only woman to become a Seeker After Truth. Of Polish origin, very beautiful, with "kind, honest eyes, which sometimes became diabolically cunning," Vitvitskaïa developed into a woman "remarkable in every aspect" and who could serve as "an ideal for every woman."

And yet Vitvitskaïa had lived an early life that had brought her to "the brink of moral ruin." At Gurdjieff's first sight of her he said there was aroused in him "a dual feeling towards her—now of hate, now of pity." Simply in hearing her life story, Gurdjieff felt" something like hatred for this "worthless woman." It seemed to him that "the Thaïs of history must have been such a type.[2] There was no helping such a person, and he quoted a Russian proverb— "What falls from the wagon is lost!"

The early death of Vitvitskaïa's mother, followed by the death of her father when she was fourteen, and the impoverishing circumstances which ensued, had resulted in her becoming the mistress of an old senator in St. Petersburg. Later, descending still further into this type of life, she worked for a doctor, walking the grand boulevard of the Nevsky, using her great beauty to lure admirers into following her back to the doctor's office where, in the hopes of meeting her, they would become his patients. She was about to be sold into the white slave trade, when Prince Yuri Lubovedsky[3] rescued her.

The Prince, Gurdjieff's great friend, told him that despite the life she had led Vitvitskaïa's "nature was unspoiled and that she had many excellent qualities" and so he had decided "to put her on the right path." He asked Gurdjieff to accompany her from Constantinople to his estate in Russia where both he and his sister would work to bring her under a higher influence. In time the subconscious depression she felt over the life she had lived lifted. Her interest grew in the esoteric ideas which had helped her and she began work on herself in earnest.

Four years later, by chance, Gurdjieff and Vitvitskaïa met again. The change in her was so remarkable that while Gurdjieff felt he knew her, he could not place her and had to ask her who she was. Vitvitskaïa told him—

"I am the person whom you once so hated that the flies which came into the sphere of the radiations of your hate perished."

Her work on herself had been so earnest that Gurdjieff said, "one could feel the result of that work."

Within a year, Gurdjieff said, she became "a permanent member" of the Seekers After Truth and as the now "inimitable and fearless Mme Vitvitskaïa ... [she] participated in all our perilous

2.   Thais is a semi-historical Athenian courtesan said to have accompanied Alexander the Great on his Asiatic campaign. (Thais, incidentally, is one of the roles Georgette played and for which she was famous.)

3.   Gurdjieff said of the Prince that he was "a man who, according to my notions, represents in contemporary conditions of life an ideal worthy of imitation."

expeditions into the depths of Asia, Africa and even Australia and its neighboring islands." Her work on herself had increased her vibration to a point that on these expeditions she "could discern at a distance of almost twenty miles the monuments [dolmens] indicating the direction of our route."[4] Where once she had "stood on the brink of moral ruin," now, Gurdjieff stated, she "might serve as the ideal for every woman." She was a woman who "had become sacred for us all," said Gurdjieff speaking for himself and the other Seekers After Truth. So sacred that when Gurdjieff believed, erroneously, that a fellow seeker had injured her he declared—"I wished to find out who the scoundrel was, in order, without dismounting and without words, to shoot him down like a partridge."[5]

While awaiting their last major expedition through the Pamir region and India, Gurdjieff and Vitvitskaïa came across one another on the same train but traveling to different destinations—Gurdjieff on his way to Ashkhabad to make money, Vitvitskaïa returning to Poland to rest. En route, they argued over how much money Gurdjieff could make in Ashkhabad[6]. The result was a wager: Gurdjieff had to make 12,500 rubles, an enormous sum of money,[7] within three months time. Gurdjieff said the wager so interested Vitvitskaïa that "she not only decided to

4. There is an interesting parallel here for Gurdjieff said in the *Third Series* that he could amass enough force in himself to kill a yak at the same distance. So, Vitvitskaïa can *see* and Gurdjieff can both *see* and *do* at incredible distances.

5. In terms of intensity and resort to violence there is an interesting parallel here with the artillery range "duel" he has with Karpenko in Kars as a young man.

6. Ashkhabad is one of the two major cities of Turkmenistan. It lies near the edge of the vast desert of Kara-Kum. Five miles north of the city is Tolkuchka Bazaar which today is the largest remaining outpost on the ancient Silk Road, the 8,000 mile necklace of trading centers that linked Europe and China for more than twenty centuries. It is at this bazaar, in all likelihood, that Gurdjieff set up his "Universal Travelling Workshop" which would repair, install, mend, remove, restore and stamp just about anything.

7. The sum represented "a real fortune," said Gurdjieff, as in those days, the salary of a Russian public official was thirty-three rubles thirty kopecks a month; a high-ranking officer, from forty-five to fifty rubles per month.

stay with me to see how I would fulfill it, but even undertook to help me." As for Gurdjieff, the task so involved him that it "fired [me] with a passionate obstinacy to carry it out whatever the consequences, and even to surpass the set conditions."

The two stayed together in Ashkhabad where with Vitvitskaïa's help, in the allotted time, Gurdjieff made 50,000 rubles—four times the amount of the wager. It was a super effort,[8] for which Vitvitskaïa, by first provoking and then helping him, acted as a catalyst, an archetypal role for women. The winning of the wager must have been a factor when Gurdjieff years later prepared for his momentous mission of bringing the teaching of the Fourth Way to the West and set himself the task of earning more than one million rubles to fund his mission—twenty times that earned in Ashkhabad!

A remarkable man, said Gurdjieff in *Meetings with Remarkable Men*, was "He who stands out from those around him by the resourcefulness of his mind, and who knows how to be restrained in the manifestation which proceed from his nature, at the same time *conducting himself justly and tolerantly towards the weaknesses of others.*" [Emphasis added] After Gurdjieff's extreme and negative initial reaction to Vitvitskaïa, her subsequent spiritual development may have helped to bring him to the understanding he expresses in the italicized part of his definition.

But his relationship with her may have brought him to an even deeper understanding. In the portrait he paints of Vitvitskaïa, there are two curious things that don't seem to fit, that stand out like inexactitudes. The first is that in *Meetings with Remarkable Men*—a book about men not in quotation marks, that is, *real*

8.   It should be pointed out that the intensity of purpose to which he had to commit to win the wager with Vitvitskaïa gave him an unexpected bonus. "During that period," he said, "a change in the functioning of my common presence took place, inexplicable from the standpoint of ordinary science and repeated more than once in the course of my life. There was a change in the regulation of the tempo of the in-coming and out-going of energy...." Did Vitvitskaïa play any part in this? Her primary interest, Gurdjieff told us, was in the science of music, or actually the science of vibrations because, as she told Gurdjieff, "the sounds of music are made up of certain vibrations which doubtless act upon the vibrations which are also in a man...."

men—he presents a woman, Vitvitskaïa. He must be telling us that in some way she is a man. But how? The second is that he said "she always dressed like a man." These two facts would seem to be connected but how to understand them? What is the context and criteria—the place of Gurdjieff's perception? We don't know. So we can only hope to reason more deeply with the material he gives us.

Certainly Vitvitskaïa did not dress so before meeting the Prince so it must refer to the period *after* she has worked on herself. For a woman to dress like a man in that time would certainly be to call blame upon themselves, make themselves objects of derision. One can understand her wearing men's clothes on expeditions—but why *always*?

Only three reasons, or some combination of them, seem possible. Perhaps she dressed so because it gave her power and entry to places from which she would otherwise be excluded. (Chopin's lover, the French writer Amandine Aurore Lucie Dupin, who adopted the *nom de plume* "George Sand," dressed as a man and even smoked cigars.) But this reason is entirely societal. Her development had passed well beyond that. Perhaps her dressing like a man (which today would be called "cross dressing") may have had to do with sexual identity: could she be bisexual or lesbian? If this is so, how is it that Gurdjieff speaks of her as being "an ideal for *every* woman"? [Emphasis added] Clearly, the sexual specificity of her being bisexual or lesbian would preclude her being an ideal for every woman. Lastly, perhaps Vitvitskaïa wanted to hide her beauty. She no longer sought, or needed, the ordinary sexual vibrations her beauty would have elicited from men. Or, could it be that she wanted to call blame to herself as an act of penance for her earlier life and a way of remembering herself. But this "acting otherwise" is specific to an early stage of self-transformation.

The first two reasons, given the objections stated, are unsatisfactory. Only with the third—dressing as a man so as not to attract sexual attention—is there promise of deeper insight. Together with this fact let us remember that Vivitskaïa's great interest and area of experimentation was the vibratory effect of music. She speaks to Gurdjieff about this so sincerely that he says, "Each of her words was so strongly imprinted on my brain that it seems to me I hear her at this moment." Gurdjieff then told her of how, during a stay among the Essenes, "by means of very ancient Hebraic music and songs they had made plants grow in half an hour, and I described [to her] in detail how they had done this. She became so fascinated by my story that her cheeks even burned. The result of our conversation was that we agreed that as soon as we returned to Russia we would settle down in some town where, without being disturbed by anyone, we could really seriously carry out experiments with music. Unfortunately, Vitvitskaïa died beforehand in Russia "from a cold she caught while on a trip on the Volga." Catching a cold disrupts, of course, one's breathing and a river is a symbol of the river of life which in one's person is represented by the spinal column. The word "volga" in Russian means sacred or holy.

In the context we are now considering let us return to the first "inexactitude" that struck us—that Vitvitskaïa, a woman, is part of a book about remarkable men, men who have consciously become active. This is the context in which the remark about her dressing occurs. Perhaps the deep reason Gurdjieff tells us she wears men's clothes is to indicate that she has developed to a point where she no longer identifies herself in terms of gender and its attendant worldly sexuality, but rather as a Seeker After Truth. In this way, Vitvitskaïa can certainly be an ideal for all women, for she is the highest of all types of women—a woman without quotation marks.

When Gurdjieff met Solita Solano, Kathryn Hulme and Louise Davidson he might easily have judged them as he had once judged the Vitvitskaïa he first met... but this time, like the Prince, Gurdjieff would not hate and pity but instead see that *their natures were unspoiled and that they had many excellent qualities.* ✗

Notes

INTRODUCTION

xi *Numbers.* The third sex represents itself as comprising 10% of the US population, or some 25 million of 250 million population. However, according to a *Time* magazine study, the percentage of homosexuals and lesbians is 1.8% to 2% or about 10 million. This is only a little higher than the seven and a half million given in the textbook *Our Sexuality* by Robert Crooks and Karla Baur (Benjamin Cummings Publishing, Redwood City, California, 1993).

xi *Societal silence.* John Boswell, in his Introduction to *Same-Sex Unions in Premodern Europe* (Villard Books, New York, 1994), points out that "the vast majority of premodern historical sources were written by men, for men, about men; women figure in them either as property or as objects of sexual desire. Women who chose to form and maintain permanent unions with other women fell in neither of these categories.... Most male writers probably did not regard lesbianism as worth worrying about.... The disproportion reverses itself from the late Middle Ages on, as male writers who were more and more disturbed by the possibility of male homosexuality found it less threatening to describe lesbian relationships." With the exception of Sappho and a few others, lesbianism, when written about at all, was written about by men.

xi *Changing times.* In the June 19, 1998, edition of the *San Francisco Chronicle*, its society columnist notes that "Architect Maria Dolores McVarish and business partner Deborah Ann Chaisty (they own buildings together) became partners for life June 13."

xi *Sign of the times.* The nexus of the dispute is moving from societal discrimination to legitimacy. Long seen as a disease, its origin debated in terms of nature or nurture, the third sex is seen more and more as being genetic. If genetic, and in the great majority of cases this seems more likely, then it is not a question of choice, but of being born so. The place and legitimacy of the third sex within society is a question that only society can answer. The deeper question is, of course, what is the criteria is to be used in terms of ascertaining legitimacy. The debate seems to have not yet reached this point.

PROLOGUE

1 *Prieuré.* It was purchased on September 31, 1922.

3 *Prehistoric Egypt.* See *Telos,* volume 2, issues 2, 3, and 4.

4 *Embryo of the group.* It is not clear when Jane Heap began to teach. Some say as early as 1927 but, as she was still in America then, that date seems unlikely. In any case, it is documented that she was teaching in 1930.

THE FIRST GROWL

8 *The Cordon.* The meaning of the word is "rope." Interesting that many years later the women who had been in Jane Heap's study group would also take that name.

12 *Life story.* Jane Heap's comments to Georgette in regard to Maeterlinck are sourced. See References.

12 *Types of love.* Gurdjieff had first spoken of these types of love to A. R. Orage at the Prieuré. Orage later wrote an essay, "On Love."

12 *Idea and experience of love.* For Gurdjieff's ideas about love see *All and Everything, First Series,* pp. 198, 309–1, 321, 355, 358, 361, 566, 568. Especially see the "objective impulse of Divine-Love," pp. 124, 370; and "resplendent Love, concerning the teaching of Jesus Christ," p. 702.

13 *Janet Flanner's pregnancy.* She either miscarried or aborted the birth. She said she thought heterosexual sex "vulgar."

15 *Salita and Solita.* The beginning of her first name "Sal" in Spanish means salt; the second, "Sol," sun. "Solita" also means "alone," something that Gurdjieff would later tell her.

19 *Jessie Anderson.* Margaret's attitude toward her mother is so extreme it would be interesting to know how her other two sisters viewed their mother.

19 *Arthur Anderson.* Not only did Margaret revere her father but her sister Lois did as well, naming her son "Arthur Peters," later nicknamed "Fritz," after her father.

21 *Theodore Dreiser.* Margaret's comments about Dreiser show how she regarded men like him and "sex display."

31 *Djuna Barnes.* She had been largely raised by her father's mother, Zadel, Djuna's own mother favoring her sons. Wald, the father, was too preoccupied with bedding all the local woman to pay much attention to any of his offspring. Both Zadel and Wald championed free love as a means for remedying poverty and increasing social stability. Humans were animals and animals were not sexually exclusive, they preached. And they practiced it. At the age of sixteen either Djuna's father himself, or a neighbor with the father's consent, had violently raped her. Understandably, it put a rage in Djuna that never died. Zadel harbored equally novel ideas. From early childhood, fearing her father's strange ways, Djuna had looked to Grandmother Zadel for emotional support. Zadel, in her sixties, welcomed the child into her bed, where they slept together for the next fifteen years. The many sexually explicit letters and drawings that Grandmother Zadel was to write Djuna strongly suggest incest; if so, a very rare form. More certain is that Djuna was bisexual. She once said she would make love to a horse if it interested her. When she met Margaret and Jane she was still on the mend from a torrid two-year affair with six-foot-four Ernst "Putzi" Hanfstaengl. She had expected to marry him but he returned to Germany telling her he couldn't marry a non-German. Putzi later became Hitler's secretary. For a more detailed picture, see Phillip Herring's *Djuna: The Life and Work of Djuna Barnes.*

32 *Margaret Anderson and Conversation.* Janet Flanner would later say of her, Margaret had "a will of tempered steel, specifically at its most resistant when she was involved in argument, which was her favorite form of intellectual exercise... conversation was her real passion." See Brenda Wineapple's *Genêt: A Biography of Janet Flanner,* p. 320.

32 *Djuna Barnes and Jane Heap.* Apparently Djuna's affair with Jane did not go well, for she complained that as a lover Jane wanted to include other women. See Phillip Herring's *Djuna,* p. 127.

NEW YORK, PARIS & THE PRIEURÉ

47 *Gertrude Stein.* The question which most interested her was "identity" which is central to the Fourth Way teaching. She met Gurdjieff once.

49 *Hemingway as heartsick.* Whether Margaret was speaking of herself as the object of his affections, or of Lady Duff Twysden, the woman who was the model for Lady Brett Ashley in Hemingway's novel *The Sun Also Rises* is unclear.

45 *Olgivanna Ivanovna Hinzenberg.* She would later marry the architect Frank Lloyd Wright. She remained a devoted follower of Gurdjieff all her life. When her husband died in 1959, she became the head of his architectural school, Taliesin.

59 *Lois' new husband.* In Margaret's extended letter blaming Lois' husband for what she calls her sister's "insanity," she gives an intimate portrait of how she views a certain type of man.

60 *Jane and Fritz.* When Jane and the two boys had returned to New York in the winter of 1925, Jane had enrolled them both in a private school. Later, in Peters' autobiographical novel *Finistère,* the principal character Matthew Cameron—young, impressionable and needing love—is seduced by Michel, a school teacher. Was Fritz at the Prieuré trying to influence other children in this way? If he was, given Gurdjieff's strong traditional perspective, Gurdjieff would have been the first to get rid of him. If not true, why would Jane blacken the boy's name with such a serious and damming accusation? Was it revenge? Projection? And where was Margaret in

all this? Why didn't she speak up? Why didn't Fritz appeal to her? Did he see her as so wrapped up in her own life that she would have no empathy for his dilemma. It was a puzzle and remains so.

CREATION OF THE ROPE

77 *Alice's car.* It is unclear why Alice would want to sell her Citroën. She and Kathryn had just arrived from America and, presumably, either had brought the car with them or had it garaged in Paris from a previous trip. In any event, they either wanted to buy another car or planned to take trains.

82 *Meeting Gurdjieff.* His meeting Kathryn and Alice at the Café de la Paix, inviting them to spend the night at the Prieuré, and then disappearing the next morning shows that he had no intention of forming a ladies-only group at this time. It would seem that his meeting with Solita in the autumn of 1934 was the catalyst.

83 *Tippy and Margaret.* Sometime after the letter episode, Margaret convinced Tippy to go with her on holiday to Vienna. Despite Margaret's ardor and argument, the actress managed to stay out of her bed which, of course, to Margaret, only made the chase all the more interesting. Margaret's later novella *Forbidden Fires* fictionalizes her great unrequited love for Tippy. It is interesting that Margaret, always a dominating presence, was attracted to Jane, Tippy and Georgette, women who all dominated in their own way. Only with Dorothy Caruso was she attracted to the mothering quality of which she had been so deprived as a child.

85 *Going to Gurdjieff's hotel room.* This invitation must have put Kathryn in "galoshes," as it would most women. That she was a lesbian perhaps made it even more a threat. Of course nothing happened. But it can be seen that Gurdjieff immediately ascertained a seeker's degree of interest with a test.

86 *The toasting to Idiots.* The toasts were said to rarely go beyond the first nine Idiots and often ended earlier. Still, this is a lot of drinking, especially as Gurdjieff demanded that the Armagnac not be sipped but be drunk "honestly." That is, at a single draught. [See *First Series*, p. 46] No doubt it was difficult to stay present when the body

had to absorb a series of alcoholic shocks to its system. It demanded a vigilant attention and discrimination. It was also a quick method of seeing people's mechanicality and inner animal.

89 *Emanations and radiations.* The definition of these two words sometimes differs in Gurdjieff literature. Here, emanate is a vibration everyone gives off. Radiate is a refined vibration which is the result of long work on oneself.

91 *Time and Good and Evil.* In working with Solita and the group, Gurdjieff specifically had them read chapters 16 and 34 of the *First Series*, "The Relative Understanding of Time" and "In the Opinion of Beelzebub, Man's Understanding of Justice Is for Him in the Objective Sense an Accursed Mirage." One of his aims in having them read these chapters perhaps is to counter their feeling of, as Solita expressed it, "I'm too old to begin this work—it's too late," and also that being "dirty" does not mean being evil.

95 *Gurdjieff's Definition of "I."* This is actually a much more precise definition than Xenophon's. It includes the relativity, the non-permanence, of the "I." Without recognizing the relativity of the "I", a stability is assumed which makes all such definitions, and the systems derived from them, false. Ouspensky quotes Gurdjieff as having introduced the concept of man being many "I"s in Russia in 1915–16 (and Gurdjieff likely spoke about it when he first arrived in 1912). In the 1920s the psychologist William James validated this concept for himself through the use of drugs. It may be that he heard about the idea from someone who knew Gurdjieff. Of course, the idea is ancient and is also given in the statement by Jesus Christ in the *New Testament* that "Man's name is legion."

95 *Gurdjieff's birthday.* By our current calendar, the Gregorian, established in 1592 by Pope Gregory XIII, his birthday is 12 days *ahead* of the older Julian calendar. As to the year of his birth, there is no general agreement. Gurdjieff said it was 1877, some put it earlier at 1866. Madame de Hartmann, his personal secretary and the person he called "the first friend of his inner life," said it was 1872, as did Louise March, who also acted as his secretary, and J. G. Bennett. After a careful examination of the facts as Gurdjieff

gives them in his *Meetings With Remarkable Men*, this author, independently, came to the 1872 date. For the reasoning, see my *Struggle of the Magicians*, pp. 273–74.

100 *High sex.* Laziness of organism is associated with prostitution. "High sex" is never explained and intonation is not given but, given his other comments, sarcasm was likely.

111 *Active element.* Solita noted that "Since I have come to you, even bones in hands are changed. Everyone has noticed I no longer have the same hands." Because of her opening to Gurdjieff and her doing the exercises he gave her, a new life had arisen within her.

113 *Nicolai Stjoernval.* According to Nicolai he is not Dr. Stjoernval's son, but Gurdjieff's.

116 *Heptaparaparshinokh.* A fundamental cosmic sacred Law. Gurdjieff said that present-day objective cosmic science formulates it as: "the-line-of-the-flow-of-forces-constantly-deflecting-according-to-law-and uniting-again at-its-ends."

119 *Butter and Miss Gordon.* Much later, after Miss Gordon had died, Solita reminded Gurdjieff of how he had tortured Miss Gordon about the butter he used on those baked potatoes. He smiled and said gently, "Even she believed me."

120 *Dionne quintuplets.* While the Dionne quintuplets were an act of nature, modern drugs make these "miracle births" much more common. Gurdjieff was also against mixed marriages as he said, "Mixed blood gives less chance of individuality." Presumably, the idea is that the blood of various races has different qualities, tempos, and that a mixture of such makes spiritual development, coming to one's true individuality, that much more difficult.

124 *Margaret's impudence.* In reading Solita's notes of the luncheons with Gurdjieff years later, Margaret said that she was "much perturbed by this completely false, and certainly unauthorized, report of my reactions. I said I realized I had been stupid; I could never *feel* (let alone *know, realize*) that I had been impudent. Everyone knew my reverence for Gurdjieff. I could never even imagine I could have been impudent to him. Such was my 'idiocy' in those days.... And ever after, I suppose."

DANCING WITH DEATH

131 *Electricity.* For Gurdjieff's ideas on this subject see the *First Series*, chapter 35, "In the Opinion of Beelzebub, Man's Extraction of Electricity from Nature and Its Destruction During Its Use, Is One of the Chief Causes of the Shortening of the Life of Man."

132 *Frank Lloyd Wright.* In June 1934 Gurdjieff had visited Wright and Olgivanna at Taliesin (The Shining Brow), their 1000-acre estate in Spring Green, Wisconsin. Said Wright after Gurdjieff's death, "In the work of this remarkable man ... we have for the first time a philosopher distinguished from all the others; a man ... sacrificing much during his life time to make the ancient wisdom of the East not only intelligible to the thought of the West but to make it a way of *Work.*"

143 *Man is man.* That, in terms of the body, we cannot be other than we are but that we can "educate our mind and with this control his animal body and not be its slave" is seminal in Gurdjieff's teaching. That a great struggle will ensue "is good thing, it makes for more struggle."

144 *Solita's Notes.* There of course could be many reasons why her notes end in March 1938, but one reason may be that the work had become too personal to be reported.

140 *Corset.* Gurdjieff likely wore a corset to help him with abdominal pain due to illnesses which he suffered from the numerous "local delicacies" he picked up on his many travels. These "delicacies" may also be the reason for his frequent drinking. What is not generally noted by his biographers is the great physical strain he was under from the exotic illnesses he had contracted in his travels, the three bullet-wounds he had endured, and several auto crashes.

148 *I am cynic.* According to *The Cambridge Dictionary of Philosophy* (Cambridge University Press, 1995) the cynic is "the classical Greek philosophical school which is characterized by asceticism and an emphasis on the sufficiency of virtue for happiness (*eudaimonia*), boldness in speech, and shamelessness in action. The Cynics were strongly influenced by Socrates and were themselves an

important influence on Stoic ethics." One of its most famous exponents is Diogenes of Sinope (400-325 B.C.) who is reported to have carried a lighted lamp in broad daylight looking for an honest man. He was called a Cynic, from the Greek word *kuon* (dog) because he was thought to be as shameless as a dog.

THE MAGUS DEPARTS

174 *Göring's Profile.* Like her earlier profile of Hitler some ten years before, Janet's coverage showed again her uncanny ability to connect the surface that life presented with its depths. Her portrayal of Göring in the dock and his astonishing, funny and shrew twenty-one hour defense he mounted of his and the Third Reich's actions was matchless. "He undeniably looked the bravura personality," she said, "in his vast, sagging, dove-colored jacket and his matching voluminous breeches, with his fine, high maroon boots and his maroon neckerchief, and above it his hard, blue eyes and what is left of the familiar fleshiness of his mobile, theatrical face...What he offered his judges was no *mea culpa* but a dissertation on the technique of power. On the witness stand, he didn't wait to be asked questions by the Allied prosecution; he told them the German answers first. The Reichsmarschall made Machiavelli's Prince look like a dull apologist; Goring was decidedly more amoral, and funnier. The horrifying weakness in everything he said was that it took no account of the destruction it had caused in other men's or nations' lives. What he offered, essentially, was the Teutonic fallacy that the divine right of kings, which used to be limited to one individual, had been bestowed upon the entire German nation, which was therefore free to do anything to anybody." See *Janet Flanner's World,* pp. 114–115.

177 *Gertrude Stein's will.* Written the month Gertrude died, her will stipulated that Carl Van Vechten was to receive whatever moneys he should need to assure publication of her unpublished manuscripts. The remainder of her estate was to be left to Alice B. Toklas "to her use for life ... insofar as it may become necessary for her proper maintenance and support." Upon her death, the collection was to go to Allan Stein, only child of Gertrude's oldest brother, Michael, and

then pass to his children. Permission for the sale of any of the art works was to be obtained from the executor appointed by the Baltimore court who, it turned out, was the great-nephew of Edgar Allan Poe. The executor sent Alice the least allowance he could and not always regularly. In 1951 Allan Stein died and, now upon Alice's death, his children were the inheritors of Gertrude's art collection. Stein's wife Roubina kept a vigil on the paintings for her children. In 1954 Alice, desperate for money and without informing the executor, sold forty Picasso drawings. Seven years later when Alice returned home from Italy, where she took an annual mud-bath cure for arthritis, she found her walls empty. Roubina had found out about the sale of the drawings and gotten a court order to have the paintings taken from Alice's apartment and stored in a Paris bank vault. When Alice, almost ninety, who spent her last years bedridden, partially deaf and almost blind, died on March 7, 1967, a major selection of the collection was sold to the Museum of Modern Art (a museum which Gertrude and Alice unequivocally hated) for $6.5 million, the proceeds going to Allan Stein's children. See *Janet Flanner's World*, "Memory is All: Alice B. Toklas," pp. 339–342.

186 *Idiocy and Madame de Salzmann.* Louise March, once Gurdjieff's secretary, quotes Gurdjieff in her book *The Gurdjieff Years*, p. 76, as saying that Madame de Salzmann was the only person "going out of idiocy." This is odd in that Gurdjieff said that everyone has an Idiot. He may have meant that at the higher levels of idiocy one becomes an individual Idiot, such as Gurdjieff, who said he was a Unique Idiot.

187 *Gurdjieff and Solita.* Early on when Solita worked with Gurdjieff in Paris he told her, "And you must see what your old friends are like. No one who liked you before must like you now— must hate you. Your friends all are special *merde*. Seeing their *merdeness* will help you see your own." Later, Gurdjieff told Solita, "I know you give me all your heart. Soon you must decide if all give up in world." He is acknowledging she has given him *all* her heart—but this is not enough. More was at stake, more was demanded. Could it be that Gurdjieff was asking her to give up her lesbian practices? If so, like A. R. Orage with Jessie Dwight, she couldn't give up the "love" of

a woman for a higher, objective love? Gurdjieff said to Solita at one point: "Also another constatation I make. Something wrong your sex. Sex very important thing is, like light, like air you breathe, food you eat. If you are in five parts, two of your five parts depend from sex. You must more normal live." Answered Solita: "Cannot even think about such things. I do not wish, I have no time. In twenty-four hours I have only four hours for myself and I must use them for sleeping." Answered Gurdjieff—"Then lopsided you will be and I can nothing do, for this depends only from you." Of all the women of the Rope, it would seem that Solita had the greatest possibility. That he confronts her in this way is only because in her long and close work with him she had developed to a point where this could be said. But understandably this is such a charged issue for Solita that she can't even think of it. Is this, at heart, the reason why Solita's notes stop so abruptly in New York and why she waits until the end to come to Paris? Another possibility is that there may have been some tension between her and Madame de Salzmann, Gurdjieff's new secretary.

185 *Poor little girl story.* Hulme puts the event after she returned from seeing her mother. Louise March, however, puts the telling of the story on Gurdjieff's birthday. Inasmuch as there were so many children present, March's dating seems more likely. See *The Gurdjieff Years: 1929–1949*, pp. 83–84.

WORKING WITH LIFE

201 *Janet Flanner as a writer.* Mary McCarthy, the novelist and a friend of Janet's, said of Janet as writer. "One couldn't be an intense admirer of Prime Minister Mendès and of de Gaulle at the same time. Janet regarded these men as if they were actors, saw these people as if they were stars, in which case there would be no conflict between liking one and another. But this is not on the highest intellectual level and helped keep Janet a journalist." See *Genêt* p. 247

202 *Janet Flanner's relationships.* She was able to maintain these with Solita, Noel, and Natalie, no doubt, because as a foreign correspondent she was able to travel easily. After the war, Janet continued to make Paris her home base so she could visit Noel in Orgeval whenever she was there. Natalie had long since moved back to New York

from Rome, always urging Janet to spend more time there. In 1953, a possible complication to their relationship developed when Natalie took a job as press agent for the volatile and sensuous Italian actress Anna Magnani. The following year, when Magnani was cast in the film depiction of Tennessee Williams' *The Rose Tattoo*, Natalia accompanied her to Hollywood. An affair between them seems likely. Five years later, when Magnani arrived in New York to star in the film *Orpheus Descending* (later retitled *The Fugitive Kind*), Natalie urged Janet to write a profile on Anna. Needless to say, Janet did not.

204 *Lesbianism.* Margaret gave an interesting summation of her perception of herself as a lesbian. In a letter to Jane Heap, April 1936, (see *Forbidden Fires*, p. 17) she wrote:

> As I grew up I never felt that my position in love involved any sexual confusion. I realized that I was in the minority but I was already accustomed to the idea of the important minority in all major concerns of life—I had always known that the majority was wrong. My situation seemed to me unique. There was nothing masculine about me from bracelets to ruffles. I suppose "Androgyny" covers the condition I am describing. I can feel like a child, a girl, a boy, or a man, but I cannot feel like a woman. I haven't the remotest connection with this alien race. The need I understand is to bestow passion to receive tenderness.
>
> I have never spoken these words to any human being, for one reason because it is inconceivable to me that anyone could love me as much as I love "them."

209 *Audrey Hepburn.* Filming *The Nun's Story* took Audrey to Africa, which made such and impact on her that after she retired from her career, she devoted herself to working for UNESCO and, on its behalf, often visiting Africa.

215 *The Nun's Story.* It was a big box office success. It's $14 million gross was the highest up to that time for any of Warner Brothers' films.

THE ROPE'S LAST DAYS

223 *Isak Dinesen.* Born Karen Christentze Dinesen, by marriage to the Swedish Baron Bror von Blixen-Finecke she had become Bar-

oness Karen Blixen. Upon returning from Kenya in 1931, she took her maiden name of Dinesen and added a masculine pseudonym. She had fallen in love with a second cousin of hers, Hans Bror Blixen. He being uninterested, she married his brother Bror. The two went to Kenya to manage a coffee plantation, thus she eluded—like Margaret, Solita, Alice and Janet Flanner (though Janet was escaping from Indianapolis at large)—a stifling family environment. Her new husband, having many liaisons, became infected with syphilis and passed it on to his wife. Though the disease was treated, she ever after suffered its effects. Her condition became known only after her death. Hannah Arendt wrote of the young woman's arrogant self-will in her forward to Dinesen's *Daguerreotypes and Other Essays* (University of Chicago Press, 1979) saying that in later life she became aware of her "'sin' of making a story come true, of interfering with life according to a preconceived pattern, instead of waiting patiently for the story to emerge." Dinesen had thought and written a great deal about human relationship and marriage in particular. While she believed that love had to be the basis of all genuine relationship, the unity that was thus formed had to be between a man and a woman. As she wrote in *Shadows on the Grass* (Random House, New York, 1961) p. 408:

> In order to form and make up a Unity, in particular a creative Unity, the individual components must needs be of different nature, they should even be in a sense contrasts. Two homogeneous units will never be capable of forming a whole, or their whole at its best will remain barren. Man and woman become one, a physically and spiritually creative Unity, by virtue of their dissimilarity. A hook and an eye are a Unity, a fastening; but with two hooks you can do nothing. A right-hand glove with its contrast the left-hand glove makes up a whole, a pair of gloves; but two right-hand gloves you throw away. A number of perfectly similar objects do not make up a whole—a couple of cigarettes may quite well be three or nine. A quarter is a Unity because it is made up of dissimilar instruments. An orchestra is a Unity, and may be perfect as such, but twenty double-bases striking up the same tune are Chaos.

That Solita would agree with this does not seem likely, but she may have felt more in concert with what Dinesen had written in her essay "Oration at a Bonfire, Fourteen Years Later." Wrote Dinesen: "A man's center of gravity, the substance of his being, consists in what he has executed and performed in life; the woman's, in what she is." In short, men have to do; women to be. See Dinesen's *Daguerreotypes and Other Essays*, p. 83.

224 *Meetings with Remarkable Men, the film.* In 1970 Kathryn met with Madame de Salzmann and her son Michel to discuss developing a film script for the book. Kathryn wrote a treatment but it was not used. Madame de Hartmann worked on a script until her death in 1979. The original idea was to make a film that would appeal to large numbers of people. Though the scenery was magnificent, as were many scenes such as the opening, those with Gurdjieff's father, and the Sarmoung, the editing of the film stripped it of all popular appeal and it was a failure at the box office, though it continues to have video store rentals. Peter Brook, a student of Madame de Salzmann's, directed the film which was released in 1979.

224 *"You don't have the talent for it."* Solita's judgment must have been terribly cutting, given Kathryn's accomplishments as writer of *The Wild Place* and *The Nun's Story.* It is wondered whether in the sub-text of what Solita was saying was embedded the idea that Kathryn had not attained a high enough level of understanding. The word "talent," then, actually meant something deeper.

246 *Other deaths.* Of those women close to the Rope, Elizabeth Jenks Clark would die in Narragansett, Rhode Island, in March 1989, and Marie-Louise Hâbets on the island of Kauai in 1991. Djuna Barnes died in New York on June 19, 1982. Nancy Cunard died in Paris in March 1965. ✗

Chronology

1869	February 8. Rouen, France. Georgette Leblanc born.
1872	January 13. Alexandropol, Russia. George Ivanovitch Gurdjieff born.
1874	February 3. Allegheny, Pennsylvania. Gertrude Stein born.
1876	October 31, Dayton, Ohio. Natalie Clifford Barney born.
1877	April 30. San Francisco. Alice B. Toklas born.
1879	February 12. Stanton, Michigan. Florence Reynolds, friend and lover of Jane Heap's, born.
1883	November 1. Kansas. Jane Heap born.
1885	Georgette Leblanc's mother dies.
	April 17. Isak Dinesen born.
1886	November 24. Youngstown, Ohio. Margaret Carolyn Anderson born. Eldest of three daughters.
1888	October 30. Troy, New York. Solita Solano (Sarah Wilkinson) born.
1892	March 13. Indianapolis, Indiana. Janet Flanner born.
	June 12. Cornwall-on-Hudson, New York. Djuna Barnes born.
1893	Paris. Georgette Leblanc sings Opéra Comique.
	August 6. New York. Dorothy Park Benjamin (Caruso) born.
1896	Nancy Cunard born.
1900	July 6. San Francisco. Kathryn Hulme born.
1901	Chicago. Jane Heap enrolls at the Lewis Institute.
1903	Solita Solano's father dies.
1904	Solita Solano elopes with Oliver Filley to the Philippines.
1905	January 14. Belgium. Marie-Louise Hâbets born.
1908	Fall. Margaret Anderson leaves home for Chicago.

269

New York. Solita Solano leaves her husband and moves from Malaysia to New York to make a living as an actress.

1910   Europe. Florence Reynolds and Jane Heap travel.

Solita Solano moves to Boston to work as a reporter.

1911   Paris. Georgette Leblanc acts in Maeterlinck's play *The Blue Bird.*

Renée Dahon, eighteen years old, gets a small part in the play and later moves in with Maeterlinck and Georgette.

1912   February 17. Indianapolis, Indiana. Frank Flanner, Janet's father, commits suicide.

1913   Chicago. Margaret Anderson appointed Book Editor of *Chicago Evening Post.*

Boston. Solita Solano's marriage annulled.

Madison, Wisconsin. Arthur (Fritz) Peters born.

1914   March. Chicago. First issue of Margaret Anderson's *Little Review.*

1916   Chicago. Margaret Anderson and Jane Heap meet.

1917   New York. Margaret Anderson and Jane Heap move to Manhattan.

Ezra Pound becomes the *Little Review*'s foreign editor.

1918   New York. *Little Review* begins serialization of James Joyce's *Ulysses.*

April 25. Indianapolis. Janet Flanner marries William Lane Rehm. The couple moves to New York's Greenwich Village.

December 21. New York. Solita Solano arrives from Boston to become drama critic for the *New York Tribune.* Solita Solano and Janet Flanner meet.

August 20. New York. Dorothy Park Benjamin elopes with Enrico Caruso.

1919   Paris. Georgette Leblanc and Maeterlinck separate. He marries Renée Dahon.

New York. Janet Flanner becomes pregnant and either miscarries or has an abortion.

December 18. New York. Gloria Caruso, daughter of Dorothy and Enrico, born.

1921   Greece and Turkey. Solita Solano sent to do articles for *National Geographic.* Janet Flanner accompanies her.

August 2. Italy. Enrico Caruso dies.

1922   New York. Kathryn Hulme settles in Manhattan.

Fall. Paris. Solita Solano and Janet Flanner arrive and decide to make it their home.

1923   Illinois. Margaret Anderson's sister Lois has nervous breakdown. Her two boys, Tom and Arthur (Fritz), go to New York to live with Margaret and Jane.

New York. Margaret Anderson has nervous breakdown.

Winter. London. Dorothy Caruso marries a second time. The marriage lasts three months.

1924   February. New York. Margaret Anderson and Jane Heap meet A. R. Orage and G. I. Gurdjieff.

Paris. Solita Solano's first novel *The Uncertain Feast* published.

June. Prieuré. Margaret Anderson, Jane Heap, Georgette Leblanc, Monique Serrure, and Tom and Fritz Peters (and possibly Louise Davidson) live at Gurdjieff's Institute for the Harmonious Development of Man at Fontainebleau-en-Avon.

July 8. En route to Prieuré from Paris. Gurdjieff's car crashes into tree. Suffers severe concussion.

Fall. Jane Heap, Tom and Fritz Peters leave the Prieuré and return to New York. Jane legally adopts the boys. Margaret stays in France with Georgette and Monique.

September 18. New York. Dorothy Caruso gives birth to her second daughter, Jacqueline.

1925   Paris. September. Janet Flanner hired as foreign correspondent for *The New Yorker.*

Paris. Solita Solano's second novel *The Happy Failure,* published.

Prieuré. Spring. Jane Heap, Tom and Fritz Peters return. Gurdjieff agrees that the boys should continue to live there. Jane returns to New York.

August 25. New York. Kathryn Hulme marries Leonard D. Geldent.

1926   Janet Flanner and William Lane Rehm divorce.

Janet Flanner's *The Cubical City* published.

Marie-Louise Hâbets enters convent.

1927   February 19. Paris. Margaret Anderson and Solita Solano meet and begin love affair. Solita Solano introduced to Gurdjieff by Margaret Anderson. Not impressed, she says—"I rather disliked him."

Solita Solano's third and last novel *This Way Up* published.

1928   San Francisco. Kathryn Hulme divorces Leonard D. Geldent.

Paris. Djuna Barnes' novel *Ryder* as well as her lesbian satire *The Ladies Almanack* published.

1929   New York. Final issue of *Little Review.*

Late October. Fritz Peters leaves the Prieuré to live with his mother and stepfather in Chicago.

1931   Margaret Anderson publishes first volume of her three-volume memoirs, *My Thirty Years War.*

Georgette Leblanc publishes *Souvenirs: My Life with Maeterlinck.*

April. Paris. Kathryn Hulme and Alice Rohrer meet Solita Solano, Janet Flanner and Djuna Barnes at the Café Flore.

Christmas Day. Paris. Georgette Leblanc gives musical reception at the château La Muette. Included among the guests are the playwright Luigi Pirandello, the pianist Allen Tanner, Solita Solano, and Kathryn Hulme.

1932   Paris. Solita invites Kathryn Hulme and Alice Rohrer to join Jane Heap's study group.

February. Kathryn Hulme and Alice Rohrer unexpectedly meet Gurdjieff at the Café de la Paix. He invites them to return with him to the Prieuré where they spend a night.

Janet Flanner begins a relationship with Noel Haskins Murphy.

1933   Georgette Leblanc stricken with pneumonia. She, Margaret and Monique move to Vernet-les-Bains in the Pyrénées Orientales and rent a little peasant's house.

Dorothy Caruso marries a third time, living with her husband on his property bordering the forest of Fontainebleau.

1934   France. Margaret Anderson's romance with Solita Solano begins to cool. She becomes attracted to the English actress Josephine Plows-Day. Solita finds correspondence between the two and writes to Day telling her that Margaret is a lesbian. Day writes back and advises Solita to "die to your sin." Margaret, discovering Solita's betrayal, becomes enraged.

Autumn. Paris. Solita Solano meets Gurdjieff and becomes his pupil.

November 6. London. Alfred Richard Orage dies.

1935   October 18. Gurdjieff sends Jane Heap to London to lead C. S. Nott's group. She and Elspeth Champcommunal live together.

October 21. Paris. Origin of the Rope. Solita Solano, Elizabeth Gordon and Louis Davidson meet in Gurdjieff's hotel room above the Café de la Paix to hear chapters of his unpublished *First Series* read.

1936   May. Paris. Margaret, Georgette and Monique move from Vernet.

Paris. Djuna Barnes' novel *Nightwood* published.

1937   May. Alice Rohrer and Kathryn Hulme return to America.

August. Gurdjieff's brother Dimitri dies.

September. New York. Alice Rohrer has a five-hour emergency operation for intestinal blockage.

November. Europe. Jane Heap and Elspeth Champcommunal have auto accident.

1938   July. Paris. Kathryn Hulme visits Gurdjieff for three weeks. Alice stays behind.

1939   April. Gurdjieff and Solita Solano, who has become his secretary, sail for New York. Despite the worsening international situation and the protestations of American students, Gurdjieff and Solano return in mid-May.

June. Paris. Georgette Leblanc diagnosed with cancer.

June. Fontainebleau. Dorothy Caruso divorces her third husband.

September 1. Hitler invades Poland.

September 3. France and Britain declare war on Germany.

September 12. Paris. Georgette operated on.

October 5. Janet Flanner and Solita Solano return to America.

October. Georgette's incision fails to completely heal.

November. Georgette's *Story of the Blue Bird* published.

1940   February 10. Le Cannet. Margaret, Georgette and Monique move to a tiny house three kilometres above Cannes.

September 1. Second World War begins with Germany's invasion of Poland.

1941   October 26. Le Cannet, Chalet Rose. Georgette Leblanc, seventy-two years old, dies of cancer and is buried in the Cimitière des Anges, Le Cannet.

1942   June. Margaret Anderson meets Dorothy Caruso aboard a ship bound from Lisbon to New York and a new companionship begins. Solita Solano meets Elizabeth Jenks Clark in the American Women's Voluntary Service and also begins a new companionship.

July. New York. Janet Flanner begins a new companionship with Natalia Danesi Murray.

1943   Spring. Oakland, California. Kathryn Hulme becomes welder at the Kaiser Shipyards.

1944   August. Belgium. Marie-Louise Hâbets leaves convent for Belgian underground and soon becomes a nurse for British forces.

August 15. Oakland. Kathryn Hulme quits her job as a welder and makes application to UNRRA, hoping to get back to Europe and Gurdjieff.

1945   April 30. Berlin. Adolph Hitler commits suicide.

May 7. Reims, France. Germany surrenders.

June. Jullouville, France. Kathryn Hulme, posted there by UNRRA meets the former Belgian nun and nurse Marie-Louise Hâbets.

New York. Dorothy Caruso's *Enrico Caruo, His Life and Death* published.

June. Paris. Janet Flanner visits Gurdjieff.

July. Paris. Kathryn Hulme visits Gurdjieff.

August 4. Wildflecken. Kathryn Hulme and Marie-Louise Hâbets posted to displaced persons center.

August 6. Hiroshima. United States drops the first atomic bomb.

Late Summer. Paris. Fritz Peters visits Gurdjieff.

Elizabeth Gordon dies either this year or the next, having been interned during the war in a German camp since 1943 or 1944.

1946   June. Paris. Kathryn Hulme and Marie-Louise Hâbets visit Gurdjieff.

July 27 Paris. Gertrude Stein, seventy-two years old, dies of cancer.

1947   Paris. Georgette Leblanc's *La Machine à Courage* published.

Paris. Janet Flanner receives French Legion of Honor for her "Letter from Paris" in *The New Yorker.*

October 2. London. P. D. Ouspensky, sixty-nine years old, dies.

1948   June. New York. Margaret Anderson and Dorothy Caruso sail for France. On June 30 they visit Gurdjieff at his apartment.

December. Gurdjieff visits New York, and Mar-garet Anderson and Dorothy Caruso follow.

1949   January 13. At Gurdjieff's birthday celebration Kathryn Hulme tells story of "the poor little girl."

Mid-February. Gurdjieff returns to France.

October. Paris. Solita Solano returns.

Mid-October. Paris. Margaret Anderson and Dorothy Caruso sail for New York.

October 28. Paris. Kathryn Hulme arrives.

October 29. Paris, France. George Ivanovitch Gurdjieff, seventy-seven years old, dies.

December 2. Hollywood, California. Florence Reynolds, seventy years old, dies, leaving her inheritance to Jane Heap.

1950   New York. Gurdjieff's *Beelzebub's Tales to his Grandson* published. It is the *First Series* of three series of books which will comprise his magnum opus, *All and Everything.*

1951   Margaret Anderson's *The Fiery Fountains* published.

February. Rotterdam. Kathryn Hulme and Marie-Louise Hâbets leave for America. Take up residence in Phoenix, Arizona. Hulme writes *The Wild Place* which details her experiences at Wildflecken, and converts to Catholicism.

1952   New York. Dorothy Caruso's *A Personal History* published.

Baltimore, Maryland. Dorothy Caruso diagnosed with cancer. Undergoes radical mastectomy.

1953   Hulme's *The Wild Place* published. Hulme wins *The Atlantic Monthly's* Non-Fiction prize.

1955	December 16. Maryland. Dorothy Caruso, sixty-two years old, dies.
1956	Kathryn Hulme's *The Nun's Story* published.
	May. Le Cannet. Margaret Anderson returns to the Chalet Rose to live with Monique Serrure.
	Orgeval, France. Solita Solano and Elizabeth Clark return to France and rent a house from Noel Murphy.
	Autumn. Margaret Anderson begins her lesbian novella *Forbidden Fires*.
1957	Los Angeles. Warner Brothers buys film rights to *The Nun's Story*. Audrey Hepburn is cast as Sister Luke (Marie-Louise Hâbets). Kathryn Hulme and Marie-Louise Hâbets meet Audrey Hepburn and become good friends.
1958	January. Los Angeles. Alice Rohrer builds a house near Kathryn Hulme's and Marie-Louise Hâbets' home.
	March 12. San Francisco. Alice Rohrer dies of coronary thrombosis and ruptured myocardium.
	New York. Djuna Barnes' *The Antiphon* published.
1959	Film version of *The Nun's Story*, starring Audrey Hepburn and Peter Finch, is released. It is nominated for an Academy Award.
	Durango, Mexico. Audrey Hepburn falls from horse while making John Huston's *The Unforgiven* and Marie-Louise Hâbets cares for Hepburn for three weeks in her and Kathryn's home.
1960	Kauai, Hawaii. Kathryn Hulme and Marie-Louise Hâbets buy a home.
1961	June 18. Le Cannet. Monique Serrure dies and is buried next to Georgette Leblanc in the Cimitière des Anges, Le Cannet.
1962	June. Copenhagen. Solita Solano visits Baroness Blixen, the Danish novelist Isak Dinesen.
	September 7. Copenhagen. Baroness Karen Blixen, seventy-seven years old, dies.
	Margaret Anderson's *The Unknowable Gurdjieff* published.
	Kathryn Hulme begins writing *Undiscovered Country*.
1963	New York. Gurdjieff's *Second Series, Meetings with Remarkable Men* published.
1964	Fritz Peters' *Boyhood with Gurdjieff* published.
	June 18. London. Jane Heap, eighty-one years old, dies.
	June 22. London. Elspeth Champcommunal, Jane Heap's companion, dies.
1965	March 16. Paris. Nancy Cunard, alcoholic and insane, dies.
	December 31. Kathryn Hulme finishes manuscript of *Undiscovered Country*. Solita Solano edits.
1966	Kathryn Hulme's *Undiscovered Country* published.

1967	February 8. Le Cannet. Margaret Anderson, suffering from emphysema and heart trouble, writes a suicide note but reconsiders.
	Cannes. Margaret Anderson moves from the Chalet Rose to the Hotel Reine des Prés.
	March 7. Paris. Alice B. Toklas, ninety years old, dies.
1969	Margaret Anderson's third and final volume of memoirs, *The Strange Necessity*, published.
1970	September. Paris. Madame de Salzmann asks Kathryn Hulme to do a film treatment of *Meetings with Remarkable Men*.
1971	January. Kauai, Hawaii. Kathryn Hulme completes film treatment.
	Fritz Peters' *Gurdjieff Remembered* published.
1972	Paris. Natalie Barney, ninety-five years old, dies.
1973	May. Cannes. France. Margaret Anderson enters Sunny Bank Anglo-American Hospital.
	October 19. Cannes. Margaret Anderson, eighty-seven years old, dies of heart failure. She is buried in the Cimitière des Anges, Le Cannet, alongside Georgette Leblanc and Monique Serrure.
1975	New York. Gurdjieff's *Life is real only then when "I Am"* published.
	November 22. Orgeval. Solita Solano, eighty-seven years old, dies.
1976	September. Orgeval. Elizabeth Clark, living alone, falls and breaks hip.
	New York. Elizabeth Clark returns.
1977	Kingston, Rhode Island. Elizabeth Clark and Mathilda M. Hills share a house together.
1978	November 7. New York. Janet Flanner, eighty-six years old, dies of heart attack.
	Fritz Peters' *Balanced Man* published.
1979	New York. Film version of *Meetings With Remarkable Men* released. Peter Brook directs.
	December 19. Las Cruces, New Mexico. Fritz Peters dies.
1981	August 25. Kauai, Hawaii. Kathryn Hulme, eighty-one years old, dies.
1989	Kingston, Rhode Island. Elizabeth Jenkins Clark dies.
1990	June 18. Patchin Place in Greenwich Village, New York. Djuna Barnes, ninety-eight years old, dies.
1991	Kauai, Hawaii. Marie-Louise Hâbets, eighty-six years old, dies. ⋈

Selected Bibliography

G. I. Gurdjieff
>	*All and Everything, First Series* (1st edition, unrevised,
>	Two Rivers Press, Aurora, Oregon, 1991)
>	*Meetings with Remarkable Men* (E. P. Dutton and Co.,
>	New York, 1963)
>	*Life is real only then, when "I Am"* (Triangle Editions, New
>	York, 1978)

Margaret Anderson
>	*The Unknowable Gurdjieff* (Arkana, New York, 1991)
>	*My Thirty Years War* (Horizon Press, New York, 1951)
>	*The Fiery Fountains* (Horizon Press, New York, 1969)
>	*The Strange Necessity* (Horizon Press, New York, 1969)
>	*Forbidden Fires* (The Naiad Press, Inc., Tallahassee, Florida,
>	1996, edited with introduction and postscript by
>	Mathilda M. Hills)

J. G. Bennett
>	*Idiots in Paris* (Coombe Springs Press, England, 1980)

Shari Benstock
>	*Women of the Left Bank: Paris, 1900-1940* (University of
>	Texas Press, Austin, 1986)

Dorothy Caruso
>
> *Enrico Caruso: His Life and Death* (Simon and Schuster,
> New York, 1945)
>
> *Dorothy Caruso: A Personal History* (Hermitage House, New
> York, 1952)

Natalia Dansei
>
> *Darlinghissima: Letters to a Friend* (Random House, New
> York, 1985). Edited and with commentary by Natalia
> Danesi Murray

Janet Flanner
>
> *Paris Was Yesterday 1925-1939* (Viking Press, New York,
> 1972)
>
> *Janet Flanner's World* (Harcourt Brace, New York, 1979)
> Edited by Irving Drutman. Introduction by William
> Shawn

Hugh Ford
>
> *Four Lives in Paris* (North Point Press, San Francisco, 1987)

Jane Heap
>
> *The Notes of Jane Heap* (Two Rivers Press, Aurora, Oregon,
> 1994)

Phillip Herring
>
> *Djuna: The Life and Works of Djuna Barnes* (Penguin Books,
> Inc., New York 1995)

Kathryn Hulme
>
> *The Nun's Story* (Little, Brown and Co., Boston, 1956)
>
> *Undiscovered Country: In Search of Gurdjieff* (Little, Brown
> and Co., Boston, 1966)

John Lester
>
> *Jane Heap Remembered: As remembered by some she taught*
> (Two Rivers Press, Aurora, Oregon, 1988)

Louise March
>
> *The Gurdjieff Years: 1929-1949* (Work Study Association,

BIBLIOGRAPHY

Walworth, New York, 1990)

C. S. Nott
Teachings of Gurdjieff (Samuel Weiser Inc., New York,
1961)
Journey Through This World (Routledge & Kegan Paul Ltd.,
London, 1966)

P. D. Ouspensky
In Search of the Miraculous (Harcourt, Brace and Co.,
New York, 1949)

William Patrick Patterson
Struggle of the Magicians (Arete Communications, Fairfax,
California, Second Edition, 1998)

Fritz Peters
Boyhood with Gurdjieff (Penguin Books Inc., Baltimore;
E. P. Dutton & Co., New York, 1964)
Gurdjieff Remembered (Samuel Weiser Inc., New York,
1971)
Balanced Man (Wildwood House Ltd., London, 1978)

Andrea Weiss
Paris Was A Woman (Harper, San Francisco, 1995)

Brenda Wineapple
Genêt: A Biography of Janet Flanner (Ticknor & Fields,
New York, 1989)

Of special interest are the papers of Solita Solano and Janet Flanner, Library of Congress; the papers of Margaret Anderson, Golda Meir Library, University of Minnesota; the papers of Kathryn Hulme, Beinecke Library, Yale University; and the papers of Florence Reynolds/Jane Heap, University of Delaware.

References

GUIDE TO THE REFERENCES

Each quotation or significant fact is designated by the code for the source material and the page upon which it appears. Thus:

3 Let every one of you. ISM, 247

means that the material referred to on page 3 of this book will be found in *In Search of the Miraculous* on page 247.

KEY TO TITLES

BG . . . . *Boyhood with Gurdjieff.* Fritz Peters
BM. . . . . *Balanced Man.* Fritz Peters
D . . . . *Djuna: The Life and Works of Djuna Barnes.* Phillip Herring
DC. . . . . *Dorothy Caruso: A Personal History.* Dorothy Caruso
FF. . . . . *Forbidden Fires.* Margaret Anderson
FLP . . . . *Four Lives In Paris.* Hugh Ford
FS . . . . *First Series of All and Everything.* G. I. Gurdjieff
G . . . . *Genêt. A Biography of Janet Flanner.* Brenda Wineapple
GR. . . . . *Gurdjieff Remembered.* Fritz Peters
ISM . . . . *In Search of the Miraculous.* P. D. Ouspensky
JH. . . . . *Jane Heap Remembered: As remembered by some she taught.* John Lester
JTTW . . . . *Journey Through This World.* C. S. Nott
MG . . . . *Memories of Gurdjieff.* A. L. Staveley
MTYW . . . . *My Thirty Years' War.* Margaret Anderson
SS . . . . *Second Series of All and Everything.* G. I. Gurdjieff

Material from archives is designated as:

PROLOGUE

THE FIRST GROWL

20 .... The virtues of Christian Science. MTYW, 57
20 .... Moved to kiss me. MTYW, 31
21 .... Dreiser was never any good. MTYW, 39
21 .... Curiously depressed all day. MTYW, 35
21 .... I didn't consider intellectuals intelligent. TFF, 104-05
22 .... I was born to be an editor. MTYW, 58
23 .... He was at least "conscious."
23 .... Her ultimatum. MTYW, 65
24 .... I donated a page. MTYW, 80
24 .... What have I been so unreal about? MTYW, 3
24 .... I was often up at sunrise. MTYW, 89–90
25 .... It isn't a question of words. MTYW, 105
26 .... The first full-blown Lesbian case. THC, 279
26 .... Fighting cock. MTYW, 187
26 .... The sardonic pleasure. THC, 279
26 .... Martie, you should know more. TFF, 3
27 .... My mind was inflamed. MTYW, 116 and 122
27 .... I had chosen her mind. MTYW
27 .... The process of encouraging Jane. MTYW, 110
28 .... For me challenge. MTYW, 123–24
28 .... My object in talking. MTYW, 151
29 .... An official organ. FLP, 242
29 .... It was time to touch. MTYW, 136
31 .... Post Office: Burned. MTYW, 175
31 .... I feel a bondage. TFF, 5
32 .... Djuna would never talk. MTYW, 181
32 .... Djuna took me over to a table. D, 127
33 .... A damned attractive woman. THC, 277
33 .... By 1922 I knew. MTYW, 230
34 .... Lois is really me—only less so. MA/GML, 8/14/24
34 .... To this day, I am not at all sure. BG, 20
35 .... Like pieces of unwanted luggage. BG, 61-62
38 .... Photo of Margaret Anderson. MA/GML
38 .... Photo of Jane Heap. MA/GML
39 .... Photo of Solita Solano. SS/LOC
39 .... Photo of Georgette Leblanc. SS/LOC

New York, Paris, & the Prieuré

42 .... By midnight. UG, 110
43 .... A seer, a prophet, a messiah? UG, 111
43 .... A supreme science of God. UG, 112
43 .... I saw this man in motion. STM, 103

73 .... Photo of G. I. Gurdjieff. SS/LOC
73 .... Photo by author.
74 .... Photos of Café de la Paix. Private collection
75 .... Photo of Noel Murphy and Janet Flanner. SS/LOC
75 .... Photo of Nancy Cunard. SS/LOC
75 .... Photo of Solita Solano. SS/LOC
76 .... Photo of Château Tancarville. Private collection
76 .... Photo of Georgette Leblanc. SS/LOC
76 .... Photo of Margaret Anderson at Château Tancarville. SS/LOC

CREATION OF THE ROPE
87 .... A la santé de tous les idiots ordinaires. UC, 78
100 .... If I am to live. UG, 144
105 .... I am living a springtime. UG, 148
115 .... I tried to stop living. UG, 153
118 .... God helps me. UG, 149
119 .... Mystical Body of Christ. UC, 113
120 .... Man begins to breed like mice. UC, 119–20
131 .... Photo of Margaret Anderson. MA/GML
132 .... Photo of Kathryn Hulme. KH/BL

DANCING WITH DEATH
153 .... Just a little swelling. TFF, 165–66
161 .... Cinema stars? TFF, 216
163 .... Our fear of death. TFF, 231
163 .... Mourir sans mourir? TFF, 236–37
163 .... Georgette will never perish. TFF, 239
165 .... Must feel more comfortable now. G
165 .... In this year everything. G, 176
166 .... Grieve about my infidelity. G, 179

THE MAGUS DEPARTS
167 .... My state was beyond loneliness. EC, 282
168 .... I was returning. UG, 174
168 .... As if through revelation. UG, 176
171 .... As if propelled by powers. DC, 156
171 .... What is inner work? DC, 156
172 .... What comes afterward? UG, 169–70
173 .... Dorothy write a book. DC, 156–57
173 .... Judgment, justice and observation. DC, 168
174 .... Accepts without question. G, 185
175 .... It's Crocodile, Mr. Gurdjieff. UC, 213–14

233 .... She hates most all. MA/GML

234 .... Katie darling. KH/BL

235 .... Darling, during the last years. MEWA/GML

235 .... I have no more courage. MA/GML, 2/8/67

237 .... I refuse to be a burden. MA/GML

237 .... What am I doing. MA/GML, 1/13/67

239 .... He walks into my room. MA/GML

240 .... And now I've just. MA/GML, 10/14/71

240 .... I miss him greatly. MA/GML

241 .... Solita drank too much. SS/LOC

242 .... I experienced Death. MA/GML, 1/23/72

242 .... I don't want to write. MA/GML

243 .... Now I am living. MA/GML

244 .... I prefer to stay. MA/GML, 8/22/73

244 .... The reason I did not. SS/LOC

244 .... You said you could. MA/GML, 8/30/73

244 .... I no longer dare. MA/GML, 9/13/73

245 .... Long long suffering. SS/LOC

245 .... A Life on a Cloud. JF, *The New Yorker,* 1/3/74

246 .... I wonder why. TFF

246 .... Life has been bleak. KH/BL

Appendix:

Personas & the Inner Animal

Some preliminary exploration concerning Gurdjieff's teaching of the inner animal.

S itting at the Café de la Paix with the Rope, Gurdjieff pointed out the personas, the societal masks, of the people passing. The persona is a primary image, along with subordinate images, rooted in personality—that which one has acquired and learned in life. Identity and persona are usually confused. When people say someone is "looking for their identity, who they really are," more often than not what is being sought is a persona mask. The young and inexperienced crave experience, but all experience leaves its mark. To avoid that "marking"—to have the experience but not be marked by it—the young often try on a number of masks.[1] Whatever the mask, one thing is certain: *in no case do they want to look like or be like their parents.*

There is confusion here in that there is no discrimination between image and being. Gurdjieff says, "Exterior play role, inte-

1. It is likely that living in the image-dominated world of film, TV, and advertising—all as suggestive and shocking as "public decency" permits—the young of our contemporary time adopt more and a greater variety of masks than their predecessors.

rior never." The persona is adopted in reaction to experience, be it fear, or a resistance; or in desire, a full-blooded drive to be, participate in, the experience. With most people, image and being become so entwined over time that image, like a sybaritic vine, sucks the life out of being.[2] A person becomes all persona, no substance.

The concept and experience of the inner animal is quite different. Gurdjieff speaks of scratching a person to see what they are like. Scratch the persona image and reaction is usually instant. That which reacts is one's inner animal. It doesn't live in the head but in the instinctual center. It would seem to be a part of, or closely connected to, essence—what a person is *before* they acquire, learn from, and react to experience. One's inner animal wants what it wants when it wants it. It has no higher aspiration. Its desires are basic, primitive. In this sense, one is ever in contention with it. But, as Gurdjieff says, one must make a friend of it, for without its motive force one cannot make a soul. One must know one's animal, work with it, feed it when it performs well, pet it—but keep it always under watch.

When one hears their inner animal named it often evokes Solita's reaction—"Canary? Oh, Mr. Gurdjieff ... *not* canary!" Or Kathryn's, confusion. One simply doesn't think of oneself as an animal. We are human beings, "three-centered beings," as Gurdjieff said. But if the three centers are occupied only in a mechanical way, then do we really represent the species? Unawakened to our full potential, asleep, we are perhaps subhuman, something between human and animal. Not an endearing idea but how else to account for the continual wars, savagery and crime that mark human history—how else to account for, as it was once formulated, "the ghost in the machine"?

Whatever one's inner animal, according to Gurdjieff it has seven aspects.

2. An evocative image of this is the medieval Apprentice Pillar at Roslyn Chapel, south of Edinburgh, Scotland. The sculpted pillar—all the others are not dressed—has a vine wrapping around it with animals sucking at the roots.

"Kanari," he said, "one of your seven aspects[3] is fly-mice (bat). Even exterior is such for me, can see even when look at your face."

"Oh, dear, bat is a squeamish animal," said Solita.

"Bat squeamish? Or man?"

"Man, of course. All mankind hate bat."

Replied Gurdjieff, "Not when I tell what means."

Which, of course, in true Gurdjieffian fashion he never does.

Along with the seven aspects, there seems to be a hierarchy of inner animals. The animals evolve—he says *transformate*—with our understanding. Gurdjieff told Solita that while her inner animal started as a Kanari (canary), it could become a crow, perhaps even a peacock. (Or, conversely, devolve into a turkey.) He said a small crow was better because it has *merde* of a better quality. His use of the word *merde* is shocking, crude. That he is speaking to women in this way offends. But Gurdjieff could also be indicating something deeper?

Merde represents the negative distillation of the three foods one has digested—physical food, air and impressions. The condition of one's *merde* is a concrete example of the state of one's digestive process. The science of scatology deals with this. And *merde,* of course, isn't just physical, but mental, emotional and instinctual as well. The popular phrase "don't give me any of that shit" is a personal statement, as opposed to the maxim "Shit happens"[4] which is impersonal. The first is psychological, the second, cosmic. So *merde* itself is suggestive of three categories of meaning—functional, psychological, cosmic. To write off Gurdjieff's use of the word as simply obscenity and not as a possible teaching in itself is a limitation.

One might suppose that whatever one's inner animal, it will evolve within its species. However, Gurdjieff told Kathryn that

---

3. According to the Law of *Heptaparaparshinokh,* every thing has seven aspects.

4. The Buddha said that life is suffering, a more elegant phrase than "shit happens." One point at which the Fourth Way differs from Buddhism is that "when shit happens, we will use it." That is, learn to correctly absorb and creatively process its impressions for the creation of our higher being-bodies.

her crocodile might become an elephant, so that presupposition is not necessarily true. There also appears to be some confusion between inner animals and tapeworms. When Alice asked, "Is my animal really boa constrictor?"[5] Gurdjieff's replied: "Yes. It was easy for me to put serpent in her because she already had by heredity a capacity for great swallowing.[6] Now what suffering she will have. Because I put the serpent in her, she will always wish to swallow. And sometimes there will be nothing to swallow and so she will double suffer."

But earlier, Gurdjieff had said her interior animal was a tapeworm, the dictionary definition of which is "any of various cestode flatworms that live in the intestines." Later, at one of the luncheons, he will say, "We have three tapeworms. One organic, one in feeling center and one in mental." If we think of all three centers having "digestive functions" then in each there would be these parasitic "worms" which eat our impressions and energy.[7] And later, "When tapeworm is satisfied it have beautiful smile like bird of paradise. When angry and wants something, he makes so—angry face, angry noise."

Fortunately, tapeworms, as adjuncts to the inner animal, or as the inner animal itself, can evolve. For example when Solita asked—after noticing that the bones in her hands had changed— "Can active elements change bones?" Gurdjieff said, "Yes, of course. Can change even tail in man. Active element makes everything. Even the kind of breath you have depend from active ele-

5. Gurdjieff told her: "Now you not look on me like cow, but like *boa constrictor*—not like empty snake, but full one. You not have poison, you swallow whole. Like crocodile." Alice, presumably, had a very strong mind capable of great concentration. When Gurdjieff speaks of "swallowing," perhaps it is to this that he refers.

6. While Alice was a self-made wealthy entrepreneur—that is, she could "swallow" a lot of people—she had intestinal problems throughout her life.

7. Could addiction and all excesses have to do with these "tapeworms," these parasitic entities that attach themselves to us? One way to get rid of them might be to starve them. Gurdjieff warns in his *First Series* about "guarding the purity of our [three] brains." This makes one think of Colin Wilson's book, *The Mind Parasites*.

ments.... Now my tapeworm sing—not 'Marseillaise' or 'Internationale.' He would only sing 'God Save King,' never would he be Communist—only monarchist or republican. Tapeworm of man is lazy and spoiled. He not have, like man, possibility of denying himself or wishing to suffer and make sacrifice for future."

Gurdjieff said also that tapeworms are of two kinds. "One—eat all but no satisfaction have. Other, eat all—but have satisfaction." And then there is this statement: "Not only is tapeworm in stomach of man, other worms also. Well, worms, such snakes as I tell about, is different kinds in stomach of man and of them all, *one is always chief* in this universe of stomach. He commands all and from him this chief in struggle of stomach-universe, *from him depends of what consists the psyche of this man and what is his animal.*[8] [Emphasis added]

So the psyche of man and his inner animal are the products of the chief tapeworm that lives in his gut. Reciprocal maintenance is a key part of Gurdjieff's teaching, but who ever would suspect that it could be so personally applied? Besides the "tapeworm" and "inner animal," there is an "interior animal" also. So there are four levels. One is psychological, the persona, or mask. Then on an instinctive level (and each center is divided into intellectual, emotional and instinctive), there is the inner animal, interior animal, and tapeworm.

Apparently, as with animals per se, there is no "peaceable kingdom. " When Solita brought Janet Flanner's love, Noel Murphy, to meet Gurdjieff, he told her: "You are combination[9] camel and sparrow. I not understand why Kanari call you friend. I know very well psyche Kanari. Also I have made special study of camel properties during forty years. Never can two such animals be friends—is not basis of friend. Now I look to see if you are male camel or female[10] camel. I not know yet. But I know even what kind of

8. Luncheon, February 23, 1937.

9. Having inner animals in combination, of course, only adds to the complexity of the teaching.

merde you make. You ever see camel *merde*? Small hard rounds, no scientist ever understand why *merde* like that. But I know. I also study strange sex organ female camel have." So friendships, rivalries, attractions and repulsions, predator and prey would seem to all be based on one's inner animal, or combination of animals. Which, in turn, is based on one's chief tapeworm.

Did Gurdjieff's inner animal teachings have an extension beyond what he gave? The relationship of animals and human beings in an initiatory context is quite ancient. In Siberia, for example, where Gurdjieff made a number of expeditions, the shamanic use of animals as "helping spirits" is quite common. As Mircea Eliade points out in *Shamanism: Archaic Techniques of Ecstasy,* "The presence of a helping spirit in animal form, dialogue with it in a secret language, or incarnation of such an animal spirit by the shaman (masks, actions, dances, etc.) is another way of showing that the shaman can forsake his human condition, is able, in a word, to 'die.'" Joseph Epes Brown in *Animals of the Soul* says that for the Lakota Indians "When the word for an animal is placed within a human's personal name, the name has then power to establish for the bearer a kind of relationship with the qualities of that animal. This relationship is personal, private, and takes on the character of the sacred." Henri Frankfurt in *Ancient Egyptian Religion* says that "In human beings individual characteristics outbalance generic resemblance. But the animals exist in their unchanging species, following their predestined modes of life, irrespective of the replacement of individuals. Thus animal life would appear superhuman to the Egyptian in that it shared directly, patently, in the static [being] life of the universe. For that reason recognition of the animals' otherness would be, for the Egyptian, recognition of the divine." When Gurdjieff speaks of maintaining a friendship with one's animal for one cannot create a soul without its help perhaps there are many levels on which his statements can be taken.

There is a great deal more that might be touched upon but this should provide a brief introduction to the subject of the inner animal.

10. Still another differentiation. Inner animals can be either male, female or, presumably what Gurdjieff called "middle sex," or "third sex."

Index

Eating The "I":

A Direct Account
of The Fourth Way—
The Way of Self-Transformation
in Ordinary Life

by William Patrick Patterson

"Most books on the Work, while quite valuable, are too dry. *Eating The "I"* is a major step in changing that: here we have a real human being, like you and I, struggling with Gurdjieff's teachings, sharing moments of despair and moments of insight and liberation."

> —Charles T. Tart, Ph. D.
> Author of *Waking Up*

"*Eating The "I"* gives as full a picture of the Work as it may be possible to get without joining it. The book comes from a great depth and carries much conviction."
> — *Gnosis*

"Patterson has two fine Irish gifts: a vivid memory and a storyteller's ear. Paced like a novel and filled with colorful characters, this spiritual autobiography is certain to appeal to those who want a rare and engaging inside glimpse of the Gurdjieff Work."
> — *Yoga Journal*

"Patterson's work is in a class with Christopher Isherwood's devastatingly frank, and brilliant, story of his spiritual quest, *My Guru and his Disciple*. Writers in the Gurdjieff tradition tend to do autobiography. There are the classic accounts of life with Mr. Gurdjieff by Ouspensky, de Hartmann, Peters and others. *Eating The "I"* will find an honored place in that series."
> —Robert S. Ellwood, Chairman, Dept. of Religious Studies
> University of Southern California

Eating The "I" is available at all serious bookstores.

Or write the publisher: Arete Communications, 773 Center Boulevard #58, Fairfax, CA 94978-0058; Fax: (510) 848-0159. Add $3.50 for postage within continental U.S.A. Outside, add $9.00 for surface; $14 for air mail.

Four-color cover. 6 x 9. 370 pp. Acid-Free Paper. Bibliography. Softcover. ISBN: 1-879514-77-X. $19.95.

Distributors: *Partners, Bookpeople, New Leaf, Samuel Weiser, Baker & Taylor.* In Australia: *Banyan Tree,* 13 College Road, Kent Town 5067, South Australia

STRUGGLE OF THE MAGICIANS

Exploring the Teacher-Student Relationship ·

by William Patrick Patterson

Yes, what an excellent book—full of things I didn't know. A real contribution to our understanding of Gurdjieff and Uspenskii."

—**Colin Wilson**, author,
The War Against Sleep

Struggle of the Magicians will fascinate anyone interested in the Fourth Way. I could hardly put it down."

—**Charles T. Tart**, Ph.D., Prof. Psychology, UC Davis; author, *Waking Up*

"For many of us, Gurdjieff and Uspenskii have remained mysteriously attractive but dauntingly difficult to grasp. *Struggle of the Magicians* is a hard to put down' exception to much of the literature available about Gurdjieff, presenting his life and work almost like a play against the panoramic backdrop of his turbulent times, from World War I and the Russian Revolution through World War II."
—*Light on Consciousness* Magazine

Struggle of the Magicians is an important contribution to the history of alternative spirituality in the West. The tension between the richly contrasting personalities of Gurdjieff and Uspenskii is a cameo of the problems with which the personal transformation tradition has had to contend, while at the same time their story illumines in real life context the powerful vistas its visions have opened. It is the finely-told chronicle of a classic event in occult history, set against the backdrop of overwhelmingly dramatic historical events, effectively set into the narrative as datelines.
—Robert S. Ellwood, Chairman, Dept. of Religious Studies
University of Southern California

Struggle of the Magicians is available at all serious bookstores.

Or write the publisher: Arete Communications, 773 Center Boulevard #58, Fairfax, CA 94978-0058; Fax: (510) 848-0159. Add $3.50 for postage within continental U.S.A. Outside, add $9.00 for surface; $14 for air mail.

Second Edition. 5.5 x 8.5. 336 pp. Acid-Free Paper. Bibliography and Index. Softcover. ISBN: 1-879514-80-8. $19.95.

Distributors: *Partners, Bookpeople, New Leaf, Samuel Weiser, Baker & Taylor.* In Australia: *Banyan Tree,* 13 College Road, Kent Town 5067, South Australia

Taking with the Left Hand

Origin of the Enneagram,
Fellowship of Friends,
& Spritual Theft

by William Patrick Patterson

"William Patrick Patterson's *Taking With the Left Hand* deals with esoteric teachings in a modern context. In this collection of three essays about various aspects of the legacy of the influential spiritual teachings of G. I. Gurdjieff, the author tackles the enneagram craze, the teachings of Boris Mouravieff and a Gurdjieff splinter group, expanding his discussion of these relatively parochial issues to raise more universal questions about the nature and transmission of spiritual truth."
—*Publishers Weekly*

"*Taking With the Left Hand* is quite remarkable. I have read it with great pleasure. Patterson always writes absorbingly, and there is no one in the field of Gurdjieff/ Ouspensky studies that I respect more, or regard as having more authority."
—Colin Wilson, author, *From Atlantis to the Sphinx*

"A lucid and compelling account of conflict and charlatanism surrounding one of the most important alternative spiritual movements of our day. Indeed, one sees the crisis unfold before one's eyes, for the author does not hesitate to charge those he finds responsible for debasement of the message of George Gurdjieff with opportunism and self-inflation. This book is important as a 'white paper' for those concerned about the broader Gurdjieff movement, and as a case study for all students of contemporary spiritual movements."
—Robert S. Ellwood, Chairman, Chairman, Dept. of Religious Studies University of Southern California

Taking With the Left Hand is available at all serious bookstores.

Or write the publisher: Arete Communications, 773 Center Boulevard #58, Fairfax, CA 94978-0058; Fax: (510) 848-0159. Add $3.50 for postage within continental U.S.A. Outside, add $9.00 for surface; $14 for air mail.

5.5 x 8.5. 176 pp. Acid-Free Paper. References, Notes, Appendices, Bibliograph,y and Index. Softcover. ISBN: 1-879514-10-9. $12.95.

Distributors: *Partners, Bookpeople, New Leaf, Samuel Weiser, Baker & Taylor.* In Australia: *Banyan Tree,* 13 College Road, Kent Town 5067, South Australia

EXPLORE TELOS

If the ideas and perspectives of the Fourth Way teaching are of interest, explore *Telos*.

The sole focus of *Telos* is inquiry into self-transformation in our contemporary world. An international twenty-eight-page quarterly, *Telos* publishes interviews, essays, book excerpts, and book and film reviews. It does not, and will not, carry advertising. For its publication, it relies solely on the support of its readership.

If you would like a complimentary copy, please send the enclosed postcard, or write:

Telos
773 Center Boulevard, Box 58
Fairfax, California 94978-0058

E-mail: Telos9@aol.com
Website:
members.aol.com/Telos9

William Patrick Patterson

Biography

A longtime student of John Pentland, the man Gurdjieff chose to lead the Work in America, Mr. Patterson has actively practiced the principles of the teaching for over twenty-five years. He is the founder and editor of *Telos*, the first international quarterly devoted to the Fourth Way. A seasoned public speaker, Mr. Patterson regularly lectures on transformational themes, leads seminars, and conducts applied research.

For many years he worked as an editor in publishing and advertising in New York City, and later in Silicon Valley and San Francisco. His work in journalism won many awards including the Jesse H. Neal Award, considered the Pulitzer Prize of business press journalism. While in New York, he founded and edited his own magazine, *In New York*. He lives in a small town in Northern California with his wife and two sons. An avid traveller, he has visited Egypt, Israel, Greece, Turkey, India, Ireland, England, Mexico and Japan, as well as Europe and Scandinavia. He looks forward to visiting Antarctica.